LCAAM

Asset Management and Investor Protection

Asset Management and Investor Protection

An International Analysis

JULIAN FRANKS, COLIN MAYER, AND
LUIS CORREIA DA SILVA

OXFORD
UNIVERSITY PRESS

OXFORD
UNIVERSITY PRESS

Great Clarendon Street, Oxford OX2 6DP

Oxford University Press is a department of the University of Oxford.
It furthers the University's objective of excellence in research, scholarship,
and education by publishing worldwide in

Oxford New York

Auckland Bangkoká Buenos Aires Cape Town Chennai
Dar es Salaam Delhi Hong Kong Istanbul Karachi Kolkata
Kuala Lumpur Madrid Melbourne Mexico City Mumbai Nairobi
São Paulo Shanghai Taipei Tokyo Toronto

Oxford is a registered trade mark of Oxford University Press
in the UK and in certain other countries

Published in the United States
by Oxford University Press Inc., New York

British Library Cataloguing in Publication Data
Data available

Library of Congress Cataloging in Publication Data
Franks, Julian R.
  Asset management and investor protection / Julian Franks, Colin Mayer, and Luis
  Correia da Silva.
    p. cm.
    1. Portfolio management. 2. Investment advisors. 3. Asset-liability management.
  4. Capital assets pricing model. I. Mayer, C. P. (Colin P.) II. Da Silva, Luis Correia. III. Title.
  HG4529.5 .F743 2002   332.6—dc21   2002074859

ISBN 0-19-925709-4 (hbk.)
ISBN 0-19-926193-8 (pbk.)

10 9 8 7 6 5 4 3 2 1

Typeset by Newgen Imaging Systems (P) Ltd., Chennai, India
Printed in Great Britain
on acid-free paper by
Biddles Ltd., Guildford and King's Lynn

CONTENTS

LIST OF FIGURES

LIST OF TABLES

LIST OF ABBREVIATIONS

AEX	Amsterdam Exchanges Index
AFG-ASFFI	Association Française de la Gestion Financière
AMA	Advanced Measurement Approach
AUTIF	Association of Unit Trusts and Investment Funds
BAKred	Bundesaufsichtsamt für das Kreditwesen
BAV	Bundesaufsichtsamt für das Versicherungswesen
Bte	Besluit toezicht effectenverkeer
BVI	Bundesverband Deutscher Investment Gesellschaften
CAC40	Compagnie des Agents de Change 40 index
COB	Commission des Opérations de Bourse
Consob	Commissione Nazionale per la Società e la Borsa
CNMV	Comisión Nacional del Mercado de Valores
CR	concentration ratio
DAX	Deutscher Aktienindex
DGSFP	Dirección General de Seguros y Fondos de Pensiones
D&O	Directors and Officers
EAMA	European Asset Management Association
EdW	Entschädigungseinrichtung der Wertpapierhandelsunternehmen
EI	exposure indicator
EL	expected loss
EU	European Union
E&O	Errors and Omissions
FEFSI	Fédération Européenne des Fonds et Sociétés D'Investissement
FMA	Fund Managers' Association
FSA	Financial Services Authority
FTSE 100	Financial Times Stock Exchange 100 Index
IAIM	Irish Association of Investment Managers
ICI	Investment Company Institute
IIC	Instituciones de Inversión Colectiva
IMRO	Investment Management Regulatory Organisation

Inverco	Asociación de Instituciones de Inversión Colectiva y Fondos de Pensiones
ISA	investment savings account
ISEQ	Irish Stock Exchange Equity Overall Index
KAGG	Gesetz über Kapitalanlagegesellschaften
KWG	Kreditwesengesetz
LGE	loss given that event
MFI	monetary financial institution
MGAM	Morgan Grenfell Asset Management Ltd
MGIFM	MG International Fund Management
MGUTM	MG Unit Trust Managers
MIBTEL	Milano Italia Borsa
NASD	National Association of Securities Dealers
NASDAQ	National Association of Securities Dealers Automated Quotation System
NYSE	New York Stock Exchange
OECD	Organization for Economic Cooperation and Development
ONS	Office of National Statistics
OPCVM	organismes de placement collectif en valeurs mobilière
OPEX	operating expenditure
OXERA	Oxford Economic Research Associates
PE	probability of loss event
RMG	Risk Management Group (of the Basel Committee)
RP	repurchase agreement
SEC	Securities and Exchange Commission
SICAV (France)	société d'investissement à capital variable
SICAV (Italy)	società di investimento a capitale varabile
SRO	self-regulating organization
STE	Stichting Toezicht Effectenverkeer
UCITS	undertaking for collective investment in transferable securities
VAG	Versicherungsaufsichtsgesetz
Wte	Wet toezicht effectenverkeer

....

ACKNOWLEDGEMENTS

A large number of individuals and institutions in financial centres around the world have assisted in the preparation of this report.

First and foremost among these is the European Asset Management Association (EAMA), and, in particular, the members of the Advisory Panel for this project. They have devoted an immense amount of time in commenting and advising on all aspects of the study. They provided detailed comments on a first version of this report that have been invaluable in its redrafting. We would particularly like to thank the members of the Panel, who include Lindsay Tomlinson, Barclays Global Investors; Robin Clark, AXA Investment Managers; Carlos Pardo, AFG-ASFFI; Angel Martínez Aldama Hervás, INVERCO; Tim Boyle, Fidelity Investments; Sean O'Dwyer, Bank of Ireland Asset Management; Fabio Galli, Assogestioni; Michael Haag, EAMA; Klaus Mössle, Deutsche Asset Management; Pim Poppe, Robeco; and Gillian Richardon, Merrill Lynch Mercury Asset Management.

Secondly, the regulatory authorities in four countries and the European Commission have provided invaluable guidance. Thirdly, in addition to members of the Advisory Panel, other European associations have been interviewed at length, including the Fund Managers' Association (FMA), Association of Unit Trusts and Investment Funds (AUTIF), Irish Association of Investment Managers (IAIM), Asociación de Instituciones de Inversión Colectiva y Fondos de Pensiones (Inverco), Assogestioni, Association Française de la Gestion Financière (AFG–ASFFI), Investment Company Institute (ICI), and asset managers in France, Germany, Ireland, Italy, the Netherlands, the UK, and the USA, as well as custodians and insurers. We are grateful to all of the above for the considerable assistance that they have provided in the completion of this report.

In addition, the authors owe considerable thanks to the staff at OXERA, without whom the book would not have been written. In particular, we are very grateful to Jacqueline O'Reilly, Leonie Bell, and Katherine Vickers for outstanding research assistance and support on the project.

1

Introduction

1.1 BACKGROUND

In April 2000, the European Asset Management Association (EAMA) commissioned Professors Franks and Mayer and Oxford Economic Research Associates Ltd. (OXERA) to extend their 1989 study of the regulation of the UK investment industry to an analysis of the European asset management business (Franks and Mayer 1989). The objectives of the study were to determine the risks inherent in asset management businesses in so far as they affect:

- the owners;
- the employees;
- the clients of the business;
- other parties with which the businesses have a relationship; and
- the financial system;

and to determine the extent to which legally imposed capital requirements ('regulatory capital') are capable of eliminating or mitigating these risks.

This book summarizes the results of that study, which was completed in December 2000.

1.2 ASSET MANAGEMENT

Asset management is a major industry. In 1999, global assets under management amounted to €33 trillion (British Invisibles 2000). Asset managers provide services to individuals, governments, public agencies, banks, pension funds, insurance companies, and charities, to name a few. They are the interface between investors, on the one hand, and financial markets and companies, on the other. As securities markets, insurance companies, and funded pension schemes grow in significance relative to deposit taking and bank lending, asset management will play an increasingly important role in economic activity around the world.

Traditionally, asset management has been associated primarily with the 'stock market' economies of the UK and the USA. It has been much less significant in Continental Europe, the Far East, and other 'bank-dependent' countries, where savings have been primarily through deposits and debt instruments, in particular pay-as-you-go pension schemes. However, as this book documents, it is not just in the UK and the USA that there has been a substantial growth in assets under management. Some of the most spectacular growth in activity has occurred in Continental Europe.

This has presented opportunities and challenges. New forms of financial instruments and institutions have emerged in countries that have traditionally relied on debt and non-market forms of intermediation. Competition has intensified, and entry has occurred both within and across national markets. However, this growth has been accompanied by potential problems: while investors enjoy a wider range of products and services, they face more complex instruments and transactions. Therefore, the potential for failures, such as misdealing and fraud, may have increased.

The natural response is to strengthen regulation. Regulation is critical to the successful operation of financial markets. Without it, ill-informed investors may face unwarranted risks from those asset managers who are incompetent or dishonest. In the absence of adequate regulation, they will choose either not to invest, or to transfer their investments to financial centres that offer stronger protection. However, regulation can also undermine financial markets by imposing excessive costs on firms and investors, and potentially driving them elsewhere. There is therefore a fine balance to be struck between inadequate and excessive regulation of asset managers.

This is particularly complicated in the context of European capital markets. Different European countries have traditionally had very different financial systems. As is documented in this book, this is reflected in the structure and operation of their asset management businesses. Not surprisingly, this in turn is mirrored in the different approaches used in regulating asset managers. The starting-point is, therefore, heterogeneous forms and regulations of asset managers. How should the European Commission respond to this diversity? Should it seek to create greater uniformity through the imposition of common regulatory rules? Is this necessary to diminish the fragmentation of European capital markets and to create a greater degree of financial integration?

The particular focus of this book is financial resource requirements. Capital requirements play a central role in the regulation of financial institutions. They are fundamental to the enhancement of financial stability and a basic requirement of deposit-taking institutions around the world. There is currently an active debate about the role that they should play in asset management, particularly in the European context. Are they relevant? If so, at what level should they be set and should they be equalized across Member States?

A prerequisite to answering these questions is to understand the nature of the asset management business in different countries and the risks that it faces. A primary function of this study has been to do exactly that, with the aim of understanding:

- how the asset management business operates;
- how it is organized;
- the nature and size of risks in the business, who bears them and how they are financed; and
- what the alternative forms of investor protection are, together with their associated costs and benefits.

It is important to appreciate that this study is not concerned with investment risks that investors face on their portfolios. Instead, it is concerned solely with *operational risks*—that is, the risks that arise from the operations of the asset management business itself (for example, failures in the purchase, execution, and reconciliation of transactions, and fraud). Furthermore, the book refers to the management activities of assets held through collective investment schemes (mutual funds or undertakings for collective investments in transferable securities, UCITS), and reports one failure, in a collective investment scheme, that may have important implications for asset management in general. However, its main focus is on the regulation of discretionary asset management under mandates. Collective investment schemes raise their own sets of issues that warrant a separate study.

Five forms of analysis were undertaken, as follows:

1. *An evaluation of the nature and structure of the asset management businesses in Europe.* The study focuses on seven European countries—France, Germany, Ireland, Italy, the Netherlands, Spain, and the UK—and contrasts these with the largest and most developed asset management market in the world, namely that in the USA. A survey of most published data was undertaken and approximately 50 asset managers in seven different markets were interviewed about the nature of their businesses. In addition, interviews were conducted with insurers and custodians of assets in Europe and the USA.

2. *A survey of the regulation of asset management in the seven countries and the USA.* Relevant published sources of information were collected, and regulators in four countries were interviewed. An interview was also held with the European Commission.

3. *An assessment of the risks in the asset management business.* A pilot questionnaire was circulated to 10 asset managers in different European countries. On the basis of this, the questionnaire was extensively revised and sent to 83 asset managers in seven countries. Completed responses were received from 39 asset managers from six European countries. Total assets under management for the sample amounted to approximately €2.3 trillion domestically (or over €5 trillion globally). The respondents to the survey were not named and remain confidential to the authors of this study.

4. This assessment of risks was supplemented by a *prominent case study of a failure in the unit trust asset management process.* All of the information on this case was obtained from publications of the relevant regulatory authority, complemented with interviews. The objective of the case study was to gain a better understanding of how investors can be safeguarded by different forms of investor protection.

5. Finally, an *extensive review of the academic literature on the regulation of financial institutions and professional firms* was undertaken.

1.3 THE STRUCTURE OF THE BOOK

The book is structured as follows:

- Chapter 2 summarizes the conclusions of the analysis, including the costs and benefits of different forms of protection.
- Chapter 3 presents a summary of the research findings.

- Chapter 4 describes the activities of the asset management industry in the seven European countries and the USA.

- Chapter 5 contrasts the structure of the industry in the different countries.

- Chapter 6 summarizes the regulatory framework in Europe and the USA; with further details provided in the appendix to the chapter.

- Chapter 7 reviews in more detail the regulation of the industry in the USA.

- Chapter 8 discusses the Basel Committee's proposal for a capital charge for operational risk.

- Chapter 9 reports the results of the survey.

- Chapter 10 describes a case study of failure in the asset management process.

- Chapter 11 surveys the academic literature on the regulation of financial institutions and the professions.

2

The Policy Implications

This book provides a detailed analysis of the structure and regulation of asset management businesses in seven European countries and the USA. It evaluates the operational risks that asset management firms incur in running their businesses, and estimates the size of losses sustained by the industry from these risks in 1999.

This chapter assesses the appropriate response of regulators to the risks of the asset management business and the way in which regulation should be framed at the European level. Different forms of investor protection give rise to different costs and benefits, including their impact on entry and competition. A key result of this study is that:

- industry structures differ markedly across countries;
- there is a close relationship between industry structures and regulation in different countries; and
- attempts to harmonize regulation across countries must be sensitive to these institutional differences.

The chapter begins by setting out the goals of regulation in Section 2.1, followed by a description of the institutional setting in Section 2.2. Section 2.3 describes the regulatory systems in the European countries included in this study and the USA, and evaluates alternative responses to the risks of the asset management business. In Sections 2.4 and 2.5, financial requirements and other responses are discussed. Section 2.6 evaluates the costs and benefits of the alternative forms of investor protection, and Section 2.7 concludes the chapter.

2.1 THE GOALS OF REGULATION

As noted in the review of the literature in Chapter 11, the goal of regulation for banks is clear; it is to provide stability to the financial system and to limit the risks of systemic failures. However, the analysis of the risks of the asset management industry in this book indicates that systemic risks are of much less significance. Unlike commercial and investment banks, and brokers and dealers, asset management firms do not, for the most part, take large positions on their own account. They invest on behalf of others. This is consistent with the results of the survey, which show that the levels of own positions are low and that financial insolvency is ranked as one of the lowest risks that asset management firms face.

One caveat to this is the rise of guaranteed products over the last decade, particularly in Continental Europe. Unless they are adequately hedged or provided by a third party such as a credit institution (as in the case of France), like own positions they expose firms to the risks of financial failure. To date, there have only been occasional failures to meet guarantees, and the results of the survey suggest that these guarantees are largely hedged. Nevertheless, guaranteed products are growing rapidly in significance and have not been fully tested in a bear market. Serious consideration needs to be given as to how investors should be protected in the future from failures to fulfil guarantees.

In the absence of systemic risks, Chapter 11 suggests that the regulation of asset managers is closer to that of professional firms than that of banks. For example, in the legal profession, some of the principal risks are fraud against client funds and professional negligence. These are similar to the risks in the asset management industry. The literature regarding the regulation of the professions points to an important trade-off, enhancing quality by restricting entry and competition. In exactly the same way, an important issue arises as to how regulation of asset managers can improve the quality of service (that is, investor protection) without having an undue effect on competition in the supply of services.

Inadequate or excessive investor protection can be costly. The costs of inadequate investor protection include the following:

- uninformed investors, fearing that they might be exploited, will be reluctant to invest, or will invest in other financial centres;

- shrinkage of the asset management business. 'Good' firms will be tainted with the failure of 'bad' firms and will withdraw from the market or migrate to other centres;
- small, uninformed investors will be particularly exposed, giving rise to large welfare losses; and
- political opprobrium resulting from financial losses may give rise to expensive and inappropriate regulation.

The disadvantages of over-regulation are:

- higher costs for firms and investors;
- the costs of entry and competition are altered; and
- loss of competitiveness of financial centres, leading to a migration of firms from over-regulated to better (or less) regulated markets.

The form and amount of regulation are therefore crucial in determining the success or otherwise of financial institutions and financial centres.

2.2   THE INSTITUTIONAL SETTING

The most striking feature of the structure of the asset management business reviewed in Chapters 4 and 5 is its diversity. Countries at similar stages of economic development have very different asset management businesses. This manifests itself in several different forms. The size of the business varies markedly across countries. Assets under management by pension funds in the UK comprise more than half of all pension fund assets in the seven European countries, and assets under management by insurance companies comprise just under half of all insurance companies' assets. However, the pension fund business in the USA is more than five times that of the UK, and the insurance company business is more than twice that of the UK.

One of the reasons for these disparities is that Continental Europe has traditionally had less well-developed stock markets and therefore had less need for a substantial asset management business. That may well be changing as stock markets expand, but, at present, asset management remains a more substantial component of the Anglo-American financial systems than that of the Continental European ones.

A second aspect of this diversity is that the nature of the asset management business differs appreciably across countries. While the UK dominates the European pension fund and insurance asset management business, it is a smaller player in mutual funds. Differences in the size of pension-managed funds reflect the greater emphasis on funded pension schemes in the UK than in other European countries, where state pensions, pay-as-you-go, and in-house corporate pension schemes predominate. The distinction in asset management businesses is not simply an Anglo-American versus Continental European one; there are significant variations within Continental Europe. For example, insurance companies are dominant in Germany, whilst the number of mutual funds and insurance company funds in France is similar. Also, mutual funds are now growing rapidly in many Continental European countries (for example, in France, profiled funds, issued mostly by insurance companies, are sharply rising, and are one of the main components of the flows to the mutual funds market).

One implication is that both the business that is being regulated and the type of investor differ significantly across countries. In some countries, clients of asset management firms are predominantly large institutional investors, and, in others, they are private clients. In some countries, most investments are through pooled funds—the survey reports that this is a particular feature of France and Italy—and, in others, through mandates (for example, in Germany, the Netherlands, and the UK). Regulation, therefore, has a potentially different impact on investor protection across countries because of differences in the nature as well as the size of asset management businesses.

Third, countries differ in the ownership as well as the activities of asset management firms. In the survey, 87 per cent of respondents reported that they were part of a larger group. Outside the UK and the USA, asset management firms are predominantly owned by banks and insurance companies, many of which may be classified as parts of large financial conglomerates. While this is the case in some of the largest asset management firms in the UK, there are also a large number of small independent firms, and, in the USA, there are nearly six times as many investment management firms as in the UK. Concentration of ownership is therefore appreciably higher in Continental Europe than in the UK and the USA. Furthermore, there are differences within Continental Europe, where France has seen a rapidly increasing number of small, independent asset management firms.

The significance of this observation is that the organization and ownership of firms crucially affect investors' exposure to loss. Firms that are part of large groups have more financial resources upon which to draw than independent firms, and may have more incentive than independent firms to provide protection to investors in the event of failure. If parent firms believe that either the intrinsic value of their asset management firms or the loss of their own reputations outweigh the cost of compensating investors, they will protect investors against loss. This was the case in Morgan Grenfell Asset Management (MGAM), reported in Chapter 10, where Deutsche Bank spent more than £210 m protecting investors against a loss in one of its fund management companies. The value of the earnings stream of that particular fund to Deutsche Bank was probably less than the cash injection to compensate investors. However, the impact of loss in reputation on profits in other parts of its funds management business and its non-asset management business may have exceeded the difference and justified the injection. Contrast that with the case of Barlow Clowes, a UK asset management firm that failed in the latter part of the 1980s. In that case, there was no rich parent with a reputation to bail out the investors, and losses of £150 m were sustained.[1] Where asset management firms are large and part of larger groups, investor exposure to loss is appreciably reduced by the ability of one part of a group to bail out another.

However, this presumes that losses across different parts of groups are uncorrelated and insufficiently large to threaten the solvency of the entire group. In the case of the Barings Group, the failure of the Bank and uncertainty about the scale of the losses prevented the company from raising sufficient funds to avoid the collapse of the entire group, including the fund management business. In this case, the company was acquired quickly and investors did not lose money; in other cases, however, the transfer might not have been effected so painlessly.

In summary, the design of regulation has to be sensitive to the fact that the size, clients, activities, and ownership of asset management businesses differ appreciably across countries, and that this affects the desired pattern of regulation.

2.3 THE RESPONSES IN DIFFERENT COUNTRIES

How have regulators responded to these very different institutional structures? Not surprisingly, the answer is that they have done so in

[1] In this particular case, the British government ended up compensating investors.

diverse ways. Chapter 6, including the appendices, and Chapter 7 report regulatory rules and arrangements in seven countries. There are seven main forms of regulation that are employed: financial resource requirements; conduct-of-business rules; separation of clients' assets requirements; disclosure rules; enforcement; auditing; and investor compensation schemes. Some of these differences are illustrated below in relation to France, Germany, the UK, and the USA.

There are expenditure-based capital requirements in all three European countries. The broad rule is 25 per cent of annual expenditures for these countries, but adjustments to take into account exposure to position risk, foreign-exchange risks, and separation of clients' monies, etc., are also present. Furthermore, in France, Germany, and the UK, there are initial capital requirements. In contrast, in the USA, there are no capital requirements at the federal level, but there may be at the state level.

There are extensive conduct-of-business rules in the UK and self-regulatory (professional ethics) rules of conduct in France. Conduct-of-business rules are far fewer in the USA and include 'fair execution', which is also common in other countries.

In France, the assets of clients and those of the asset management company must be kept strictly separate. In Germany, asset managers must keep securities at a credit institution or be regulated as credit institutions themselves. In the UK, firms that hold clients' monies or assets are subject to more extensive capital requirements and conduct-of-business rules. In the USA, investment advisers that hold clients' securities are subject to more rigorous and random auditing. Also in the USA, there are extensive disclosure rules, auditing by private as well as public auditors, and enforcement through the courts.

There have been significant calls on the compensation fund in the UK, amounting to more than £130 m over the past five years. However, it is worth noting that firms regulated by Investment Management Regulatory Organisation (IMRO)—and, in particular, asset management companies—account for only a small proportion of total compensation paid. A limited compensation scheme for investment firms was recently introduced in Germany. There are no (direct) compensation schemes in France or the USA.

In summary, France emphasizes conduct-of-business rules and custody requirements for collective investment schemes and mandates; Germany, capital requirements and separation of clients' assets; the

UK, capital requirements, conduct-of-business rules, and a compensation scheme; and the USA, disclosure, auditing, and enforcement.

The various forms of regulation are complementary to the structures of asset management business in the four countries. In Germany, investors are in general institutional and asset management firms are part of large institutions. Investors are therefore for the most part relatively well informed and can be compensated in the event of failure by parent institutions wishing to preserve their own reputations. As a result, the cost of a mandatory compensation scheme is likely to be lower than in the UK, which has a higher number of small retail investors. The imposition of large capital requirements is consistent with the concentration of the German asset management business in large organizations.

In some countries, for example France, an asset management business has emerged over the last decade outside of the banking system and insurance companies, in particular in the form of mutual funds. Investor protection has therefore focused mainly on these institutions—for example, the imposition of depositary (trustee) requirements in France on the UCITS or mutual fund management business, but not on mandated portfolio management. The separation of clients' assets has, however, been imposed on UCITS as well as on individual mandates. The UK has a significant independent private client business but a relatively small mutual fund business.[2] Regulation has therefore sought to protect investments made through mandates as well as collective schemes. This has been done through a combination of capital requirements, conduct-of-business rules, incentives to employ separate custodians, and a compensation scheme.

The USA has the largest independent asset management business both in mandates and collective schemes. However, its approach to regulation is quite different from that of the UK. It does not rely on capital requirements, custody rules, or compensation schemes; instead, it emphasizes disclosure, auditing, and enforcement. The UK regulation relies heavily on public contracting—the screening and monitoring of firms according to prespecified rules by public agencies—while the USA emphasizes private contracting—the provision of information to investors and their ability to enforce contracts through the courts. The difference in emphasis is clearly in part a consequence of a greater reliance on the judicial process—in particular,

---

[2] The UK government initiatives to subsidize saving through schemes such as ISAs may be giving a large boost to sales of mutual funds.

Table 2.1. The institutional and regulatory structure of asset management in France, Germany, the UK, and the USA

	Institutional	Regulatory
France	High proportion of mutual funds	Conduct-of-business rules, capital requirements, and custodianship
Germany	Reputational capital of parent institution	Capital requirements, and custodianship
UK	—	Capital requirements, conduct-of-business rules, compensation schemes, and custodianship
USA	—	Disclosure, auditing, and enforcement through the courts

the ease with which private investors are able to litigate in the two countries.

Table 2.1 summarizes the institutional and regulatory forms of investor protection in the four countries.

Investor protection should therefore be considered in the context of institutional arrangements in different countries, as well as in formal regulatory rules.

2.4   FINANCIAL RESOURCE REQUIREMENTS

The alternative responses described above are evaluated in this and the next section. This section begins, however, with financial resource requirements.

Capital requirements in asset management vary from substantial amounts in Germany to nothing in the USA, with the UK and France somewhere in between. What is the appropriate level of capital requirements for asset management firms?

Capital requirements are primarily considered in the context of banks. As noted in Section 2.1, while the main function of the regulation of banks is to promote financial stability, asset management firms are not for the most part subject to systemic risks, except potentially in regard to guaranteed products. Only eight of the 39 firms that completed the questionnaire reported having capital at risk, and the levels of capital at risk averaged €47 m. This is fundamental to a consideration of the merits or otherwise of capital requirements.

In the case of asset management firms, capital provides clients with a cushion against losses sustained from operating failures of the business. Losses can be covered up to the value of the reserves of the business. The cost of providing the capital is therefore the value of the 'put option' that the capital gives investors to protect their investments from the effects of operating losses. The mean cost of capital reported by firms in the survey is 15.7 per cent, with a range from 7 to 30 per cent. This large range possibly reflects variations in the values of the put options across firms.

The benefit of providing capital is that investors value this protection in terms of the price at which they are willing to transact with the asset management firm. In exactly the same way as capital of banks reduces the cost of raising deposits, so the capital of asset management firms raises the price at which clients will purchase asset management services. In determining the optimum amount of capital to employ, asset management firms will trade off the cost of the put option against the enhanced value of their business. Firms therefore voluntarily choose to hold capital for commercial reasons. The survey of asset management businesses reports that firms in general hold capital well in excess of regulatory requirements. The median ratio of capital held to requirements is 2.7 and the mean ratio is 5.7.

However, there is an important reason why the amount of capital that an institution chooses to hold might fall short of what is deemed to be 'socially desirable'—that is, what a public agency might seek. The institution may fail to recoup all of the benefits from holding capital that investors derive. There are three factors that could cause a deviation between the optimal levels of capital that institutions privately choose to hold and what is collectively in the interest of investors and institutions as a whole.

The first is that some of the benefits from one firm's financial resources may accrue to other firms. There is, in the parlance of the economics literature, an 'externality'. The most pertinent example is the contagious failure of financial institutions—the instability of financial systems resulting from the failure of one institution spilling over to others. That is, the fundamental justification for the imposition of capital requirements on banks in excess of what they might privately choose to hold (see Chapter 11). According to the literature, individually, banks do not take adequate account of the extent to which holding capital reduces the exposure of other institutions as well as their own, and some collective enforcement by a public agency is required. That is why it is of fundamental importance to appreciate that the regulation of asset management firms is not primarily concerned with systemic risks. The primary justification for the imposition of capital requirements on banks does not apply to asset management firms. However, there are other reasons why firms may not hold enough capital.

The second is that investors may not be well informed about risks to which they are exposed and therefore do not value them fully. There may be 'information asymmetries' in the parlance of the literature, leading to incorrect valuations. Regulators may therefore feel justified in imposing higher capital requirements on the grounds of the better information about investor risks that they possess.

The third is that asset managers have no interest in the value that clients attach to their services because they are intent on defrauding them. Levels of capital are not then chosen on the basis of 'fair' commercial criteria at all, and regulators may feel justified in imposing what they regard as fair levels.

While these last two justifications are superficially appealing, they both have serious pitfalls. First, they assume a considerable degree of information on the part of regulators, both in terms of the risks of businesses and more significantly in terms of how private levels of capital deviate from the optimal level. Even if they are fully informed about risks, regulators have little information about the costs of imposing capital requirements. As a result, regulators will find it difficult to set capital requirements across firms that are optimal from a social-welfare perspective. Put more prosaically, they will find it increasingly difficult to justify levels of capital requirements that are more easy for some firms.

Second, there is often a confusion of symptoms with causes. Fraudulent firms may hold little capital, but firms that do not hold much capital are not necessarily fraudulent. Requiring potentially fraudulent firms to hold capital raises the same problems as requiring potential thieves to hold more money. Firms would be required to hold very substantial amounts in order for the capital to provide effective protection against fraud. But, then, this would create formidable barriers for new entrants. If capital requirements are set at modest levels then the entry of dishonest and incompetent firms is not avoided; if they are set at high levels then entry of the honest and competent is discouraged. If information asymmetries and fraud are the two main 'market failures' that afflict asset managers then capital requirements are very poor solutions. These failures require very different responses.

2.5 OTHER FORMS OF PROTECTION

The most serious failures reported in Chapter 9 in the survey of asset management firms were misdealing and breach of client guidelines. This was consistent with the frequency of failures, their impact when they occurred, and actual losses sustained by firms. In terms of reported complaints, the most significant items were IT systems failure, misdealing, and breach of client guidelines. Most losses were below €1 m, although there were occasional losses of, for example, €3 m for breach of client guidelines and €7 m for misdealing. The interviews indicated that losses from these operational failures could occasionally be as much as €20 m. The characteristics of operational risks are that they primarily relate to securities transactions and internal systems, and involve not infrequent modest losses.

Provided that investors are informed, they will be able to price these risks appropriately and will only be willing to purchase asset management services at an appropriately reduced price. However, if investors are ill informed about the operational risks, they will not be properly priced. In this case, good firms will be unable to charge the premium over poor firms that they should be able to command. Information problems are therefore a primary source of market failure in asset management. The response in the USA has been to require extensive disclosure of information to investors and regulators.

In their 1989 study of the UK asset management business, Franks and Mayer (1989) record that fraud was the main threat to investors. Subsequent to their analysis, the Robert Maxwell pension case reinforced the potential exposure of investors to this risk. However, risks of fraud now appear to be appreciably lower. While there was some reference to fraud by respondents in the survey, it was by no means regarded as the primary risk. Incidents of losses were small, perceived frequency was low, and there were no reported complaints about fraud.

One of the significant changes since the 1989 study is the growth of custody. Separation of client funds and the growth of custodianship have contributed significantly to enhanced investor protection and, in particular, to the avoidance of fraud. In 1989, the use of separate custodians by investment management firms in the UK was rare. Possibly in response to the Maxwell affair or possibly as a consequence of the development of the custodian industry, non-group custodians (that is, outside the group to which the asset manager belongs) now hold over

80 per cent of UK firms' assets under management.[3] The survey reports that the use of non-group custodians is in general lower on the Continent than in the UK. This may reflect the greater use of custodians within the same group of firms on the Continent.

As noted above, most operating losses are of modest scale. As a consequence, respondents to the survey report that they are able to finance most operating losses from internal earnings. However, occasional large losses do occur. The case reported in Chapter 10 is a clear example of this. The MGAM suffered losses amounting to more than £210 m. The case also illustrates the limitations of custodianship and trusteeship. While there was no theft of securities or monies, there were irregularities in the management of the funds that were not detected either internally or externally by the trustees. As a consequence, the regulator, IMRO, imposed fines of nearly £400,000 on the two trustees. It is unclear to what extent the trustees or custodians would have compensated investors for losses, had the Deutsche Bank not injected £180 m to rescue the asset management firm. In particular, it is unclear whether investors would have been fully protected from loss by the existence of both a trustee and custodian, had the MGAM not been part of a large group. Therefore, while custodianship and trusteeship can go a long way to mitigate the market failures of information asymmetries and fraud, they may not provide complete protection. Regulators may wish to improve custody contracts to clarify the degree of investor protection.

Further protection can come from insurance markets. In the sample, 19 firms have indemnity insurance, 15 employee fidelity and fraud insurance, and nine other insurance, including civil responsibility, real estate, and directors' and officers' insurance. Firms regard insurance as particularly relevant to areas where substantial losses can occur as a consequence, for example, of fraud and failures in IT systems. However, some firms have expressed doubts about the promptness and reliability with which claims are met by insurers. Insurance markets, both private and mutual, are better developed in the USA than in Europe. This has led to greater standardization of contracts, a higher level of protection, and lower costs. The greater degree of disclosure of information and auditing of companies in the USA may have contributed to this result.

---

[3] This is confirmed by a recent study (British Invisibles, 2000), which reports a striking increase in custodianship in the UK, from 50% in 1997 to 71% in 1999.

In the absence of well-functioning insurance markets, there is more emphasis on compensation funds in Europe, in particular in the UK. Over the past five years, the Investors Compensation Scheme in the UK has paid out more than €100 m. Since 1988, more than 12,000 people have received compensation and more than 700 firms have been declared in default. Of these totals, ten IMRO-regulated firms were declared in default by the scheme. In the case of eight of these companies, compensation, amounting to almost £14 m, was paid to 317 investors.[4]

Compensation schemes encourage (discourage) entry and competition where they are large (small) in relation to the regulatory burdens imposed on firms. In general, they subsidize high-risk firms at the expense of low-risk firms or the taxpayer. They therefore, at least in part, make entry easier by mitigating the consequences of other forms of regulation, in particular capital requirements. However, like state aid, they distort competition between countries. The imposition of a common European compensation scheme might be thought to reduce this risk. In fact, differences in industry structures across countries mean that harmonized compensation schemes can be highly distorting. For example, a particular level of compensation will, on average, benefit the UK asset management industry, with its comparatively large number of small firms relative to the more highly concentrated German industry.

In addition, compensation schemes encourage firms to hold too little capital. Since clients of asset management firms do not bear all the costs of the firms' failure where compensation schemes are in operation, they do not value the full benefits of capital—compensation funds create externalities. While this might be thought to justify the imposition of capital requirements, regulators cannot readily establish the extent to which compensation schemes influence firms' capital structure decisions. The relationship between required levels of capital and the scale of compensation schemes is therefore unknown, and, for the reasons mentioned above, will be dependent on the structure of a particular country's asset management business.

Instead, distortions to competition from compensation schemes can be avoided by having risk-based fee structures. Since such structures reflect firms' holdings of capital, they automatically induce firms to choose optimal capital structures. Again, the question is, how can regulators determine fee structures? One approach might be to encourage

---

[4] IMRO, 'Report and Accounts'.

Table 2.2. The alternative forms of investor protection and their impact on entry and competition

Responses	Investor protection	Impact on entry/competition
Capital requirements	Poor, unless when set at very high levels	Significant entry barrier
Custody/depositary	Reduce risks of fraud and operational failures	Low if markets are competitive
Disclosure/auditing	Promote awareness of risks	Enhance competition and entry
Insurance	Protection against large losses	High for small firms
Compensation schemes	High if schemes are generous	Subsidize entry and competition

private insurers to offer standard contracts equivalent to those of compensation schemes. Since systemic risks are not a substantial problem in asset management, the market failures that cause insurance contracts to fail in relation to bank deposits should not be present in asset management. The feasibility of having privately supplied standard compensation contracts is worth further investigation.

Table 2.2 summarizes the impacts of different responses on investor protection and entry/competition.

2.6 AN EVALUATION OF ALTERNATIVE FORMS OF INVESTOR PROTECTION

This book has emphasized the important interaction between institutional structure and forms of regulation. It has argued that investor protection comes both from specific institutional arrangements and from formal systems of regulation. In particular, in Section 2.3 of this chapter, four forms of investor protection were identified: two institutional and two regulatory in nature. The institutional forms were the reputational capital of firms that are parts of groups (of which asset management in Germany is the best example), and the protection that custodians and trustees provide in mutual funds (for example, in France). The regulatory forms were the promotion of private contracting through rules regarding information disclosure, auditing, and enforcement (as observed in the USA), and public contracting by regulatory bodies through capital requirements, conduct-of-business rules, and compensation funds (which is particularly significant in the UK). Clearly, these distinctions are highly stylized, and there are elements of all forms of institutions and regulation in all countries. However, they serve to illustrate the different institutional and regulatory responses. The key question that they raise is what is their comparative performance?

This chapter began by stating that the goals of regulation are to promote financial stability and to provide investor protection while avoiding adverse effects on competition—in particular, the entry of new firms. It has been argued that, for the most part, systemic risk is not relevant to asset management firms, but significant potential problems have been highlighted that may be created by the growth of guaranteed products offered by asset managers. The risk to asset managers associated with guaranteed products is mitigated to some extent in France, where guarantees are only offered by institutions external to the asset manager, such as credit institutions specially authorized by the regulator to fulfil this function. These activities are subsequently regulated. Leaving this aside, the different systems of regulation should be judged against two benchmarks: the degree to which they provide effective investor protection; and their impact on competition.

The private contracting system of the USA emphasizes the operation of markets through information disclosure and auditing. It encourages high levels of entry and competition, but relies on the legal system to enforce contracts through private as well as public litigation. It is therefore essentially a system of caveat emptor.

The public contracting system of the UK offers investors greater protection through a compensation scheme, but at the expense of limiting competition through the imposition of capital requirements and conduct-of-business rules. The scale of protection is therefore primarily determined by the size of the compensation scheme, and the effect on competition by the size of capital requirements and the nature of conduct-of-business rules. The results of the survey confirm that the cost of capital varies greatly across firms, indicating that the costs of an extra unit of capital are potentially high for some companies.

The parent-firm system of Germany places less reliance on public agencies; to that extent, it is less interventionist than the UK. However, it limits entry to firms that have access to substantial amounts of capital and are in general parts of large organizations. So long as asset management firms have deep pockets on which to draw, and can rely

Table 2.3. The characterization of regulatory systems in the USA, Continental Europe, and the UK

System	Degree of investor protection	Entry and product variety
Private contracting (USA)	Low—caveat emptor	High
Parent firms, mutual funds (France, Spain, and Germany)	Medium	Medium
Public contracting (UK)	Determined by compensation fund	Determined by capital requirements

on the reputation of the parent firm to bail them out in the event of failure, they offer investors high degrees of protection.

Where investments occur largely through mutual funds, as in France and Spain, protection comes primarily from 'depositaires' or 'depositarios', respectively. Where the parent-firm system is not dominant, there is a greater potential for entry, but also greater possibility of contractual disagreements between asset managers, custodians, and trustees, as illustrated in the UK case study in Chapter 10. Investors may therefore be exposed to greater risks than under the parent-firm system.

A summary of the forms of protection in different countries, the degree of investor protection they provide, and their effect on entry and competition is provided in Table 2.3.

2.7 SUMMARY

There are several implications of the results reported elsewhere in this study.

Attempts to harmonize regulatory rules across countries are inappropriate. Regulation and institutional arrangements are complementary. So long as the pronounced institutional differences that have been reported in this study persist, then so, too, should different forms of regulation.

There is, in general, a trade-off between investor protection and competition, as suggested at the beginning of this book. High levels of investor protection can be achieved through large compensation funds and high capital requirements, but at the expense of competition, product variety, and entry. Responses to the survey suggest that the costs of higher capital requirements are large for some firms and could therefore have significant effects on competition.

The market failures that occur in asset management are different from those that occur in banks. They arise from information asymmetries and fraud, not in general from systemic risks. They should be corrected directly by a combination of disclosure, auditing, enforcement, insurance, custody, and trustees, rather than indirectly through capital requirements.

The development of insurance markets, greater clarity of investor protection in custody arrangements, auditing, and enforcement through the courts are all key components of a move towards a more market-oriented system. The creation of an integrated financial market in Europe would benefit from such a development, but requires careful consideration of the way in which information, insurance, and legal structure can be strengthened.

A move towards raising capital requirements would be counterproductive. It would discourage the necessary development of markets in information and insurance, as well as having a direct impact on competition and entry. High capital requirements may place the European asset management industry at a competitive disadvantage in relation to other countries, most notably the USA. Unless capital requirements are set at unrealistically high levels, they could also provide a false sense of security.

CHAPTER

3

Summary of Research Findings

The purpose of this book is to identify the operational risks inherent in the asset management business and to evaluate the role of capital in mitigating these risks.

3.1 THE NATURE OF THE ASSET MANAGEMENT BUSINESS (CHAPTERS 4 AND 9)

There are significant differences in the nature of asset management businesses across Continental Europe, as well as between the UK and Continental Europe, and between the USA and Europe.

In France, collective investment schemes dominate, but mandates are growing in importance. In Germany, insurance companies have been the largest investor group, but investment funds are catching up. In Italy and Spain, collective schemes and asset management by banks are the largest investor groups. In the Netherlands and Ireland, pension funds and life insurance funds dominate.

In the UK and the USA, pension funds and life assurance companies are the largest investor groups.

Japanese and US equities account for about one-half of equity and bond transactions by European asset managers. European equities and bonds account for most of the remainder, with emerging markets accounting for around 5 per cent of equity transactions and 1 per cent of bond transactions.

3.2 INDUSTRY STRUCTURE (CHAPTERS 5 AND 9)

There are substantial differences in the ownership of asset management businesses across countries.

In Continental Europe and Ireland, asset management is dominated by banks and insurance companies. Levels of concentration are high and increasing in many countries.

In the UK and the USA, concentration levels are modest and there is a larger number of small investment management firms.

3.3 REGULATORY FRAMEWORK (CHAPTERS 6 AND 7)

Capital requirements are broadly similar in European countries. In the USA, there are no federal capital requirements imposed on investment advisers and state capital requirements are small.

There are custody requirements in all European countries under consideration. In the USA, an investment adviser with the custody of clients' assets is obliged to supply the client with additional information.

There are greater disclosure requirements in the USA than in Europe.

There is a high level of enforcement in the USA through auditing, administrative proceedings, and civil actions.

Compensation schemes have been implemented in most European countries under consideration. There is no compensation scheme in the USA.

An investment company operating in the USA is required to have insurance against larceny and embezzlement; this is not the case for European firms. There is mutual insurance available in the USA that provides a significant fraction of the company assets.

In Europe, regulators emphasize capital requirements, custody, and compensation schemes to a varying extent. The US regulators focus on disclosure, auditing, insurance, and enforcement.

3.4 OPERATIONAL RISKS IN THE ASSET MANAGEMENT BUSINESS (CHAPTERS 9 AND 10)

Most asset managers offer discretionary services to their investors, although a significant fraction in Germany and Italy operate on an advice-only basis.

There has been a substantial growth in guaranteed products offered by asset managers.

Most transactions are conducted with firms outside of groups.

The main operational risks to which investors are exposed are from misdealing and breach of client guidelines.

The case study reported in Chapter 10 illustrates how potential failures of internal control systems can create large losses.

Operational risks arising from new business acquisition were significant.

Losses arising from fraud can have a significant financial impact.

The largest operating loss reported by the sample of firms was €7.2 m arising from misdealing. This corresponded to 17 per cent of annual operating expenditure (OPEX) of the firm in question. The next largest loss was €3 m arising from a breach of client guidelines, corresponding to 7.5 per cent of annual expenditure.

For the most part, losses incurred have involved average amounts of €1.3 m. The interviews indicated that these occasional losses could be up to €20 m in a particular year.

Total losses identified for the whole sample amounted to approximately €40 m.

3.5 FORMS OF PROTECTION IN ASSET MANAGEMENT (CHAPTERS 9 AND 10)

Most losses are financed out of internal profits.

About 29 per cent of firms that were parts of groups had specific guarantees from their parents.

In all the countries analysed, separation between client assets and firms' own assets is widespread. Furthermore, the survey indicated an increasing degree of non-group custodianship. In the UK, for example, the median proportion of assets held by non-group custodians is 100 per cent. The median for all countries in the sample is 85 per cent.

The case study reported in Chapter 10 raises questions about the extent to which the role of trustees/custodians can provide adequate investor protection.

Approximately 50 per cent of the sample of firms had indemnity insurance, and 37 per cent had employee fidelity and fraud insurance.

Claims on insurance were primarily as a result of misdealing and failure to collect income.

Insurance may be appropriate for certain large exposures to fraud. However, concerns were expressed about the reliability of recouping losses from insurers.

Most firms hold capital well in excess of regulatory requirements. The mean ratio between the actual to the required capital was 5.7 and the median was 2.7.

The average cost of raising capital cited by firms was 15 per cent, but there was a wide range across the sample, from 7 to 30 per cent.

3.6 MARKET FAILURES IN THE ASSET MANAGEMENT BUSINESS (CHAPTERS 9 AND 11)

The market failures arising in the asset management business are different from those in banks. Asset management firms do not in general take own positions. Where asset managers took own positions in the sample of firms, the median value of capital at risk was €10 m. The financial risks that justify the imposition of capital requirements in banks are less relevant to asset management firms.

The main market failures that arise in asset management come from imperfect information on the part of investors and risks of fraud. Capital requirements do not provide an appropriate correction for either form of market failure.

One caveat is the growth in guaranteed products over the last few years. Careful consideration needs to be given to the financial exposure created by these innovations, including consideration of which parties bear the risks arising from this exposure. Capital would play a role if risks of such products were inadequately hedged.

3.7 ALTERNATIVE FORMS OF PROTECTION (CHAPTER 2)

Regulation should seek to neutralize the market failures in asset management in much more direct ways than capital. Alternatives considered in the study are custody, information disclosure, enforcement, auditing, compensation schemes, insurance, and conduct-of-business rules.

Countries employ these forms of regulation to varying degrees. There is a close complementarity between the form of regulation and institutional arrangements in different countries. Investor protection is provided in some countries primarily through institutional arrangements, and, in others, through formal systems of regulation.

The USA emphasizes disclosure, auditing, insurance, and enforcement.

The UK emphasizes capital requirements, conduct-of-business rules, and compensation schemes.

Investor protection in Continental Europe comes primarily from a combination of capital requirements, conduct-of-business rules, and institutional arrangements—in particular, the deep pockets and reputational capital of parent firms.

There has been a growth of independent firms, in particular those managing mutual funds, in some Continental European countries. Investor protection relies considerably on the role of the independent custodian and trustee.

These forms of institutional and regulatory protection offer investor protection and affect competition and entry to quite varying degrees.

The US system promotes the greatest degree of competition and entry in asset management. However, it relies in large part on caveat emptor and the operation of the judicial system in enforcing contracts at low cost.

The UK system is more prescriptive. Under this system, the degree of investor protection and effects on competition depend on the size of the compensation scheme and on the level of entry barriers created by regulatory rules, including capital requirements.

The traditional reliance on the deep pockets of parent firms in Continental Europe provides high levels of investor protection, but at the cost of serious barriers to entry in some countries.

The emerging institutional solutions (through, for example, mutual funds) open up markets to more competition. However, the case-study analysis suggests that protection from custodian and trustees may in practice be limited by the complexity of contractual relations between the parties. The effectiveness of this form of protection is therefore yet to be clarified.

The use of insurance markets in the asset management business is more prevalent in the USA than in Europe. The more highly developed insurance markets in the USA may reflect the greater degree of information disclosure.

3.8 THE CURRENT REGULATORY PROPOSALS (CHAPTER 8)

The Basel proposals on capital requirements are related to operational risk.

There are three measures of operational risk: a single indicator based on income; a standardized approach dividing banks into standardized units and providing indicators for each unit based on a beta factor; and an internal measurement approach, where the bank determines a probability and potential size of loss, and capital requirements are based on expected sizes of losses.

The effect of these requirements on capital is uncertain and dependent on the size of assets under management.

Based on simulations dividing firms into four size categories, capital requirements are similar to current requirements in two categories, higher in one and smaller in the fourth.

There is a proposal to include insurance against operational losses.

3.9 REGULATORY CONVERGENCE (CHAPTER 2)

In framing regulatory rules in Europe, the European Commission should be sensitive to the significant differences in regulatory and institutional arrangements that exist across countries.

Attempts to harmonize regulation may not be appropriate and may be counterproductive. For example, harmonization of compensation schemes may, in the face of different institutional structures, distort competition rather than promote level playing fields.

Instead, greater integration of financial markets may be more effect- ively realized through improved information and disclosure, auditing (including by private agencies), and enforcement of contracts. Consideration should also be given to improving the functioning of insurance markets.

4

Assets under Management:
Europe and the USA

This chapter begins by comparing the assets under management for eight countries—France, Germany, Ireland, Italy, the Netherlands, Spain, the UK, and the USA. Detailed country-by-country analyses follow.

4.1 CROSS-COUNTRY COMPARISON

Global assets under management during 1999 have been estimated at a value of €33 trillion (British Invisibles, 2000). This represents an increase of almost 95 per cent since 1995, when the same source estimated global assets under management to be over €17 trillion. In 1999, pension funds, insurance companies, and mutual funds accounted for roughly equal proportions of total assets. Assets managed on behalf of private individuals have been estimated to be worth €23 trillion. There may be some overlap between private wealth and institutional assets under management; for example, private individuals may have invested in pension funds.

Table 4.1 reports the assets managed on behalf of pension funds, insurance companies, and mutual funds for the seven European countries and the USA in 1999. This table allows a comparison between the size and the main components of the asset management industries for these countries. Figures for assets managed on behalf of private clients are reported in subsequent sections.

Table 4.1. The assets under management for eight countries, 1999 (€ billion)

Country	Pension funds	Insurance companies[1]	Mutual funds
France	66	830	705
Germany	129	673	515
Ireland	47	32	150
Italy	65	169	412
Netherlands	397	220	83
Spain	32	62	219
UK	1270	1266	345
Total	2006	3252	2429
USA	7225	2403	6388

Note:
[1] The latest available figures arc from 1998, and include life and non-life insurance companies.

Sources: InterSec Research Corp., CCF Charterhouse, OECD, Investment Company Institute, Fédération Européenne des Fonds et Sociétés D'Investissement (FEFSI), Association Française de la Gestion Financière (AFG–ASFFI), Inverco, De Nederlandsche Bank, Central Bank of Ireland, and British Invisibles (2000).

Funds managed on behalf of institutional clients (pension funds and insurance companies) represent a higher proportion of total assets managed in the UK. Pension funds in the UK are at least four times larger than any of the other European countries considered, and account for 65 per cent of the total pension fund assets for the European countries considered. Germany, Ireland, Italy, and France have comparatively low levels of pension fund assets. Therefore, in this case, part of the reason for the difference in the sizes of pension fund assets may be the different sizes of the industries.

The difference between assets managed for insurance companies in Europe is less pronounced than that for pension funds. Assets managed for insurance companies in the UK account for a significantly lower proportion (40 per cent) of the European total when compared to that for the UK pension fund assets. Of the total for the seven European countries, the assets of insurance companies in Germany represent 21 per cent and of those in France 26 per cent. Furthermore, approximately the same value of insurance companies' assets is managed in the USA and Europe.

However, the European ranking, by size, of pension funds' and insurance companies' assets is reversed when mutual funds are considered. According to Table 4.1, France, Italy, and Germany dominate the market for mutual funds of the seven European countries considered. In these countries, mutual funds are typically managed by institutions such as banks, insurance companies, or other financial conglomerates. However, in the UK, the mutual fund market is largely based on retail business, which is relatively small-scale. The mutual fund market is over two and one half times larger in the USA than the total for the European countries reported in Table 4.1.

To conclude, the structure of the asset management business differs appreciably across countries, particularly between the UK, with its emphasis on pension funds and insurance companies, and Continental Europe, with its emphasis on mutual funds and, in some countries, such as France and Germany, on insurance companies.

The following sections analyse in detail the asset management industry in each of the countries listed in Table 4.1. Three aspects are detailed for each country analysis:

- total assets under management;
- sources of assets under management; and
- portfolio allocation of assets under management.

Consistency across countries has been maintained as far as possible. In particular, country-by-country statistics report assets managed for pension funds and insurance companies for all countries. However, in Germany, there is only a breakdown of assets into insurance companies and investment funds available, but not pension funds. Furthermore, there are differences in the breakdown of statistics obtained for each country, which have led to more detailed disaggregation in particular countries.

4.2 FRANCE

The French asset management industry mainly consists of portfolio management companies (sociétés de gestion de portefeuille) and UCITS management firms (sociétés de gestion d'organismes de placement collectif en valeurs mobilière, OPCVMs). The former undertake the management of financial assets on behalf of third parties, including all types of discretionary asset management, as well as the management of UCITS. The latter exclusively manage UCITS.

UCITS, or OPCVMs, are as defined in the 1985 European UCITS Directive. In France, they are divided into two main categories that differ with respect to their legal form: SICAVs (sociétés d'investissement à capital variable), which are open-ended investment companies, and 'fonds communs de placement', which have a contractual form and represent 'co-ownerships' of transferable securities.

In 1998 and 1999, portfolio and UCITS companies managed about 95 per cent of total assets in France. The remaining 5 per cent are managed by investment service providers, which offer a range of investment services and do not have asset management as their main activity.

Table 4.2 reports that, by the end of 1999, portfolio and UCITS management companies managed total assets equal to €1223 billion. This represents an increase of over 18 per cent on the previous year and almost 63 per cent on 1997. The growth in the assets managed by portfolio management companies is responsible for this increase in the total assets managed. As shown in Table 4.2, in 1998 and 1999 the share of assets managed by portfolio management companies increased relative to that of companies which exclusively manage UCITS.

AFG–ASFFI provides a breakdown between mandated portfolio management and UCITS management for the years 1996–9 (Table 4.3). While mandates made up only 13 per cent of assets in 1996, their share increased to 40 per cent in 1999. This is largely a consequence of the spin-off of asset management activities by insurance companies.

The net assets of institutional investors, such as OPCVMs, life insurance companies, and pension funds, are reported in Table 4.4.

Table 4.2. The total assets under management by portfolio and UCITS companies, 1997–9

	1997		1998		1999	
	€ bn	%	€ bn	%	€ bn	%
Portfolio management companies	662.2	88.2	983.3	95.1	1158.3	94.7
UCITS management companies	88.5	11.8	50.3	4.9	65.0	5.3
Total	750.8	100.0	1033.6	100.0	1223.3	100.0

Source: Commission des Opérations de Bourse (COB).

Table 4.3. The total assets under management, 1996–9 (€ billion)

	1996		1997		1998		1999	
	€ bn	%	€ bn	%	€ bn	%	€ bn	%
For individual mandates	65	12.7	328	40.3	443.8	42.9	483.6	39.5
For UCITS	446	87.3	485.4	59.7	589.8	57.1	739.7	60.5
Total	511	100.0	813.4	100.0	1033.6	100.0	1223.3	100.0

Sources: AFG–ASFFI and COB.

Table 4.4. The net assets of institutional investors,[1] 1994–9 (€ billion)

	1994		1995		1996		1997		1998		1999	
	€ bn	%	€ bn	%	€ bn	%	€ bn	%	€ bn	%	€ bn	%
Insurance companies	395	45.5	466	50.4	555	52.6	647	36.4	743	40.7	821	39.4
OPCVMs	425	48.9	410	44.3	446	42.3	485	27.3	573	31.4	708	34.0
Individual discretionary mandates	n/a[2]	n/a	n/a	n/a	n/a	n/a	589	33.1	444	24.3	484	23.2
Pension funds	49	5.6	49	5.3	54	5.1	58	3.3	64	3.5	71	3.4
Total net assets	869		925		1055		1779		1824		2084	

Notes:
[1] All categories reported at market value.
[2] In this and subsequent tables, n/a means that the information is not available.
Sources: AFG-ASFFI and Fédération Française des Sociétés d'Assurances.

According to Table 4.4, over the period 1994–9, the net assets managed for these three groups of investors more than doubled. Each category of investor experienced growth. This is particularly so for insurance companies, whose assets doubled over the period under consideration. The assets of OPCVMs and pension funds increased by 67 and 45 per cent, respectively.

In 1994, the assets of OPCVMs accounted for 49 per cent of the total net assets reported in Table 4.4. However, by 1999 this proportion had declined as a result of the increasing significance of individual discretionary mandates.

Table 4.5 provides a breakdown of the total UCITS assets by investment fund category during 1997–9. Although money market funds, and bond and debt security funds, still remained important, there was a sharp rise in balanced funds and especially in equity funds. Together, equity-related funds represented approximately 55 per cent of the total assets. Balanced funds invested in a mixture of securities, mainly including equities (55 per cent). The increase in equity funds was driven mainly by the strong performance of the main equity markets, but it also reflects positive net inflows. If adjusted by the French CAC40 index, the growth in net equity funds was as high as 9 per cent in 1998. Note also the presence of guaranteed funds accounting for approximately 5 per cent of assets held through UCITS in 1999. These funds invested an average of 60 per cent of their assets in equities in 1999. Between 1997 and 1999, they declined slightly, despite an increase in 1998.

Table 4.5. The breakdown of total UCITS assets by fund category, 1997–9

	1997		1998		1999		Change	
	€ bn	%	€ bn	%	€ bn	%	€ bn	%
Money market mutual funds	155.4	34.2	157.4	29.5	178.8	27.4	23.4	15.1
Bond and debt security funds	123.5	27.2	132.3	24.8	122.1	18.7	−1.4	−1.1
Sub-total	278.8	61.4	289.7	54.2	300.9	46.2	22.1	7.9
Balanced funds	86.3	19.0	122.4	22.9	163.7	25.1	77.4	89.7
Equity funds	63.8	14.0	91.3	17.1	153.6	23.6	89.8	140.8
Sub-total	150.0	33.0	213.7	40.0	317.3	48.7	167.3	111.5
Funds carrying minimum performance guarantee or capital loss hedge	25.6	5.6	31	5.8	33.5	5.1	7.9	30.9
Total	454.5	100.0	534.4	100.0	651.7	100.0	197.3	43.4

Source: AFG–ASFFI (1998), forthcoming for 1999.

Table 4.6. Portfolio allocation of OPCVMs

	1994		1995		1996		1997		1998		1999	
	€ bn	%	€ bn	%	€ bn	%	€ bn	%	€ bn	%	€ bn	%
Deposits	37.6	9.2	47.1	12.1	42.8	10.1	49.9	11.0	48.1	9.0	34.0	5.2
Money market instruments	103.1	25.3	85.1	21.9	84.6	20.0	73.5	16.2	77.3	14.5	85.9	13.2
Bonds and other fixed-revenue securities	214.1	52.5	205.6	52.8	223.6	53.0	222.8	49.1	256.9	48.1	279.6	42.9
Equities	52.7	12.9	52.5	13.5	68.5	16.2	106.7	23.5	154.8	29.0	258.4	39.6
Other	0.5	0.1	−0.9	−0.2	2.5	0.6	1.2	0.3	−2.6	−0.5	−5.7	−0.9
Total net assets	408.0		389.4		422.0		454.1		534.5		652.2	

Source: AFG–ASFFI.

The portfolio allocation of OPCVMs is reported in Table 4.6.

According to Table 4.6, during the period 1994–9, the proportion of portfolios invested in deposits, money market instruments, and other securities declined, although this was offset by an increase in the proportion of portfolios held in equity.

To summarize, in France, UCITS have been the prominent investment vehicle in the past, but mandates are rapidly increasing in importance. Although not the largest investment category, equity funds have grown sharply in significance.

4.3 GERMANY

Assets under management in Germany are held through collective investment schemes (investment funds) or mandates, or are funds of insurance companies. No details are available for mandated asset management, except in the survey analysis reported in Chapter 9. Table 4.7 reports the financial assets of insurance companies and investment funds under management during the period 1994–8. By the end of 1998, the combined financial assets of German insurance companies and investment funds were €1566 billion. The largest investor group was insurance companies; in 1998 they accounted for 65 per cent of total assets under management. However, over the last five years, the share of investment funds has been increasing, from 27 per cent in 1994 to 35 per cent in 1998. Investment funds are open-ended, and are either public (retail) funds or special (institutional) funds, as further explained below. By 1998, investment funds held €553 billion of financial assets.

The figures reported in Table 4.7 include the pension fund assets. The insurance statistics contain life assurance contracts and pension funds provided by insurance companies ('Pensionskassen'), which, in Germany, have been one of the traditional ways to provide privately for retirement. They also contain the pension contracts entered by employers on behalf of their employees. In addition, some pension assets are counted as investment fund assets. Since 1998, investment funds can take the form of pension investment funds (AS-Fonds), as shown in Table 4.7.

Table 4.8 shows the allocation of portfolios, as recorded in the Bundesbank's *Financial Accounts*. While funds placed in banks and bonds were the largest classes of asset held in 1994, with each asset type accounting for 28 per cent, by 1998 their share had fallen relative to

Table 4.7. The financial assets of German institutions, 1994–8 (€ billion)

	1994		1995		1996		1997		1998	
	€ bn	%	€ bn	%	€ bn	%	€ bn	%	€ bn	%
Insurance companies	615.1	72.6	681.6	71.6	758.4	69.9	915.7	67.8	1012.9	64.7
Investment funds	232.5	27.4	270.6	28.4	327.4	30.1	435.0	32.2	553.0	35.3
Total	847.6	100.0	952.1	100.0	1085.8	100.0	1350.7	100.0	1565.8	100.0

Source: Bundesbank (1994–8).

Table 4.8. Portfolio allocation by asset, 1994–8 (€ billion)

	1994		1995		1996		1997		1998	
	€ bn	%	€ bn	%	€ bn	%	€ bn	%	€ bn	%
Funds placed with banks	236.3	27.9	268.7	28.2	304.8	28.1	333.9	24.7	361.1	23.1
Money market paper	4.1	0.5	4.0	0.4	2.7	0.2	2.5	0.2	2.7	0.2
Bonds	235.9	27.8	273.2	28.7	304.8	28.1	339.5	25.1	382.2	24.4
Investment fund certificates	70.7	8.3	83.3	8.7	106.8	9.8	148.3	11.0	190.0	12.1
Equity	147.9	17.5	160.1	16.8	199.1	18.3	351.6	26.0	448.3	28.6
Other	152.7	18.0	162.9	17.1	167.5	15.4	174.8	12.9	181.5	11.6
Total	847.6	100.0	952.1	100.0	1085.8	100.0	1350.7	100.0	1565.8	100.0

Note: Funds placed in banks are mainly held in the form of time deposits. Investment fund certificates are shares in investment funds held by insurance companies.

Source: Bundesbank (1998).

corporate equity. The share of corporate equity in total financial assets rose from 17.5 per cent in 1994 to 29 per cent in 1998, while that of funds in banks and bonds fell to 23 and 24 per cent, respectively. Thus, by 1998, the largest class of asset held was equities, followed by bonds and funds placed in banks. Part of the increase in equity is due to the performance of the equity market, which doubled in value from 1994 to 1998. However, it also reflects a strong net inflow, particularly in 1997 and 1998.

However, the portfolio allocation differs widely between the insurance companies and investment funds (as shown in Table 4A.5). In 1998, the largest asset class held by insurance companies was funds placed in bank deposits (32 per cent), with the majority being held in the form of time deposits. Investment funds allocated 50 per cent of their portfolio to bonds; the balance is largely held in equities (39 per cent). This is significantly larger than the fraction of corporate equity held by insurance companies (23 per cent).

Investment funds are also more internationally diversified than insurance companies. In 1998, about 36 per cent of securities held by investment funds were overseas issues, compared with only 5 per cent for insurance companies.

In Germany, investment funds may qualify as UCITS, as defined in the 1985 UCITS directive. They fall into one of two categories:

- public funds ('Publikumsfonds'), which are retail funds that issue shares to the general public and to an unlimited number of investors.

Table 4.9. The breakdown of investment funds, 1998

Type	Public funds			Special funds		
	no.	€ bn	%	no.	€ bn	%
Securities funds of which:	718	144.1	69.68	4222	369.2	99.18
Equity-based	296	67.5	32.63	300	38.9	10.44
Bond-based	262	64.0	30.95	1203	104.6	28.09
Mixed	160	12.6	6.10	2719	225.8	60.65
Money market funds	39	18.2	8.81	2	0.1	0.03
Real estate funds	17	44.1	21.32	21	2.9	0.79
Pension funds (AS-Fonds)	31	0.4	0.19	—	—	—
Total	805	206.8	100.00	4245	372.3	100.00

Note: Mixed funds hold both equity and fixed-income securities. All funds are open-ended investment funds. Note that the combined total differs from the value of total fund assets in Table 4.6.

Source: Bundesbank (1998).

In 1998, there were 805 public funds with a value of €207 billion (see Table 4.9);

- special funds ('Spezialfonds'), which are institutional funds that issue shares to a limited group of investors (mainly banks, insurance companies, non-financial companies, etc.). In 1998, the value of the 4245 special funds amounted to €372 billion (see Table 4.9).

Under the Third Capital Markets Promotion Act, the existing range of investment fund types was broadened. In particular, since 1998, investment funds can take the form of pension investment funds (AS-Fonds), which are similar to defined-contribution pension schemes. With AS-Fonds, investors pay a certain amount each month for a minimum of 18 years or until the investor's sixtieth birthday. At the end of the savings period, investors have the choice to redeem all shares or receive monthly annuities over a longer period of time. Thus, these investment funds are solely aimed at providing for retirement. At the end of 1998, 31 AS-Fonds had been registered with a volume of €0.4 billion (see Table 4.9). These AS-Fonds are expected to grow relative to the life assurance contracts and pension funds offered by insurance companies, which have been the traditional way to provide privately for retirement.

Table 4.9 breaks down the total assets of domestic investment funds by fund category. In 1998, most were either equity- or bond-based, or mixed securities funds. Mixed funds invest in both equities and fixed-income securities. About 70 per cent of all public funds are securities funds. The fraction of special funds in securities is even higher, at 99 per cent. In particular, mixed funds account for 60 per cent of special funds. This is because these are popular for insurance companies, which are the largest customers of institutional funds. Insurers prefer a mix of investment type (equity, bonds, property), which can be tailored to match the different types of the insurers' liabilities. Real estate and money market funds are primarily public funds, and account for a share of 21 and 9 per cent, respectively.

In summary, insurance companies have been the largest investor group in Germany, but investment funds are growing in significance. The investment fund market is dominated by institutional funds rather than retail funds. Although bonds and bank finance have been the largest asset class for institutional investors, equity has grown in importance. The share of equity investment has been larger for investment funds than for insurance companies.

4.4 IRELAND

Assets under management for Irish residents and non-residents amounted to €180 billion in 1999. These assets, which represent almost the entire asset management industry, are controlled by 15 asset management companies. Table 4.10 shows the assets under management of members of the Irish Association of Investment Managers (IAIM) during the last decade.

Table 4.10 shows a substantial increase in assets under management of IAIM members during the last decade—by 1999, these were over seven times larger than those reported in 1992. It is interesting to compare the growth in assets under management with the level of growth in the Irish stock exchange.[1] Growth in the index of Irish shares (ISEQ) is reported in Table 4A.7 for 1990–2000.

The value of the ISEQ index is over four times higher in 2000 than in 1990. Taking account of this growth in the value of equities, it is not surprising that assets under management have grown substantially. Between 1992 and 1995, equities increased by 83 per cent, which is similar to the 87 per cent growth in assets under management for

---

[1] It should be noted, however, that the comparison is of limited relevance, given the increasing diversification of portfolios, of which domestic equity is just a small proportion.

Table 4.10. The assets under management of the IAIM members, 1992–9 (€ billion)

	1992	1995	1999
Pensions[1]			
Segregated	6.2	9.8	24.9
Endowment	1.6	2.7	5.1
Unit-linked	2.5	3.9	11.0
Unit trusts	0.9	2.0	5.8
Total	11.1	18.4	46.8
Charities/religious	0.6	0.8	1.6
Life funds[2]			
Unit-linked	3.3	3.8	7.7
Main fund/endowment	2.6	4.5	7.7
Shareholders	0.1	0.1	1.0
Total	6.0	8.4	16.4
Private clients			
Segregated	1.1	0.8	0.3
Unit trusts	0.2	0.5	1.0
Total	1.3	1.3	1.3
Tracker bonds	0	0	1.1
Other[3]	1.8	3.3	5.9
Total for Irish residents	20.9	32.2	73.1
Total (including non-residents)	24.7	39.0	179.7

Notes:
[1] Pension funds are classified as segregated, endowment, unit-linked, or unit trust. Segregated pension funds refer to funds that are managed for a single client and are therefore not pooled. Endowment funds refer to pension products sold by insurance companies. Unit-linked funds are also sold by insurance companies, and their value relates to that of the underlying fund. Typically, these funds do not offer a guarantee. Unit trust funds are similar to unit-linked funds, except that they are sold by companies other than insurance companies.
[2] Life funds consist of main funds, unit-linked funds, or shareholders' funds. Main funds are generally with-profits funds, or comprise life-cover premiums. Unit-linked life funds have the same characteristics as pension funds. Shareholders' funds refer to funds owned by the life company.
[3] The 'Other' category includes general insurance, corporates, and building-society funds.
Sources: IAIM and Datastream.

Irish residents over the same period. Furthermore, during the period 1995–9, the value of equities doubled, while total assets under management quadrupled (as reported in Table 4.10).

In 1992, assets managed on behalf of the resident clients accounted for more than 80 per cent of total assets under management (shown in Table 4.10). By 1999, this had fallen to approximately 40 per cent, indicating a substantial increase in assets managed on behalf of international clients.

In 1999, pension funds accounted for the largest proportion of assets under management (over 60 per cent of assets managed on behalf of residents). The substantial growth in total assets under management is reflected by growth in assets managed for the categories listed. Assets managed for institutions, such as pension funds, charities, and life funds, as well as tracker bonds,[2] have increased significantly, while those managed for private clients did not experience any growth over the past decade.[3] However, since retail funds include unit-linked, life, segregated funds, unit trusts, and tracker bonds, it is worth noting that the latter figures may also incorporate funds managed on behalf of private clients. Therefore, the growth of assets of private clients may be more pronounced than the above figures would suggest.

In conclusion, there has been substantial growth in the asset management industry in Ireland. Pension and life funds now dominate the business, while private client business remains modest.

4.5 ITALY

Table 4.11 reports the assets under management for Italy during 1994–9.

Table 4.11 shows that, in 1999, collective investment schemes accounted for 59 per cent of total assets under management. SICAVs are the company form of mutual funds, while open-ended funds represent the contractual form. Compared to open-ended funds, SICAVs represent a small proportion of total mutual funds. Following the terminology used by Assogestioni and the Bank of Italy, *asset management* is the second-largest category, accounting for 21 per cent of assets under management. In addition to managing the assets of funds, this category also contains the assets of 'managed accounts', which refers to accounts set up in banks or with securities houses on behalf of private clients. Decisions regarding the investment of monies in these accounts are made by the banks or securities houses on behalf of individual investors. Most of these companies have become società di gestione del risparmio, which are also permitted to manage assets on behalf of mutual funds.

---

[2] Statistics on assets managed on behalf of tracker bonds are not reported for other countries.

[3] Statistics on private clients are not included for other countries, with the exception of Italy.

Table 4.11. The assets under management for Italy, 1994–9 (€ billion)

	1994	1995	1996	1997	1998	1999
Mutual-ended funds and SICAV	69.6	69.1	109.0	202.9	395.6	538.9
Italian open-ended funds	67.2	65.5	101.7	189.7	371.7	474.6
Italian SICAV[1]	—	0.08	0.30	0.54	0.62	0.73
Italian closed-ended funds	—	—	—	—	0.46	1.4
Other[2]	2.4	3.5	7.0	12.6	22.8	62.2
Asset management net of investment in mutual funds and SICAV	—	—	130.0	159.0	187.5	192.6
Banks	68.7	70.0	96.8	134.5	191.5	222.4
Società di intermediazione mobiliare[3]	15.0	19.6	27.2	59.4	89.0	48.1
Investment companies[4]	9.7	9.7	10.6	—	—	91.3
Asset management total	93.5	99.4	134.6	193.9	280.5	361.9
Life insurance net of investment in mutual funds and SICAV	44.7	55.8	67.3	84.4	101.6	126.2
Life insurance total	45.0	56.3	67.6	85.2	106.1	134.9
Pension funds[5]	49.1	52.2	51.1	53.8	56.3	57.7
Total assets managed[6]	163.3	177.0	357.4	500.1	741.0	915.3

Notes:
[1] SICAV (società di investimento a capitale varabile) refers to an open-ended investment company that has its registered office in Italy and offers its shares to the public.
[2] Includes pre-1993 Luxembourg funds and post-1993 Luxembourg/Ireland funds.
[3] Securities houses.
[4] Before 1997 investment companies were known as trust companies.
[5] Pension funds include pre-1993 pension funds, which refer to defined-benefit pensions, and post-1993 defined-contribution pensions. The latter has been estimated by the Bank of Italy.
[6] Net of duplication in mutual funds and SICAV.

Sources: Assogestioni and Bank of Italy.

'Società di gestione del risparmio' can also manage assets on behalf of life insurance companies and pensions funds, which account for 14 and 6 per cent of total assets, respectively. Assets under management in 1999 were almost six times larger than those managed in 1994. This is a reflection of the growth in all categories identified in Table 4.11. However, by the end of the millennium, the market for mutual funds had grown to manage funds over seven times larger than those managed in 1994. These funds largely consist of open-ended funds. Conversely, pension funds have grown by only 2 per cent.

It is interesting to compare the growth in assets under management with that in the Milano Italia Borsa (MIBTEL) index of equities (reported in Table 4A.8).

Over the period 1994–9, the value of the MIBTEL index tripled. Taking this growth in the value of equities into account, it would appear that

Table 4.12. Portfolio allocation of mutual funds in Italy (%)[1]

	1994	1995	1996	1997	1998	1999
Net asset value (€ bn)	67.2	65.5	101.7	189.7	372.3	475.3
Domestic	60.4	68.3	75.0	64.7	63.9	46.8
Government bonds	41.8	50.2	62.2	52.0	51.9	34.2
Corporate bonds	3.0	3.2	2.4	2.1	1.4	2.6
Equities	15.6	14.9	10.4	10.6	10.6	10.0
Foreign	26.7	23.0	15.4	24.3	28.9	47.4
Bonds	11.1	8.9	7.4	13.6	17.2	21.8
Equities	15.6	14.1	8.0	10.7	11.7	25.6
Other	12.9	8.8	9.5	11.1	7.2	5.8

Note:
[1] Allocation for other assets not available.

Source: Assogestioni.

part of the growth experienced by assets under management could be explained by a general rise in the value of the stock market. However, other factors, such as an increase in the value of bonds, may also have affected growth in assets, because funds may invest in equities as well as bonds.

Table 4.12 reports the portfolio allocation of Italian open-ended mutual funds and SICAVs only. A similar breakdown is not available for the assets controlled by asset managers, life insurance companies, or pension funds. In 1999 the split between domestic and foreign assets was approximately equal. However, for the earlier period, domestic assets constituted over 60 per cent of portfolios. For domestic assets, government bonds are preferred to equities; for foreign assets, the split between bonds and equities has changed over the 1994–9 period. Figures for 1994 and 1995 show the larger proportion of asset holdings in equities. This scenario is reversed during 1997 and 1998, when a larger proportion of assets is held in the form of foreign bonds.

To conclude, there has been very rapid growth in asset management in Italy. This is particularly evident in the categories of mutual funds, SICAVs and *asset management* by banks. There has also been particularly fast growth in foreign bond and equity holdings.

4.6 THE NETHERLANDS

Limited data on asset management is available from the regulatory authorities in the Netherlands. Balance-sheet assets for insurance companies and pension funds supplied by the insurance regulator are shown in Table 4A.1, although it is not clear whether these are estimated at market or book value. Furthermore, they may incorporate assets other than financial assets.

Table 4.13 shows a breakdown of assets managed on behalf of institutions.

Table 4.13 shows that total balance-sheet assets of institutions almost doubled over the period 1994–9. This growth has been reflected in each of the categories considered above. In particular, assets of investment institutions and insurance companies have doubled over the period.

The majority of assets are managed on behalf of pension funds, although the proportion controlled by pension funds has declined over the period. In 1999, insurance companies controlled over 32 per cent of total balance-sheet assets, while investment companies accounted for more than 11 per cent.

Growth in assets under management may, in part, be attributable to an increase in the stock market (see Table 4A.9).

There have been significant annual increases in the value of the Dutch all-share index—by 1999, it had grown to over three times its 1994 value. This increase in the value of equities may explain some of the doubling of the value of assets under management reported in Table 4.13.

The aggregate allocation of the portfolios for the institutions identified above is reported in Table 4.14.

In 1994, capital market investments accounted for 95 per cent of total balance-sheet assets. Over the period 1994–9, this proportion remained

Table 4.13. The disaggregation of assets under management in the Netherlands[1] (€ billion)

	1994		1995		1996		1997		1998		1999	
	€ bn	%	€ bn	%	€ bn	%	€ bn	%	€ bn	%	€ bn	%
Insurance companies	103.7	28.0	116.0	28.5	132.7	28.8	156.3	29.5	215.4	33.0	233.8	32.4
Pension funds	225.7	60.9	244.2	59.9	274.1	59.5	309.1	58.3	365.7	56.0	404.1	56.1
Investment institutions	41.4	11.2	47.4	11.6	53.8	11.7	65.1	12.3	72.4	11.1	83.1[2]	11.5
Total	370.8		407.6		460.5		530.5		653.6		721.0	

Notes:
[1] Based on balance-sheet totals.
[2] Calculated as the average of the first two quarters of 1999 as a result of the start of a new series.
Sources: De Nederlandsche Bank (2000) and Datastream.

Table 4.14. Portfolio allocation (€ billion)

	1994		1995		1996		1997		1998		1999	
	€ bn	%	€ bn	%	€ bn	%	€ bn	%	€ bn	%	€ bn	%
Claims on monetary financial institutions (MFIs)	7.7	2.1	7.3	1.8	10.7	2.3	11.1	2.1	17.7	2.7	19.7	2.7
Short-term claims	5.5	1.5	4.5	1.1	6.2	1.4	6.9	1.3	6.8	1.0	7.8	1.1
Capital market investments												
Dutch securities	109.6	29.6	133.5	32.7	164.7	35.8	195.4	36.8	234.8	35.9	227.2	31.5
Bonds	70.2	18.9	83.9	20.6	95.6	20.8	105.8	19.9	122.0	18.7	114.4	15.9
Equities	39.4	10.6	49.6	12.2	69.2	15.0	89.6	16.9	112.9	17.3	112.8	15.6
Foreign securities	63.7	17.2	77.4	19.0	102.6	22.3	144.4	27.2	209.4	32.0	283.6	39.3
Bonds	18.0	4.9	21.3	5.2	32.2	7.0	47.9	9.0	77.3	11.8	100.0	13.9
Equities	45.6	12.3	56.1	13.8	70.4	15.3	96.5	18.2	132.1	20.2	183.5	25.5
Private loans	113.4	30.6	114.2	28.0	104.4	22.7	95.8	18.1	95.4	14.6	86.3	12.0
Mortgages	32.5	8.8	29.6	7.3	31.0	6.7	32.9	6.2	37.6	5.8	40.7	5.6
Real estate not for own use	33.6	9.1	34.7	8.5	37.8	8.2	40.3	7.6	46.8	7.2	49.5	6.9
Total capital market investments	352.9	95.2	389.4	95.5	440.5	95.7	508.7	95.9	624.0	95.5	687.3	95.3
Real estate for own use	1.0	0.3	0.9	0.2	0.9	0.2	0.8	0.1	0.5	0.1	0.6	0.1
Miscellaneous assets	3.9	1.0	5.5	1.3	2.2	0.5	3.0	0.6	4.6	0.7	5.6	0.8
Total	370.8		407.6		460.5		530.5		653.6		721.0	

Sources: De Nederlandsche Bank (2000) and Datastream.

relatively stable. The proportion of these capital market investments attributable to loans has declined over the period from over 30 per cent in 1994 to 12 per cent in 1999. This reduction in loans has been offset by an increase in Dutch and foreign securities. In particular, the latter accounted for 17 per cent of balance-sheet assets in 1994. Five years later, this percentage increased to almost 40 per cent, while Dutch securities amount to over 31 per cent of balance-sheet assets. In 1999, domestic bonds and equities are of the same importance. However, foreign equities account for 65 per cent of foreign securities.

To conclude, pension funds in the Netherlands account for over 50 per cent of total institutional assets under management. Investment institutions and insurance corporations have experienced growth. The components of portfolios have changed over the period 1994–9, with a shift away from loans to (foreign) equities and bonds.

4.7 SPAIN

The asset management industry in Spain consists mainly of UCIT management firms or 'Sociedades Gestoras de Instituciones de Inversión Colectiva', insurance companies, and 'Entidades Gestoras de Fondos de Pensiones', which primarily manage pension funds.

UCITs are divided into two main categories that differ with respect to their legal form:

• 'Sociedades de Inversión de Capital Variable', which are open-ended investment companies, and 'Sociedades de Inversión de Capital Fijo', which are closed-ended investment companies; and

• 'Fondos de Inversión', which have a contractual form and represent 'co-ownerships' of transferable securities.

The net assets of institutional investors, such as 'Instituciones de Inversión Colectiva' (IICs) (mutual funds and investment companies), life insurance companies, and pension funds, are reported in Table 4.15.

According to Table 4.15, over the period 1994–9, total net assets managed almost tripled. Each category of investor experienced growth. This is particularly the case for IICs, whose assets increased by more than three times during the period under consideration. The assets of insurance companies and pension funds doubled and tripled, respectively.

Table 4.15. The net assets of Spanish institutional investors,[1] 1994–9 (€ billion)

	1994		1995		1996		1997		1998		1999	
	€ bn	%	€ bn	%	€ bn	%	€ bn	%	€ bn	%	€ bn	%
Insurance companies	29	27	35	28	42	24	50	21	58	19	69	21
IICs	69	63	76	60	115	65	167	69	212	71	219	67
Individual discretionary mandates	1	1	2	2	2	1	3	1	4	1	5	1
Pension funds	10	9	13	10	17	10	22	9	27	9	32	11
Total net assets	109		126		176		242		301		325	

Note:
[1] All categories reported at market values.

Sources: Dirección General de Seguros y Fondos Pensiones (DGSFP), Comisión Nacional del Mercado de Valores (CNMV), and Inverco.

Table 4.16. The breakdown of total mutual fund assets by fund category, 1997–9

	1997		1998		1999		Change 1997–9	
	€ bn	%	€ bn	%	€ bn	%	€ bn	%
Money market mutual funds	61	38	51	25	42	20	−19	−31
Bond and debt security funds	49	30	53	26	42	20	−7	−14
Sub-total	110	68	104	51	84	40	−26	−45
Balanced funds	15	9	33	16	47	23	32	113
Equity funds	9	6	18	9	28	13	19	111
Sub-total	24	15	51	25	75	36	51	214
Funds carrying minimum performance guarantee or capital loss hedge	28	17	48	24	47	24	19	68
Total	162	100	203	100	206	100	44	27

Source: Inverco.

In 1994, the assets of IICs accounted for 63 per cent of the total net assets. This percentage increased to 67 per cent in 1999. Meanwhile, in 1999, insurance companies' assets accounted for 21 per cent of the total net assets, a decline of six percentage points on the 1994 level.

Table 4.16 provides a breakdown of total mutual funds' assets by investment fund category during 1997–9. Although money market funds, and bonds and debt security funds, still remained important, there was a sharp rise in balanced funds, and particularly in equity funds. Together, equity-related funds represented approximately 36 per cent of total assets. The increase in equity funds was driven mainly by strong performance of the main equity markets, but it also reflects

Table 4.17. Portfolio allocation of UCITs in Spain (%)

	1994	1995	1996	1997	1998	1999
Net asset value (€ bn)	69	76	115	165	212	219
Domestic	93	91	92	89	75	65
Government bonds	88	84	85	77	62	47
Corporate bonds	2	4	4	6	6	9
Equities	3	3	3	6	7	9
Foreign	3	2	2	5	17	28
Bonds	3	2	2	3	12	16
Equities	n/a	n/a	n/a	2	5	12
Other	4	7	6	6	8	7

Sources: CNMV and Inverco.

positive net inflows. Note also the strong presence of guaranteed funds, which accounted for approximately 24 per cent of assets held through UCITs in 1999. In the case of UCITs, government bonds account for a majority of holdings, but foreign bonds and equities have increased in significance (Table 4.17).

To summarize, in Spain, UCITs are the prominent investment vehicle. Although not the largest investment category, equity funds have grown sharply in significance.

4.8 THE UK

Table 4.18 reports the breakdown of assets under management for institutional clients in the UK, and shows how the relative components have grown over the period 1994–8.

The total assets under management for institutional clients, pension funds, and insurance companies in the UK increased by more than 70 per cent over the period 1994–8, largely owing to the growth in assets managed for insurance companies and unit trusts. Both these categories experienced growth in the funds under management of over 90 per cent.

There are two explanations for this significant increase in assets under management. First, there may be an increase in the number of funds or clients. Second, it may be a result of the increase in the stock market. The FTSE 100 index, a proxy of stock market movements, grew by 72 per cent from 1994 to 1998, which suggests that an increase in the

Table 4.18. The assets under management for the UK institutions, 1994–8 (€ billion)

	1994		1995		1996		1997		1998	
	€ bn	%	€ bn	%	€ bn	%	€ bn	%	€ bn	%
Insurance companies	512.6	41.6	586.0	43.0	698.0	43.3	993.6	44.3	1106.4	46.1
Investment trusts	50.3	4.1	51.4	3.8	63.6	4.0	77.2	3.4	67.0	2.8
Pension funds	563.0	45.7	602.5	44.2	690.6	42.8	962.9	42.9	996.7	41.5
Unit trusts	106.0	8.6	123.3	9.0	160.0	9.9	211.1	9.4	232.4	9.7
Total	1231.9	100	1363.1	100	1611.9	100	2244.8	100	2402.6	100

Sources: ONS (1994–8) and Datastream.

value of the stock market played some role in the substantial increase in assets under management (see Table 4A.10). However, because it consists of domestic equities, growth in this index can only partly explain the growth in assets under management, because assets can be invested in vehicles other than equities, such as bonds.

By 1998, insurance companies accounted for over 45 per cent of total assets managed in the UK (see Table 4.18). The percentage of assets managed for investment trusts and pension funds declined over the period under consideration. Furthermore, the proportion of assets managed on behalf of overseas pension funds and private clients fell between 1995 and 1999 (as shown in Tables 4A.2 and 4A.3).

Table 4.19 shows the allocation of assets managed on behalf of the UK institutions by type of asset.

The majority of assets under management are held in domestic assets. The division of total assets under management between domestic and overseas appears to have been stable over the period from 1994 to 1998. The substantial increase in assets under management has not led to a change in the relative market shares of domestic and overseas assets.

Most domestic and overseas assets comprise equity, although the proportion has declined over the period. The next-largest category is government securities.

Table 4A.4 reports investment in different categories of assets by institution. All institutions choose to hold the majority of their assets in equity, a trend that was reflected in the aggregate statistics in Table 4.19. Investment trusts hold more equity than any other institution.

To summarize, the UK asset management industry is dominated by insurance companies and pension funds. Mutual funds represent a modest proportion of the total assets under management. Despite a rapid rise in assets under management, the proportions allocated to

Table 4.19. Portfolio allocation of the UK institutions by asset, 1994–8 (€ billion)

	1994	1995	1996	1997	1998
Domestic					
Short-term assets	36.5	47.2	64.5	90.6	97.2
UK government securities	140.5	161.0	194.2	282.4	318.7
Corporate securities—equities	556.0	632.8	751.8	1083.4	1080.4
Corporate securities—other	45.5	55.1	63.4	97.7	124.7
Unit trust units	55.0	63.6	82.5	106.1	136.6
Property	76.6	67.6	73.7	97.5	100.2
Other	67.2	67.2	70.2	89.2	111.6
Sub-total	977.3	1094.5	1300.3	1847.0	1969.4
Overseas					
Short-term assets	2.3	2.3	2.8	5.0	3.5
Government securities	23.4	24.7	25.1	32.1	47.7
Corporate securities—equities	218.6	231.7	269.5	343.2	358.8
Corporate securities—other	9.0	7.3	11.7	15.3	20.4
Other	1.3	2.7	2.5	2.3	2.7
Sub-total	254.6	268.7	311.6	397.9	433.2
Total	1231.9	1363.1	1611.9	2244.8	2402.6

Sources: ONS (1994–8) and Datastream.

insurance companies, investment trusts, pension funds, and unit trusts have remained relatively constant since the mid-1990s. Domestic securities, particularly equities, dominate asset holdings.

4.9 THE USA

Table 4.20 contains information on the value of assets managed by asset managers, or 'investment advisers' as they are called in the USA that are registered with the Securities and Exchange Commission (SEC).[4] These figures do not include state-regulated investment advisers, which manage assets of less than $25 m.

Assets managed by the SEC-registered investment advisers almost trebled over the period 1995–2000 as reported in Table 4.20. This is partly explained by the significant growth in assets managed on behalf

---

[4] An investment adviser that generally manages assets greater than $25 m must register with the SEC. Those that generally manage less than this amount must register with the state.

Table 4.20. The assets managed by SEC-registered investment advisers (€ trillion)

Year	Total assets	Assets managed for investment companies
1995	8.1	2.2
1996	8.6	2.8
1997	11.7	4.1
1998	12.5	4.3
1999	16.7	5.9
2000[1]	22.6	9.2

Note:
[1] Estimate.

Sources: SEC Budget and Datastream.

of investment companies or mutual funds. In 2000, assets managed on behalf of investment companies are estimated to increase to be over four times their value in 1995. This increases the share of total assets managed by investment advisers from almost 30 to 40 per cent.

It is interesting to compare the growth in the value of assets under management with that in the stock exchange (see Table 4A.11).

The NYSE Composite index more than doubled from 1993 to 1999. Therefore, a significant part of the growth in assets under management identified in the table may be due to an overall increase in the stock market.

Total financial assets for various institutions are shown in Table 4.21. Since investment advisers are not required to provide information on their clients when registering with the SEC, no such information is available. The Board of Governors of the Federal Reserve System publishes 'Flow of Funds Accounts of the United States', which contains the totals for the industry. It is worth noting that these are not totals for investment advisers, but for the industry. Therefore, the divergence between the assets managed by investment advisers (as reported in Table 4.20) and total financial assets (reported in Table 4.21) may in part be explained by the exclusion of the US-registered investment advisers that are located outside the USA (see Table 4.21). There are approximately 350 registered investment advisers located outside the USA. The SEC statistics also include assets managed by foreign firms that have received authorization from the SEC to operate in the USA. In addition, state-registered investment advisers are included in Table 4.21 but not in Table 4.20.

Table 4.21. Total financial assets for the USA (€ billion)

	1994		1995		1996		1997		1998		1999[1]	
	€ bn	%	€ bn	%	€ bn	%	€ bn	%	€ bn	%	€ bn	%
Insurance companies	1995	30.3	2143	28.3	2419	26.6	3022	24.7	3048	23.3	3562	22.6
Life insurance companies	1462	22.2	1577	20.8	1802	19.8	2263	18.5	2304	17.6	2732	17.3
Other insurance companies	532	8.1	566	7.5	618	6.8	759	6.2	744	5.7	829	5.3
Pension funds	2863	43.5	3336	44.1	3986	43.7	5473	44.7	5828	44.5	6909	43.8
Private pension funds	1932	29.4	2216	29.3	2581	28.3	3477	28.4	3648	27.8	4314	27.4
State and local government employee retirement funds	930	14.1	1119	14.8	1405	15.4	1997	16.3	2180	16.6	2595	16.5
Mutual funds	1723	26.2	2085	27.6	2706	29.7	3762	30.7	4229	32.3	5294	33.6
Money market mutual funds	471	7.2	566	7.5	711	7.8	938	7.7	1106	8.4	1356	8.6
Mutual funds	1160	17.6	1416	18.7	1879	20.6	2690	21.9	3004	22.9	3790	24.0
Closed-end funds	92	1.4	103	1.4	116	1.3	134	1.1	119	0.9	148	0.9
Total	6581		7563		9111		12257		13105		15764	

Note:
[1] Calculated as the average of four quarters.

Source: Board of Governors of the Federal Reserve System (2000).

Table 4.22. Portfolio allocation (€ billion)

	1994		1995		1996		1997		1998		1999[1]	
	€ bn	%	€ bn	%	€ bn	%	€ bn	%	€ bn	%	€ bn	%
Checkable deposits and currency	14.8	0.22	11.9	0.16	16.2	0.18	24.0	0.20	22.2	0.17	19.7	0.13
Foreign deposits	12.3	0.19	15.1	0.20	18.5	0.20	20.9	0.17	25.5	0.19	42.7	0.27
Time and savings deposits	106.8	1.62	124.9	1.65	158.9	1.74	209.7	1.71	208.1	1.59	245.6	1.56
Money market fund shares	37.5	0.57	46.1	0.61	88.5	0.97	143.2	1.17	149.2	1.14	187.5	1.19
Security repurchase agreements (RPs)	150.2	2.28	175.1	2.31	192.4	2.11	245.6	2.00	261.0	1.99	290.2	1.84
Credit market instruments	3382.0	51.39	3540.5	46.81	3929.8	43.13	4738.6	38.66	4881.1	37.24	5695.2	36.13
Open market paper	262.8	3.99	295.8	3.91	341.7	3.75	464.9	3.79	519.6	3.96	656.7	4.17
US government securities	1249.5	18.99	1273.9	16.84	1359.1	14.92	1537.4	12.54	1537.8	11.73	1756.9	11.14
Treasury	653.0	9.92	649.9	8.59	690.9	7.58	762.5	6.22	710.5	5.42	793.0	5.03
Agency	586.4	8.91	615.6	8.14	659.1	7.23	765.9	6.25	819.6	6.25	956.0	6.06
Municipal securities	425.1	6.46	437.2	5.78	488.3	5.36	591.1	4.82	606.5	4.63	689.2	4.37
Corporate/foreign bonds	1006.4	15.29	1090.2	14.42	1272.8	13.97	1608.3	13.12	1696.1	12.94	1996.5	12.66
Policy loans	67.1	1.02	73.3	0.97	80.6	0.88	93.3	0.76	86.4	0.66	92.3	0.59
Mortgages	190.5	2.89	183.5	2.43	189.6	2.08	213.1	1.74	209.7	1.60	245.5	1.56
Corporate equities	2101.5	31.93	2737.2	36.19	3628.1	39.82	5406.9	44.11	6026.2	45.98	7478.3	47.44
Mutual fund shares	169.2	2.57	262.3	3.47	361.0	3.96	559.6	4.57	619.4	4.73	759.1	4.82
Trade receivables	41.5	0.63	43.8	0.58	45.9	0.50	53.9	0.44	51.3	0.39	60.4	0.38
Miscellaneous assets	565.0	8.59	606.3	8.02	672.1	7.38	854.6	6.97	861.6	6.57	985.9	6.25
Total	6580.8		7563.1		9111.3		12257.1		13105.6		15764.5	

Note:
[1] Calculated as the average of four quarters.

Source: Board of Governors of the Federal Reserve System (2000).

Throughout the 1994–9 period, private pension funds remained the largest category, despite a decline in their proportion of total financial assets of almost two percentage points, from 29.4 per cent in 1994 to 27.2 per cent in 2000. On aggregate, pension funds have fallen by less owing to the increasing significance of state and local government employee retirement funds. A comparison with the UK may be informative, where the proportion of pension funds in total assets under management has similarly declined, by four percentage points during the period between 1994 and 1998 (see Table 4.18).

The gap between private pension funds and mutual funds in the USA has been closing. The percentage of mutual funds has increased from 17.6 per cent in 1994 to 25.7 per cent in 2000. The proportion of mutual funds or unit trusts in the UK has also been growing, although mutual funds only account for 10 per cent of total assets under management in the UK, compared with almost 26 per cent in the USA. Total financial assets in 2000 are almost three times the size of the figure reported in 1994. This is a reflection of the growth in all the categories, but particularly in mutual funds.

The portfolio allocation of assets under management is reported in Table 4.22.

Credit market instruments, including government and corporate bonds, accounted for over 50 per cent of the portfolios in 1994. However, the proportion of assets invested in both the US government and corporate and foreign bonds has declined over the period 1994–9. Conversely, the proportion of portfolios held in equities has increased significantly over the period under consideration.

To conclude, pension funds are the largest component of the asset management business in the USA. Mutual funds have grown rapidly in significance. The overall portfolio allocation has shifted away from bonds and loans towards equities.

4.10 SUMMARY

The structure of the asset management business differs appreciably across countries. Particularly pronounced is the difference between the UK, with its emphasis on pension funds and insurance companies and a modest mutual fund business, and most of Continental Europe and the USA. Insurance companies have been dominant in

Germany and France. Mutual funds have been significant in France, Italy, and Spain and have grown rapidly in most Continental European countries and the USA. Assets held under mandates have grown significantly in France, and equities have risen in significance in most markets.

Appendix

4A.1 THE NETHERLANDS

Table 4A.1. The assets according to balance sheet in the Netherlands, 1989–98 (€ billion)

Year	Life insurance	Non-life insurance	Pension funds	Total
1989	71.8	10.4	154.5	236.7
1990	76.8	10.8	161.9	249.5
1991	86.9	11.4	174.5	272.7
1992	99.7	12.3	189.9	301.9
1993	116.6	13.8	217.4	347.8
1994	124.6	14.7	230.4	369.8
1995	143.1	18.0	256.6	417.7
1996	154.2	19.9	278.2	452.3
1997	150.1	22.2	314.9	487.1
1998	198.2	24.9	372.4	595.5

Sources: Verzekeringskamer and Datastream.

4A.2 THE UK

Table 4A.2. The assets under management for overseas institutional clients, 1996 and 1999 (€ billion)

	1996		1999	
	€ bn	%	€ bn	%
Insurance companies	83.95	20	90	18
Investment trusts	3.7	0.9	16.5	3
Pension funds	286.4	68	312	63
Unit trusts	44	11	73.6	15
Total	418		492	492

Source: British Invisibles (1997, 2000), 'Fund Management', City Business Series.

Table 4A.3. The assets under management for private clients, 1995–6 and 1998–9 (€ billion)

	1995–6		1998–9	
	€ bn	**%**	**€ bn**	**%**
UK	168	83	437	85
Overseas	35	17	75	15
Total	203		512	

Source: British Invisibles (1997, 2000), 'Fund Management', City Business Series.

Table 4A.4. Portfolio allocation of different institutions in 1998 (%)

	Insurance companies	Investment trusts	Pension funds	Unit trusts
Domestic				
Short-term assets	6.0	0	4.8	0
UK government securities	18.9	2.9	16.0	3.5
Corporate securities—equity	45.2	88.1	58.8	86.2
Corporate securities—other	10.2	5.1	1.4	8.6
Unit trust units	9.6	0.5	5.4	0
Property	6.8	0.2	4.3	0
Other	3.3	3.2	9.3	1.7
Overseas				
Short-term assets	1.1	0	1.1	0
Government securities	17.4	2.5	12.0	0
Corporate securities—equity	72.9	97.2	84.0	93.4
Corporate securities—other	8.6	0	3.0	3.3
Other	0	0.2	0	3.3

Source: ONS, 'Financial Statistics'.

4A.3 GERMANY

Table 4A.5. Portfolio allocation by asset in 1998 (%)

	Insurance companies	Investment funds
Funds placed with banks	31.8	7.1
Money market paper	—	0.5
Bonds	10.2	50.5
Investment fund certificates	18.8	—
Shares	22.8	39.3
Other	16.5	2.6
Total	100.0	100.0

Source: Bundesbank, *Financial Accounts*.

4A.4   EXCHANGE RATES

Table 4A.6. Euro exchange rates, 1990–2000

Year	French franc	Deutschmark	Irish punt	Italian lira	Dutch guilder	Sterling	US dollar
1990	6.90	2.06	0.77	1543.69	2.32	0.70	1.36
1991	6.98	2.05	0.77	1531.90	2.31	0.70	1.21
1992	6.66	1.96	0.75	1723.08	2.21	0.80	1.29
1993	6.72	1.90	0.81	1850.79	2.14	0.78	1.16
1994	6.56	1.91	0.80	1953.37	2.15	0.79	1.27
1995	6.56	1.86	0.83	2123.83	2.09	0.84	1.31
1996	6.50	1.93	0.78	1918.06	2.16	0.79	1.25
1997	6.61	1.97	0.75	1922.84	2.22	0.68	1.11
1998	6.56	1.96	0.79	1936.23	2.21	0.70	1.20
1999	6.56	1.96	0.79	1936.27	2.20	0.65	1.07
2000	6.56	1.96	0.79	1936.27	2.20	0.58	0.84

Note: Most firms provided responses to the questionnaire in Euros. It is therefore difficult to establish which exchange rate was used.

Source: Datastream.

4A.5   DOMESTIC INDICES

Table 4A.7. Growth in the ISEQ index, 1990–2000

Year	ISEQ index	Annual change (%)
1990	1342.7	—
1991	1437.6	7.1
1992	1148.0	−20.1
1993	1783.5	55.4
1994	1810.6	1.5
1995	2107.7	16.4
1996	2666.0	26.5
1997	3821.1	43.3
1998	4196.7	9.8
1999	4627.4	10.3
2000	5726.7	23.8

Source: Datastream.

Table 4A.8. MIBTEL index, 1993–9

Year	MIBTEL index	Annual change (%)
1993	9914	—
1994	10,191	2.8
1995	9453	−7.2
1996	10,571	11.8
1997	16,806	59.0
1998	23,695	41.0
1999	28,976	22.3

Source: Datastream.

Table 4A.9. Amsterdam Stock Exchange All-share index, 1994–9

Year	All-share index	Annual change (%)
1994	378.8	—
1995	439.0	15.9
1996	598.3	36.3
1997	838.6	40.2
1998	1000.0	19.3
1999	1296.8	29.7

Source: Datastream.

Table 4A.10. The change in the FTSE 100 index, 1994–2000

Year	FTSE 100 index	Annual % change
1994	3032.8	—
1995	3531.5	16.4
1996	4028.4	14.1
1997	4991.5	23.9
1998	5217.1	4.5
1999	6058.9	16.1
2000	6315.9	4.2

Source: Datastream.

Table 4A.11. The New York Stock Exchange Composite index, 1993–9

Year	NYSE Composite index	Annual change (%)
1993	259.1	—
1994	250.9	−3.1
1995	329.5	31.3
1996	392.3	19.1
1997	511.2	30.3
1998	595.8	16.6
1999	650.3	9.1

Source: Datastream.

5

The Industry Structure: Europe and the USA

While Chapter 4 examines the size and constituent parts of the asset management business, this chapter focuses on the structure of the industry in the eight countries studied in this book. In particular, the number and ownership of firms and the level of concentration in these industries are examined. This allows any similarities or differences between the countries to be identified, which may be relevant when the regulatory framework is considered in the following chapter.

5.1 CROSS-COUNTRY COMPARISON

Table 5.1 reports the number and ownership of firms in the seven European countries under consideration and the USA.

It is difficult to compare the size of the asset management industries within Europe because information on the number of firms is unavailable in some countries. However, comparing the sizes of the industry in the USA and the UK, the number of state- and federal-registered investment advisers operating in the USA is several times larger than their counterparts in the UK.

The InterSec 250[1] provides details on the types of institutions represented in the top 250 asset management companies. Firms are classified as banks, insurance companies, investment managers,

[1] InterSec Research Corp. conducts an annual survey of the largest, non-US-based, institutional investors. The top 250 companies are ranked by total assets under management, which is the sum of domestically and foreign-managed assets.

Table 5.1. The number and ownership of asset management companies, 1998

	Number of firms	Types of institution[1] (%)			
		Bank	Insurance company	Investment manager	Pension fund
France	473	69.2	23.1	7.7	0
Germany	21[1]	25.0	53.6	17.9	3.6
Ireland	15	66.7	33.3	0	0
Italy	55	60.0	30.0	10.0	0
Netherlands	13[1]	15.4	38.5	7.7	38.5
Spain	7[1]	85.7	0	14.3	0
UK	1160[2]	11.4	34.3	31.4	22.9
USA	18,650[3]	n/a	n/a	n/a	n/a

Notes:
[1] Details of the structure of ownership for all countries and the number of firms for Germany and the Netherlands have been calculated using the InterSec 250. These figures only represent the upper range of the industry. For example, in Germany there are more than 500 independent asset managers, in addition to the number that are subsidiaries of larger groups.
[2] This figure is the total number of firms regulated by IMRO.
[3] This figure represents the total number of investment advisers in the USA. There are 6650 investment advisers registered with the SEC and managing assets over $25 m. The remainder are registered with state securities authorities.
Sources: InterSec 250, Euromoney, IAIM, Assogestioni, IMRO, SEC, and COB.

internally managed pension funds, or independent unit trusts, or mutual fund companies. The information on the type of institution reported in Table 5.1 was based on this classification for firms according to their total assets under management. Consequently, Table 5.1 provides details of the types of institution operating at the upper end of the market, and not the total number of firms operating in the asset management industry for each country.

Table 5.1 shows that there is a higher proportion of UK firms categorized by the InterSec as investment managers than any of the other countries considered. Asset managers in France, Germany, Ireland, Italy, the Netherlands, and Spain are more likely to be subsidiaries of larger parent groups. In particular, those in France, Italy, and Ireland are more likely to be owned by banks, while those operating in Germany are owned by insurance companies. The Netherlands has the highest proportion of self-managed pension funds.

The concentration ratios for the top 5, 10, and 15 European firms listed in the InterSec 250 are reported in Table 5.2. The concentration ratios in the table show the proportion of total InterSec assets that are controlled by companies in France, Germany, Ireland, Italy, the Netherlands, Spain, and the UK.

Table 5.2. Concentration ratios (CRs) for seven European countries (%)

Year	CR5	CR10	CR15
1996	11.3	17.0	21.0
1997	12.3	18.7	22.9
1998	12.9	17.9	22.3

Sources: InterSec 250 and Euromoney.

Table 5.3. Market shares (%)

	Top 5	Top 10	Top 15
France	42	58	—
Ireland	77	—	—
Italy	—	71	—
UK	21	37	46

Sources: AFG–ASFFI, IAIM, Bank of Italy, and FMA.

These ratios suggest that the largest companies of the seven European countries listed in InterSec 250 do not control a large proportion of the total InterSec assets. However, concentration among the top 5, 10, and 15 firms did increase over the period from 1996 to 1998.

The following sub-sections provide information on the market shares of asset managers in each country. Data on the market shares of asset managers was not available for Germany, Italy, the Netherlands, or the USA. Table 5.3 reports the market shares of the largest 5, 10, and 15 companies operating in France, Ireland, Italy, and the UK.

According to the market shares reported in Table 5.3, the five largest asset managers in Ireland control the majority of the market. However, the size of the industry in terms of the number of players could have an impact on this figure. Furthermore, the asset management industries in France and Italy are more concentrated than in the UK. Taking France and Italy as examples, this would suggest that asset management industries in Continental Europe are characterized by a higher degree of concentration.

Industry characteristics are discussed at country levels in the following sub-sections. For each country, annual statistics are reported on:

- the number of companies;
- the size of companies; and
- concentration levels.

5.2 FRANCE

The French asset management industry consists mainly of portfolio management companies, which engage in all types of discretionary asset management, and UCITS management companies, which manage UCITS exclusively. As shown in Table 5.4, in 1999 there were 353 portfolio management companies and 120 UCITS management companies.

Portfolio and UCITS management companies manage about 95 per cent of total assets in France. The remaining 5 per cent of assets are managed by around 160 investment service providers, which include subsidiaries of credit institutions and insurance companies, and for which asset management is not their sole activity.

Table 5.5 considers the size of companies and reports the number of firms within different size categories as measured by their assets under

Table 5.4. The number of portfolio and UCITS management companies, 1996–9

	1996	1997	1998[1]	1999
Portfolio management companies	162	301	334	353
UCITS management companies	294	203[2]	131	120
Total	456	504	465	473

Notes: Portfolio management companies are the sociétés de gestion de portefeuille and UCITS management companies are the sociétés de gestion d'OPCVM.
[1] The 1998 figures are adjusted.
[2] This figure includes 66 companies that have not yet been certified.

Source: COB (1998, 1999).

Table 5.5. The number of portfolio and UCITS management companies by size of assets under management, 1996–8

Assets under management by company (€ bn)	1996		1997		1998	
	no.	%	no.	%	no.	%
<1.5	137	93.20	285	83.33	296	82.68
1.5–3	0	0.00	21	6.14	19	5.31
3–15.2	5	3.40	26	7.60	28	7.82
>15.2	5	3.40	10	2.92	15	4.19

Notes: The figures for 1996 include only portfolio management companies. For 1997 and 1998 only the management companies actually active in the market are included. Figures are calculated on the basis of the companies that had filed their annual accounts by 31 December 1998.

Source: COB.

Table 5.6. The largest asset managers in France, 1999 (€ billion)

	Ownership	Assets under management	Market shares (%)
CDC Asset Management	Bank	149.4	11.7
INDOCAM	Bank	140.5	11.0
AXA Investment Managers	Insurance	95.6	7.5
Société Générale Asset Management	Bank	84.0	6.6
AGF Asset Management	Insurance	62.6	4.9
Credit Lyonnais Asset Management	Bank	50.6	4.0
FINAMA Asset Management	Insurance	44.8	3.5
BNP Gestions	Bank	42.4	3.3
Victoire Asset Management	Insurance	37.2	2.9
Banques Populaires Asset Management	Bank	34.8	2.7
Paribas Asset Management	Bank	33.1	2.6
Sub-total		775.0	60.9
Total assets under management		1273.0	100.0

Sources: AFG–ASFFI (2000), COB, and companies' annual reports.

management. In 1998, the large majority of companies (83 per cent) managed a total portfolio of assets of less than €1.5 billion. About 15 companies (4 per cent) managed more than €15.2 billion each.

Table 5.6 reports the assets managed by the 11 largest asset managers operating in France.

According to Table 5.6, the largest 11 asset managers in France control 61 per cent of the market. The top five asset management companies control 42 per cent of the market. Seven of the 11 largest asset managers are part of banking groups, while the remainder are subsidiaries of insurance companies.

5.3   GERMANY

The industry structure information for Germany is taken from InterSec 250 and therefore, considers only the largest asset managers in Germany. Table 5.7 lists the 21 German managers listed in the InterSec250 and ranked by the value of their domestically managed assets.

The 21 largest players in the German asset management industry together own assets worth €881 billion. Ten (48 per cent) of the top

Table 5.7. Twenty-one largest German asset managers, 1998

Type of ownership	Institution
Bank	Deutsche Bank Group
	HypoVereinsbank
	Dresdner Bank Group
	Commerzbank Group
	Westdeutsche Land
	Sal Oppenheim
	BHF Bank Group
Insurance	Allianz Group
	Volksfursorge
	Aachener & Munchner
	Gerling Konzern
	Iduna Group
	Deutsche Kronken
	Alte Leipziger
	Karlsruher Lebensverich
	Deutsche Ring Gruppe
	Hannoversiche Lebensv
Investment management	Deka Bank
	Union Investment
	Metzler Investment
Pension fund	Siemens

Source: InterSec 250.

21 asset managers are insurance companies or part of an insurance company group, seven (33 per cent) are banks or part of a banking group, and three (14 per cent) are companies that InterSec classifies as an independent asset manager. One asset manager (Siemens) is a large industrial group that manages its own pension fund.

The Association of Investment Management Companies (Bundesverband Deutscher Investment Gesellschaften, BVI) collects asset ownership information on its members. Although the data refers to investment funds and not to mandated asset management, it allows an assessment of the degree of concentration in the German fund management industry. Table 5.8 reports the total assets of the 10 largest investment companies, as well as the companies' shares in the total market. The table refers to public (retail) funds only, and distinguishes between real estate and other funds. As can be seen, the three largest investment companies managing public funds together own more than half of all industry assets. No corresponding statistics are available for special (institutional) funds.

Table 5.8. German investment funds (public funds only), 1999

Total assets (excl. real estate funds)			Total assets (real estate funds only)		
Company	€ bn	% share of total market	Company	€ bn	% share of total market
DWS	54.3	23.1	DESPA	12.3	24.3
DEKA	40.7	17.3	DIFA	8.6	17.7
DIT	36.3	15.4	DEGI	8.3	16.6
Union Investment	26.3	11.2	DGI	5.7	11.4
ADIG-Investment	17.5	7.4	CGI	5.0	9.9
DVG	7.3	3.1	III GmbH	4.1	8.1
Frankfurt-Trust	5.7	2.4	BfG ImmoInvest	2.0	3.9
Allianz	4.5	1.9	WestInvest	1.8	3.6
Oppenheim	3.9	1.6	CS Ass Man. Immo	0.9	1.8
Zurich Invest	3.8	1.3	HansaInvest	0.6	1.2

Notes: Public funds are open-ended investment funds offered to the general public. Real estate funds are distinguished from other funds, which are mainly securities funds. The market share is calculated by the BVI with respect to the entire market in the funds.

Source: BVI.

5.4 IRELAND

The asset management industry in Ireland manages assets of approximately €180 billion, which are controlled by 15 companies. The level of concentration in the Irish asset management industry is quite high, with five IAIM members managing 77 per cent of the total assets on behalf of the Irish residents. This excludes assets managed on behalf of international clients. Three Irish firms are listed in the InterSec 250, two of which are owned by banks and one by an insurance company.

There has recently been a period of increased consolidation. Mergers and acquisitions during this period have included:

- New Ireland Investment Managers acquired by the Bank of Ireland;
- Irish Life merged with Irish Progressive;
- ESB Fund Mangers taken over by Aberdeen Asset Managers;
- Guinness Mahon taken over by Irish Life & Permanent;
- Hibernian Investment Managers taken over by Commercial General Union;
- Norwich Union merged with Commercial General Union (now Commercial General & Norwich Union); and
- Ulster Bank Investment Managers taken over by KBC Belgium.

Table 5.9. Ownership of IAIM members

	Number of firms	**% of firms**
Irish-owned	3	21
Foreign-owned	11	79
of which		
UK	6	43
EU	5	36
Total	14	100

Source: IAIM.

Ownership details of 14 members of the IAIM are reported in Table 5.9. Over 20 per cent of investment managers are Irish-owned; the remainder are foreign-owned, of which there is an almost equal split between the UK and other European Union (EU) countries.

5.5   ITALY

Table 5.10 reports the growth in the number of asset management companies in Italy.

According to the table, the number of asset management companies has more than doubled since 1985, reaching a peak in 1998. Most of this growth took place during the late 1980s. The rate of growth has since slowed and, in some years, declined, mainly as a result of increased consolidation in the industry. This may also explain the change in market shares of the largest companies with domestically managed assets listed by the InterSec. These shares, reported in Table 5.11, have been calculated for the firms listed in the InterSec with domestically managed assets, and are therefore not based on domestically managed assets for the asset management industry in Italy.

The number of firms, listed in the InterSec, which domestically manage assets has declined during the period 1996–8. However, assets managed by Italian firms listed in the InterSec increased to €127 billion by the end of 1998. Evidence of increased concentration has been reported in the 1999 Annual Report of the Bank of Italy (Banca d'Italia 1999), which finds that the 10 largest companies, in terms of assets under management, control 71 per cent of assets.

Table 5.12 reports the details of ownership of asset management companies.

Table 5.10. The number of asset management companies in Italy

Year	Number of asset management companies	Annual % change
1985	25	—
1986	34	36.0
1987	38	11.8
1988	50	31.6
1989	56	12.0
1990	58	3.6
1991	53	−8.6
1992	55	3.8
1993	51	−7.3
1994	53	3.9
1995	54	1.9
1996	54	0
1997	53	−1.9
1998	59	11.3
1999	55	−6.8

Source: Assogestioni.

Table 5.11. The largest Italian firms, 1996–8

1996		1998	
Company	Domestically managed assets (€ bn)	Company	Domestically managed assets (€ bn)
IMI	13.2	San Paolo	51.4
INA	12.8	Generali Group	28.4
Riunione	10.4	Arca	26.7
Cariplo	10.4	INA	20.8
Banca Commerciale Italiana	10.0		
Fondiaria	6.6		
Generali Group	5.7		
Total	69.1		127.3

Sources: InterSec, Euromoney, and Datastream.

Table 5.12. Ownership of asset management companies (% net assets managed)

	1993	1994	1995	1996	1997	1998	1999
Banks	63.7	66.7	74.1	80.8	83.8	93.8	94.0
Independent companies	19.3	16.5	8.7	3.7	—	—	—
Insurance	7.3	7.2	7.9	8.4	7.9	5.1	4.9
Other[1]	9.7	9.6	9.3	7.1	8.3	1.1	1.1

Note:
[1] The 'Other' category includes joint ventures, non-financial intermediaries, and individual owners.

Sources: Assogestioni and Commissione nazionale per la società e la borsa (Consob).

From 1993 to 1999, the net assets controlled by banks increased by almost 30 percentage points, at the expense of the other categories listed above. Moreover, this is consistent with the 1999 Annual Report of the Bank of Italy (Banca d'Italia 1999), which notes that, of the top 10 asset management companies, only two are owned by insurance groups, while the remainder are subsidiaries of banking groups.

5.6 THE NETHERLANDS

The number of institutions under supervision in the Netherlands is reported in Table 5.13.

The number of life insurance companies has increased by 11 per cent over the last decade, while that of non-life insurance companies and pension funds has declined, by approximately 30 and 12 per cent, respectively. Despite this fall in the number of institutions under supervision, balance-sheet assets for these institutions have more than doubled over the period from 1994 to 1999 (as shown in Table 4A.1).

Table 5.14 reports the number of institutions regulated by the securities board of the Netherlands, the Stichting Toezicht Effectenverkeer (STE).

The number of portfolio managers and securities brokers, referred to as off-exchange institutions, under the supervision of the STE increased during 1997–9. The number of such institutions that do not require a licence has also increased by a larger proportion.

Table 5.13. The number of institutions under supervision

Year	Life insurance	Non-life insurance	Pension funds
1989	93	392	1156
1990	96	385	1141
1991	96	385	1139
1992	97	391	1122
1993	98	393	1114
1994	95	314	1102
1995	96	280	1090
1996	99	288	1081
1997	107	284	1058
1998	108	294	1039
1999	103	281	1015

Source: Verzekeringskamer.

Table 5.14. The institutions supervised by the STE

Institutions	1997	1998	1999
Off-exchange institutions (portfolio managers and securities brokers)	154	181	206
Exempt off-exchange institutions[1]	3070	4384	5877

Note:
[1] Includes institutions, such as insurers, investment companies, pension funds, and credit institutions, that do not need a licence to trade securities.

Source: STE (2000).

Table 5.15. The largest Dutch companies, 1996–8

1996		1998	
Company	Domestically managed assets (€ bn)	Company	Domestically managed assets (€ bn)
Algemeen Burgerlijk Pensioenfonds	114.9	ING Group	49.2
ING Group	80.9	Algemeen Burgerlijk Pensioenfonds	48.2
Aegon	71.6	Aegon	34.0
Robeco	38.2	Achmea	28.5
ABN Amro	28.4	Robeco	18.5
PVF	19.9	PGGM	15.1
Achmea	18.7	Pens Schootse Poort	14.7
SNS Group	16.2	Bouwnijverheid Bedrijfspensioenfonds	13.6
PGGM	16.1	Shell	11.5
Delta-Lloyd	15.3	Interpolis	11.0
Philips	12.4	SNS Group	7.9
Metaalnijverheid Bedrijfpensioenfond	11.6		
Shell	11.6		
Bouwnijverheid Bedrijfspensioenfonds	9.7		
Stad Rotterdam	9.0		
Interpolis	3.5		
Total	478.1		252.2

Sources: InterSec, Euromoney, and Datastream.

Table 5.15 reports the domestically managed assets for Dutch companies listed in the InterSec at the end of 1996 and 1998.

Table 5.15 also shows that the number of Dutch firms listed in the InterSec 250 declined over the period 1996–8. In addition, domestically managed assets fell by almost 50 per cent.

Table 5.16. Ownership of largest Dutch firms

	1996	1997	1998
Bank	2	2	2
Insurance company	6	6	5
Investment manager	2	2	1
Pension fund	6	6	5
Total	16	16	13

Sources: InterSec 250 and Euromoney.

The ownership details of the Dutch firms listed in the InterSec are reported in Table 5.16.

According to Table 5.16, the largest categories of institutional investor are pension funds and insurance companies. As a consequence of the reduction in the total number of institutional investors in 1998, the number of firms in each category fell.

5.7 SPAIN

The Spanish asset management industry mainly consists of the UCIT management companies, insurance companies, and pension fund management companies. As shown in Table 5.17, in 1999 there were 127 UCIT management companies, 370 insurance companies, and 112 pension fund management companies.

The UCIT management companies and insurance companies manage about 88 per cent of total assets in Spain. The remaining 12 per cent of assets are managed by pension fund management companies and other investment service providers.

Table 5.18 considers the size of mutual funds management companies and reports the number of firms within different size categories, as measured by their assets under management. In 1998, the large majority of companies (83 per cent) managed a total portfolio of assets of less than €1.5 billion. Only three companies (2 per cent) managed more than €15 billion each.

The Association of UCITs and Pension Funds (Asociación de Instituciones de Inversión Colectiva, Inverco) collects asset ownership information on its members. Although the data refers to investment and pension funds, and not to the mandated asset management, it allows an assessment of the degree of concentration in the Spanish fund management industry.

Table 5.17. The number of UCITs, pension fund management companies, and insurance companies in Spain, 1996–9

	1996	1997	1998	1999
UCIT management companies	136	133	131	127
Insurance companies	398	392	378	370
Pension fund management companies	107	107	110	112
Total	641	632	619	609

Note:
UCIT management companies are 'Sociedades Gestoras de IIC'.

Sources: CNMV, DGSFP, and Inverco.

Table 5.18. The number of UCIT management companies in Spain by size of assets under management, 1996–8

Assets under management by company (€ bn)	1996		1997		1998	
	no.	%	no.	%	no.	%
<1.5	123	90.6	114	85.7	109	83.2
1.5–3	6	4.4	10	7.5	10	7.6
3–15	5	3.6	7	5.2	9	6.8
>15	2	1.4	2	1.6	3	2.4

Source: Inverco.

Table 5.19. The largest asset managers in Spain, 1999 (€ billion)

	Ownership	Assets under management	Market shares (%)
BSCH	Bank	54.5	22.9
BBVA	Bank	50.9	21.4
La Caixa	Saving bank	16.5	6.9
Ahorro Corporacion	Saving bank	12.0	5.0
Caja Madrid	Saving bank	10.0	4.2
Banco Popular	Bank	8.5	3.5
Bankinter	Bank	6.3	2.6
Banco Sabadell	Bank	5.5	2.3
Ibercaja	Saving bank	4.4	1.8
Deutsche Bank	Bank	4.3	1.8
Sub-total		172.9	72.7
Total assets under management		237.8	100.0

Source: Inverco.

Table 5.19 reports the assets managed (UCITs and pension funds) by the 10 largest asset managers operating in Spain.

According to Table 5.19, the largest 10 asset managers in Spain control 73 per cent of the market. The top five asset management companies control 60 per cent of the market. Six of the 10 largest asset managers are part of banking groups, while the remainder are subsidiaries of saving banks.

5.8   THE UK

The number of firms regulated by the IMRO is reported in Table 5.20.

The number of firms regulated by the IMRO has declined from a peak of 1209 in 1993/4 to 1160 in 1999/2000. This decrease of almost five per cent may be explained by an increase in consolidation in the industry, or by the excess of withdrawals over admissions. The level of entry of regulated firms increased by 80 per cent over the period from 1993/4 to 1999/2000, which was accompanied by a 70 per cent reduction in the number of resignations and terminations. However, only during 1998/9 and 1999/2000 does the number of new firms admitted exceed the number of firms resigning.

Table 5.21 reports the assets under management of the top 5, 10, and 15 members of the FMA as a proportion of the total assets managed by the FMA members. These figures were calculated on the basis of the UK operations only of 73 FMA members. These asset managers are managing clients' assets worldwide. Therefore, for Table 5.21, the market is defined as all UK fund managers managing worldwide assets. The FMA members control approximately 80 per cent of this market. Total assets under management for the 73 FMA members amount to £2071.5 billion.

The ownership of the largest firms, according to total assets under management, listed by the InterSec, is shown in Table 5.22.

Table 5.20. The firms regulated by the IMRO, 1993–2000

	1993/4	1994/5	1995/6	1996/7	1997/8	1998/9	1999/2000
Number of regulated firms at start of year	1209	1142	1153	1100	1055	1047	1090
Applications							
New firms admitted	60	98	78	55	79	108	108
Firms resigned/ terminated	(127)	(87)	(131)	(100)	(87)	(65)	(38)
Number of firms regulated at end of year	1142	1153	1100	1055	1047	1090	1160

Source: IMRO (2001).

Table 5.21. The concentration ratios of FMA members

	Assets under management (£ bn)	Market share (%)
Top five companies	550.6	26.6
Top ten companies	949.6	45.8
Top 15 companies	1196.1	57.7
Total assets under management of FMA members	2071.5	100.0

Source: FMA.

Table 5.22. The ownership of the UK firms, as listed in the InterSec 250

	1996	1997	1998
Bank	6	7	4
Insurance company	18	17	12
Investment manager	11	11	11
Pension fund	6	6	8
Total	41	41	35

Sources: InterSec 250 and Euromoney.

Of the largest fund managers operating in the UK in 1998, the majority were owned by insurance companies, despite the declining number of insurance companies listed in the InterSec 250. The number of pension funds has increased over the period, while, conversely, the number of banks has declined and the number of investment managers has remained stable.

5.9   THE USA

Table 5.23 contains information on the number of investment advisers registered with the SEC. These figures do not include state-regulated investment advisers.

The total number of SEC-registered investment advisers declined following the enactment of the National Securities Markets Improvement Act 1996, which established new requirements for an adviser to register or remain registered with the SEC. Advisers that did not meet the revised criterion are regulated by the state. It has been estimated that 12,000 investment advisers are registered with state securities authorities.

Table 5.23. The SEC-registered investment
advisers

Year	Number of advisers
1995	22,000
1996	22,400
1997	12,698
1998	8000
1999	6650
2000[1]	6850

Note:
[1] Estimate.

Source: SEC Budget.

Despite this decline of approximately 70 per cent in the number of investment advisers registered with the SEC, total assets managed by investment advisers have increased by almost 80 per cent since 1995 (as shown in Table 4.20). This would suggest that the market controlled by investment advisers registered with the SEC has become more concentrated. Between 900 and 1000 investment advisers provide services to investment companies.

5.10   SUMMARY

In all of the countries considered, with the exception of the UK and the USA, asset management is dominated by banks and insurance companies. Levels of concentration are high in these countries and are apparently increasing. Concentration is relatively low in the UK and the USA.

6

The Regulatory Framework

This chapter summarizes the regulatory framework in seven European countries and the USA. Extensive descriptions of the regulatory regime in each country are provided in the appendix to the chapter. The topics covered include the following:

- regulatory authorities;
- capital requirements;
- separation of clients' assets;
- disclosure;
- enforcement;
- audit;
- compensation;
- insurance;
- complaints;
- authorization; and
- supervision.

The next chapter provides further details on the USA.

6.1   THE REGULATORY AUTHORITIES (TABLE 6.1)

Table 6.1. Summary of regulatory authorities in seven European countries and the USA

France	COB authorizes and regulates asset managers
Germany	The Bundesaufsichtsamt für das Kreditwesen (BAKred), the federal banking supervisory authority, regulates companies that provide financial services, other than insurance companies
	Insurance companies are regulated by the Bundesaufsichtsamt für das Versicherungswesen (BAV), the federal insurance supervisory authority
Ireland	The Central Bank of Ireland is responsible for the authorization and supervision of asset management companies
	Asset management activities conducted within an insurance company or a pension fund are supervised by the Department of Enterprise, Trade and Employment or the Pensions Board, respectively
Italy	The Bank of Italy and Consob are responsible for the regulation of asset management companies
Netherlands	Portfolio managers are regulated by STE, the securities board of the Netherlands
	The Insurance Chamber (Verzekeringskamer) regulates insurance companies and pension funds that manage their own assets. Collective investment schemes are regulated by the Dutch Central Bank
Spain	CNMV authorizes and regulates asset managers and UCITS managers DGSFP authorizes and regulates pension fund managers and insurance companies
UK	The Financial Services Authority (FSA) regulates asset management
	The introduction of the Financial Services and Markets Act 2000 established the FSA as the single body responsible for the regulation of all financial services. Previously this was the responsibility of IMRO, a self-regulatory organization authorized by the FSA
USA	Investment advisers managing assets of less than $25 m are regulated by state securities authorities
	The SEC is responsible for the supervision of investment advisers with assets under management greater than $25 m

6.2   THE CAPITAL REQUIREMENTS

The capital requirements imposed on asset managers by regulators in seven European countries and the USA are summarized in Table 6.2.

Unlike their US counterparts, regulators in each of the European countries under consideration have imposed a capital requirement on

Table 6.2. Summary of capital requirements

	Initial capital	Liquid capital requirement					
		Expenditure-based	Position risk	Settlement/ delivery/ counterparty/ underwriting	Large exposure[1]	Foreign exchange[2]	Other assets[3]
France	✓	✓	✗	✗	✗	✗	✗
Germany	✓	✓	✓	✓	✓	✓	✓
Ireland	✓	✓	✓	✓	✓	✓	✓
Italy	✓	✓	✗	✗	✗	✗	✗
Netherlands	✓	✓	✓	✓	✓	✓	✓
Spain	✓	✓	✗	✗	✗	✗	✗
UK	✓	✓	✓	✓	✓	✓	✓
USA	✗	✗	✗	✗	✗	✗	✗

Notes:
[1] Large-exposure risk arises as a result of exposure to a counterparty.
[2] Foreign-exchange risk.
[3] Refers to risks arising from other assets.

asset management companies. For France, Germany, Ireland, Italy, the Netherlands, Spain, and the UK, regulators have devised a capital requirement with two components. The first is an initial capital requirement. Typically, this is fixed at three levels, as set out in the Capital Adequacy Directive—€50,000, €125,000, and €730,000, depending on the activities conducted. If the firm does not hold the clients' assets, deal for its own account, or underwrite issues then its initial capital requirement is €50,000. If the asset manager deals for its own account or underwrites issues, its initial capital requirement is €730,000. Holding the clients' assets requires an initial capital of €125,000. In the Netherlands, this middle level of initial capital has been removed and the lower requirement has been reduced to €35,000 for firms that transmit orders from the client to another firm. The other two levels of requirement (€50,000 and €730,000) remain unchanged. Asset managers in Italy face an initial capital requirement of 2 billion lire (€1033 m), irrespective of the services offered by the firm. In France, the initial capital requirement is FFr350,000 (€53,357). The initial capital requirement in Spain is set at Ptas 10 m (€60,101).

In addition to the initial capital requirement, there is a liquid capital requirement. The composition of this requirement is similar in France, Germany, Ireland, the Netherlands, and the UK. In these countries, the liquid capital consists of an expenditure-based requirement and requirements for position risk, settlement/delivery/counterparty failure, underwriting risk, large-exposure risk, foreign-exchange risk, and other assets risk. In France, Germany,[1] Ireland, and the Netherlands, the expenditure-based requirement is equal to 25 per cent of the fixed overheads in the previous year. This is similar to the '13-week' rule placed on the UK asset managers, which states that the expenditure-based requirement is equal to 13 weeks of annual audited expenditure.[2] Unusually, in Italy, the liquid capital requirement is a function of the value of assets under management and must be at least equal to 25 per cent of fixed operating costs in the previous financial year. The capital requirement is calculated as 0.5 per cent of the value of assets in open-ended funds, SICAVs, and pension funds; 2 per cent for closed-ended funds; and an additional capital charge in the case of pension funds that guarantee the repayment of principal.

A two-tier system of regulation operates in the USA. Investment advisers that manage assets of less than $25 m are regulated by the state, while advisers controlling assets over $25 m are required to register with the SEC, the federal regulator. In regulating these investment advisers, the SEC focuses on enforcement and disclosure, and does not impose regulatory capital requirements. However, capital requirements may be imposed at the state level—for example, in California, these range from $1000 to $25,000, depending on the activity conducted by the company.

6.3 THE SEPARATION OF CLIENTS' ASSETS (TABLE 6.3)

Table 6.3. Summary of rules on separation of clients' assets

France	Assets under mandate are required to be held by a company outside the asset management company. The assets of OPCVMs are held by a depositaire, which is responsible for custodianship and inspection In addition, safe-custody provisions are included in the code of conduct defined by the trade association
Germany	Portfolio managers must keep client securities in a safe-custody account at a credit institution
Ireland	Client money must be held separately from that of the company
Italy	Clients' assets are to be separated from those of other clients and from those of the company

[1] In Germany, the 25% rule has not yet been transmitted into domestic law.
[2] This may be reduced to six weeks if the company does not act as a custodian or appoint a custodian on behalf of the client.

Table 6.3. (continued)

Netherlands	Asset management companies must ensure that clients' assets are held separately from those of the firm
	The degree of separation depends on the type of activities conducted by the firm. For example, a firm that only acts as a financial intermediary must hold clients' assets in a bank account in the client's name
Spain	An asset manager must ensure that clients' assets are separately identifiable from the assets of the asset manager and from those of other clients. The assets of the OPCVMs and pension funds are held by a depositaire, which is responsible for custodianship and inspection
UK	An asset manager must ensure that clients' assets are separately identifiable from assets of the firm. The purpose of this rule is to prohibit the mingling of client and firm assets
	A firm that is a custodian, or appoints a custodian on behalf of the client, must perform a reconciliation of the client's account at least twice a year
USA	An SEC-registered investment adviser with custody of clients' assets is required to provide additional information to clients. For example, the client must be provided with an itemized statement of the securities in the possession of the firm
	All such funds and securities of clients will be examined and verified by an independent accountant at least once during each calendar year and without prior notice to the investment adviser. Following the examination, the accountant's report will subsequently be filed with the SEC

6.4 DISCLOSURE (TABLE 6.4)

Table 6.4. Summary of disclosure rules

France	Clients must be periodically notified of the value and composition of the portfolio
Germany	Regular fund reporting is required under the Investment Company Act
Ireland, Italy, Netherlands, UK	Clients must be notified of the value and composition of the portfolio
Spain	Clients must be periodically notified of the value and composition of the portfolio. Clients must also be notified when there are conflicts of interest
USA	In addition to notification of the value and composition of the portfolio, the 'Brochure Rule' requires investment advisers to disclose at least the information contained in Part II of Form ADV, the registration form. The information contained in Part II includes the education and business background of the investment adviser, and any disciplinary events

6.5 ENFORCEMENT (TABLE 6.5)

Table 6.5. Summary of enforcement actions

France	COB can impose administrative sanctions concerning practices contrary to regulations
Germany	The regulatory authority is allowed to impose sanctions and fines to punish breaches and enforce compliance
Ireland	There are several powers available to the Central Bank of Ireland, which may be imposed on firms that fail to comply with regulations. For example, authorization may be revoked or an application for authorization refused. In some circumstances, penalties, such as a fine or a term of imprisonment, may be issued
Italy	Penalties of imprisonment and fines may be imposed on individuals who provide investment services without authorization or who breach regulations
Netherlands	The STE has the power to penalize and fine companies that do not comply with regulations
Spain	CNMV can propose to the Ministry of Finance the imposition of administrative sanctions and fines concerning practices that contravene regulations, in respect of UCITS managers and individual portfolio managers. DGSFP can propose to the Ministry of Finance the imposition of administrative sanctions and fines concerning practices that contravene regulations, in respect of pension fund managers and insurance companies
UK	There are a number of actions available to IMRO to enforce regulations, such as warnings, powers of intervention, investigation, enforcement committee, and disciplinary tribunal
USA	The Division of Enforcement conducts investigations into possible violations of regulations, and is responsible for prosecuting the civil suits of the SEC in the federal court, as well as its administrative proceedings

6.6 AUDIT (TABLE 6.6)

Table 6.6. Summary of rules for audit

France	Asset managers are required to submit audited accounts. The COB and senior management within the company must be notified of any irregularities discovered by auditors during their examinations of the company
Germany	Institutions must submit audited accounts. The auditor must immediately report facts that warrant the qualification or withholding of the audit certificate
Ireland	External auditors must inform the Central Bank of any deficiencies in the financial systems, matters that affect the solvency of the company, and inaccuracies in the returns to the Bank

Table 6.6. (continued)

Italy	Any irregularities discovered by auditors during their examination of the company must be promptly reported to the Bank of Italy and Consob
Netherlands	Portfolio managers are required to submit accounts to the STE on a regular basis. External auditing is conducted annually by a company appointed by the asset manager. On average, the STE conducts a visit of a portfolio manager once a year
Spain	Asset managers, UCITS managers, and pension fund managers are required to submit audited accounts on a regular basis. External auditing is conducted annually by a company appointed by the management company. The audit must be performed in accordance with auditing standards
UK	An auditor must be appointed by a company to prepare its annual financial returns to IMRO. The audit must be performed in accordance with auditing standards. IMRO has the power to appoint a second auditor to report the financial statements
USA	The Office of Compliance and Examinations at the SEC is responsible for conducting examinations and inspections of investment advisers

6.7 COMPENSATION (TABLE 6.7)

Table 6.7. Summary of compensation schemes

France	There is no specific compensation scheme for clients of asset managers. However, a scheme operates whereby deposits, bonds, and cash are guaranteed. The investments of asset managers' clients are covered under this scheme
Germany, Ireland, Netherlands	The Investor Compensation Directive has been introduced into domestic legislation. The compensation scheme will provide payment to private investors in the event that an asset management company is unable to return securities or monies owing to the client. The amount of compensation payable is 90% of the claim, subject to a maximum payment of €20,000
Italy	There are two compensation schemes in operation: one for clients of banks and the other for clients of asset managers and securities houses. The latter has been in operation since 1991
Spain	There is no specific compensation scheme for clients of asset managers, UCITS managers, or pension fund managers
UK	The Investors Compensation Scheme was established in 1986 to provide compensation to private investors. The amount of compensation is currently set at a maximum of £48,000 (€74,146). This is calculated as the full payment of the first £30,000 (€46,404) of the claim, plus 90% of the next £20,000 (€30,936)
USA	There is no specific compensation scheme in operation

6.8 INSURANCE (TABLE 6.8)

Table 6.8. Summary of insurance

France, Germany, Ireland, Italy, Netherlands, Spain, UK	There is no compulsory insurance requirement
USA	Under the Investment Companies Act 1940, an investment company[1] is required to obtain a bond against larceny and embezzlement. No such requirement is placed on investment advisers

Note:
[1] An investment company is equivalent to a mutual fund.

6.9 COMPLAINTS (TABLE 6.9)

Table 6.9. Summary of complaints procedures

France	COB deals with complaints against asset managers. Complaints that are upheld can lead to sanctions, referral to the courts, or amicable settlement
Germany	Internal procedures dealing with complaints are required under conduct-of-business rules (for banking groups)
Ireland	Asset management companies are required to maintain a written record of all complaints. Complainants have the right to report the matter to the Central Bank, should they not receive satisfaction from the company
Italy	There is no specific ombudsman to deal with complaints concerning asset management companies. However, individual companies may complain to Consob, with the possibility of taking the complaint before the courts
Netherlands	Regulations require that companies deal with complaints within a reasonable period of time. A record of all complaints must be maintained. Complainants have the right to notify the STE of the matter, should they not receive satisfaction from the company. In addition, the Dutch Securities Institute has established a complaints committee to deal with complaints from private investors concerning firms regulated by the STE
Spain	There is no specific ombudsman to deal with complaints concerning asset management companies, UCITS, or pension funds. However, there is an ombudsman to deal with complaints regarding insurance companies. UCITS and pension fund clients may complain to CNMV or DGSFP, with the possibility of taking the complaints before the courts
UK	Companies are required to have a procedure to deal with written complaints. The Investment Ombudsman was appointed to deal with complaints relating to services provided by firms regulated by IMRO/FSA
USA	If an investor has failed to receive settlement of a complaint from a firm, the complainant may report the matter to the Office of Investor Education and Assistance at the SEC. It may then decide to refer the matter to the Enforcement Division for further investigation. The Office of Investor Education and Assistance will send a report to the firm and the investor. If the complaint remains unsettled, there is a limited time period within which the investor may commence legislative action

6.10 AUTHORIZATION (TABLE 6.10)

Table 6.10. Summary of authorization rules

France	COB's review of the application for authorization focuses on the adequacy of the asset manager's legal form, the capitalization, and the management and operational infrastructure necessary to conduct business
Germany	In addition to the minimum capital requirement and the organizational arrangements necessary for the proper operation of the business, institutions must have trustworthy managers with the necessary qualifications
Ireland	The Central Bank must be satisfied that the management of the company comprises persons of probity and competence; that the firm has sufficient capital; and that the regulations set out by the bank are likely to be met. It must also understand the risks of the business; the suitability of shareholders and directors must be assessed; the financial position of the firm must be examined; and compliance with regulations must be ensured
Italy	The management of the company must fulfil integrity and experience requirements set out by the Minister of the Treasury. The name of the company must contain the words 'società di gestione del risparmio' and it must have a registered office in Italy
Netherlands	Management must be reliable and competent, and comprise of at least two people; there must be a minimum level of shareholder equity and own resources; certain accounting procedures must be adopted and information disclosed to investors
Spain	Asset management companies and UCITS management companies must be authorized and registered by CNMV. Pension fund managers must be authorized and registered by DGSFP. Both types of managers must fulfil different capital requirements and the management and operational infrastructure necessary to conduct business
UK	An asset management company must prove that it has and will continue to have 'fit and proper' persons to undertake investment business. This criterion is judged on the basis of compliance with ten principles devised by the FSA
USA	Registration as an investment adviser with the SEC involves the completion of the registration Form ADV; compliance with the Brochure Rule; maintaining accurate and current books and records; and being subject to inspection and examination by the SEC staff

6.11 SUPERVISION (TABLE 6.11)

Table 6.11. Summary of supervision rules

France	Supervision by the COB includes on-site inspections of business premises
Germany	Supervised institutions must provide the necessary information. The authority can carry out audits, inspect business premises, and send representatives to general meetings
Ireland	An asset management company is subject to continual supervision. This includes on- and off-site monitoring
Italy	The Bank of Italy and Consob carry out inspections of authorized asset managers
Netherlands	Portfolio managers are assessed on a regular basis. Financial adequacy is investigated, and any violation of the regulations will result in the imposition of penalties and fines
	The STE must be notified of a change in the management or scope of the business
Spain	Institutions must provide the CNMV or DGSFP with the necessary relevant information. An asset management company is subject to continual supervision, including on-site inspections of business premises
UK	Asset management companies are continually monitored. Adequacy of financial resources is examined, and penalties are imposed on firms that have violated regulations
USA	The Office of Compliance and Examinations at the SEC is responsible for conducting inspections of investment advisers. Furthermore, investment advisers with custody of clients' assets are subject to examination by independent auditors without prior notification

6.12 SUMMARY

There are several significant points to be drawn from this chapter.

1. Capital requirements are broadly similar in European countries. There are no federal capital requirements imposed on investment advisers in the USA.

2. There are custody requirements in all European countries under consideration. In the USA, an investment adviser with custody of clients' assets has to supply the client with additional information.

3. There are greater disclosure requirements in the USA than in Europe.

4. Different forms of compensation schemes exist in all European countries under consideration. There is no compensation scheme in operation in the USA.

5. An investment management company operating in the USA is required to have insurance, which is not the case for European firms. Finally, a high level of enforcement occurs in the USA through auditing, administrative proceedings, and civil actions.

In some European countries, regulators emphasize capital requirements, custody, and compensation schemes. The US regulators focus on disclosure, auditing, insurance, and enforcement. Since the focus of US regulation is quite different to that of European regulation, in the next chapter we provide further detail on the US system.

Appendix

6A.1 FRANCE

The Regulatory Authorities

Asset managers in France are governed by the regulations and fall under the jurisdiction of the Commission des Opérations de Bourse (COB), which is the French securities and exchange commission. The COB is an independent administrative body, composed of a president and nine members. It is responsible for the authorization and supervision of the activity of individual and collective portfolio management. It is also the regulatory authority responsible for investor protection in France and for law enforcement, partly through the imposition of administrative sanctions in respect of breaches of its regulations.

The Financial Activities Modernisation Act 1996 allows management companies the freedom of choice of their purpose. They can either manage exclusively UCITs (sociétés de gestion d'OPCVM), or expand their purpose to cover all types of discretionary asset management, including UCITs, in which case they are called portfolio management companies (sociétés de gestion de portefeuille).

Asset managers play a role in the regulatory and supervision process through their participation in the Consultative Council of Asset Management (Comité Consultatif de la Gestion Financière) and in the Disciplinary Council of Asset Management (Conseil de Discipline de la Gestion Financière). The Consultative Council of Asset Management is to be consulted by the COB in relation to the authorization of portfolio management companies; to the approval of proposals to engage in portfolio management as part of any investment firm or credit institution's activities; and to rules and regulations relating to portfolio management. The Disciplinary Council of Asset Management is a disciplinary body with powers to sanction any breach of French legislation applicable to funds and the offer of portfolio management services.

While most assets are managed by portfolio management companies and UCIT management companies, about 5 per cent are managed by investment service providers. These fall under the regulations of the Credit Institutions and Investment Companies Commission (Comité des Etablissements de Crédit et des Entreprises d'Investissement); however, for the purposes of this report, these will largely be ignored here.

The Capital Requirements

The authorization to carry out asset management activities as a portfolio or UCIT management company may only be granted by the COB if the company shows that it has sufficient own funds to carry out the business. According to the COB, the minimum capital requirement is FF350,000, or 25 per cent of the overheads in the anticipated or previous year's profit and loss accounts.

The Separation of Clients' Assets

Clients' assets must be held separately from those of the asset management company. Assets under mandate must be held in the client's account, with a credit institution outside the asset management company. Therefore, strict separation of clients' monies and securities is compulsory in the case of mandated asset management.

The assets of OPCVMs are held by depositaires which act as custodian. This requirement was set out in legislation in 1988. In November 1993, COB also imposed a regulation regarding the functions of a depositaire of an OPCVM.

The possible lack of contractual obligations between the asset manager and the institution acting as custodian of assets, and the lack of control by the depository is considered in the 'Mandated Individualised Portfolio Management Professional Ethics', which is a set of rules of conduct defined by AFG–ASFFI. The rules of conduct for asset managers are summarized below (see 'Professional Ethics and Rules of Conduct').

Disclosure

Asset management companies are required to provide clients with periodic reports detailing the value and composition of the portfolio.

Enforcement

Under the law of 2 August 1989, the COB can impose administrative sanctions concerning practices contrary to its regulations. When the COB observes infringements of its regulations, it can pronounce a fine amounting to as much as FF10 m, or, when profits have been realized, up to ten times their amount. The fine depends on the gravity of the infringements committed and is in proportion to the advantages or profits derived. The sanction procedure is made public, and the decision is subject to appeal at the Cour d'Appel in Paris.

As a protective measure, and following a formal investigation and sanction procedure, the COB also has the right to withdraw the authorization if the company does not meet the requirements under which it was granted.

Audit

Asset managers must prepare and submit audited accounts. The COB must be notified of any irregularities discovered by auditors during their investigation of the company. Similarly, the senior management of the company must also be informed.

Compensation

There is no specific compensation scheme in operation for the clients of asset managers. However, there is a scheme whereby deposits, bonds, and cash are guaranteed. A client's investments are also covered under this scheme.

Complaints

The COB receives some 2,500 complaints every year, although the great majority are unrelated to asset management. For the most part, the investors are not acquainted with their rights and the Commission is able to provide them with the necessary information. If the complaint is well founded, the COB considers four courses of actions: a fine; referral to the Public Prosecutor, should the case reveal the existence of criminal fraud; referral to the civil courts if compensation appears justified; or amicable settlement of the dispute.

Authorization

The COB licenses portfolio management companies and the UCIT management firms, and approves the activities concerning asset management of all the investment service providers. It is required to treat an application for authorization within three months of receiving it. Prior to issuing approval of a portfolio management company, the COB undertakes to verify:

- the existence of the company's headquarters in France;
- the existence of adequate initial capital;
- the identity and status of the shareholders;
- the integrity and experience of senior executives;
- the presence of at least two persons in a position to determine the company's general policy;
- the adequacy of the legal framework; and
- the existence of a programme of activities for each of the services to be provided.

The programme of activities must indicate for the three years ahead the extent of the authorization that the company is seeking (collective investment schemes or portfolio management), the investment strategy, the marketing strategy, human resources, and technical means.

COB's review of the application focuses on the adequacy of the asset manager's legal form, capitalization, and management and operational infrastructure to conduct its business.

Supervision

The supervision carried out by the COB is designed to detect all those practices and conduct likely to be harmful to the security of the investor. In this respect, the COB is particularly concerned with prudential control and supervising the rules of conduct connected to this. It ensures that the controls and procedures that are submitted to the COB during the authorization process are put in place, that a compliance officer and an individual responsible for internal control are appointed, and that all rules and regulations are complied with. On its part, the management company is required to inform the COB of any event that may compromise the company's ability to comply with its licence.

Among the supervision rights is the right of the COB chairman to order an investigation at any point in time. An investigation is often triggered as a result of observations arising from market supervision and the follow-up of corporate activities, or as a result of complaints. The COB investigators are entitled to:

- enter all business premises;
- have made available to them all documents and to obtain a copy of those documents; and
- summon and interview any person likely to be able to supply information.

The Professional Ethics and Rules of Conduct

The 'Mandated Individualised Portfolio Management Professional Ethics', published in April 1997 by the AFG–ASFFI, contains a set of 60 rules of conduct. These recall, specify, or complete the legislative or regulatory provisions in effect, and the basic uses and practices of professional ethics usually observed in France. Observance of the rules is obligatory for members of the AFG–ASFFI who are involved in mandated individualized portfolio management. The rules may therefore be seen as a form of complementary self-regulation of the French asset management industry.

Broadly, the professional ethics concern rules and guidelines on the following.

The management and prevention of conflicts of interest—the asset management company must set up an organization that allows it to carry out its functions in the exclusive interest of the principals (clients). If asset management is performed within an institution or group that operates in several areas, the fields of activities and operations must be separated. Portfolio managers must carry out asset management for third parties as their principal activity. They should never manage at the same time the portfolio belonging to the company, to companies in the group, or to companies acting as custodian of the assets they manage.

The obligation of means—the company must have available at all times the personnel, organization, and equipment suitable for the type of services offered and the level of expansion of its activities.

The contractual relationship between manager and principals—the portfolio management mandate must contain provisions concerning the purpose of the mandate and management objectives; the authorized operations and types of products; the selected investment area; the minimum investment levels; any existence of a guaranteed result; the remuneration of the manager; the methods for informing the principal; the absence of responsibility of the mandated agent with regard to transactions carried out at the principal's request; the obligation on the part of the principal to inform the mandated agent of any event that could alter the provisions of the contract; and the duration of the mandate and the procedures required for its termination. Also confirmed in writing is the possible obligation on the part of the company to have recourse to a custodian or intermediaries chosen by the investor.

The relations with principals—for example, the manager has a duty to keep its principals informed. Any documents sent must be objective, clear, and comprehensible, particularly those sent to non-professional principals.

The relations with intermediaries—the choice of intermediaries must be made on the basis of objective criteria taking into consideration the quality of services provided. Among the criteria are the rules of professional ethics proper to intermediaries, in particular the separation of activities on their behalf from those on behalf of third parties.

The marketing of individualized management under mandate—for example, the asset management company must not engage in wrongful or misleading advertising practices.

The behaviour of the portfolio manager employed by the company— among other rules, portfolio managers are required to show reserve in the market transactions they carry out on their own behalf so as to avoid finding themselves in a situation of conflict of interest.

6A.2 GERMANY

The Regulatory Authorities

There is no single authority supervising the German asset management industry. The relevant regulatory body for asset managers and investment companies is the Federal Banking Supervisory Authority (Bundesaufsichtsamt für das Kreditwesen, BAKred); for insurance companies, it is the Federal Insurance Supervisory Authority (Bundesaufsichtsamt für das Versicherungswesen, BAV). The two authorities are responsible for authorization and solvency supervision. Solvency supervision is broadly defined as monitoring the companies' ability to safeguard their continuing existence by pursuing an appropriate business policy and by maintaining sufficient capital.

Since fewer insurance companies are managing their own funds, regulation of investment management has increasingly shifted to the BAKred, with the BAV continuing to regulate insurance companies' own funds. No statistics are published on how many insurance companies have outsourced asset management and how many continue to manage their funds in-house.

To the extent that asset managers trade in securities, they are also supervised by the Federal Supervisory Office for Securities Trading (Bundesaufsichtsamt für den Wertpapierhandel), which is responsible for market supervision. Broadly, market supervision serves to ensure the protection of depositors, the transparency of the securities markets, and the integrity of the capital market.

The legal basis for all financial services institutions, including those that provide portfolio management services, is provided by the Banking Supervisory Act (Kreditwesengesetz, KWG). The Investment Companies Act (Gesetz über Kapitalanlagegesellschaften, KAGG) regulates the operation of domestic investment companies. Investment companies manage investment funds, but can also provide portfolio management activities for third parties. Private and public insurance companies are not considered as financial services institutions, and do not therefore fall under the legislation of the KWG. Instead, they are separately regulated by the Insurance Supervision Act (Versicherungsaufsichts-gesetz, VAG).

Other relevant legislation includes:

- the Securities Trading Act (Wertpapierhandelsgesetz), which implements the prudential and conduct-of-business rules for trading with securities;
- the Safe Custody Act (Depotgesetz), which governs deposits of securities and applies to all safe-custody activities; and
- the Deposit Guarantee and Investor Compensation Act (Einlage-sicherungs- und Anlegerentschädigunggesetz), which provides for basic investor compensation in the event of losses.

The Capital Requirements

All financial services institutions, including those providing portfolio management for third parties, are subject to the capital adequacy rules laid down in the KWG. Capital requirements for investment companies are legislated in the Investment Companies Act (KAGG). Separate solvency regulation, which applies to insurance companies, including the asset management part if it has not been outsourced to a separate business, is contained in the Insurance Supervision Act.

The Banking Act

Anyone wishing to provide financial services in Germany, including portfolio management, generally needs a written licence from the Federal Banking Supervisory Authority. As laid down in the Banking Act (KWG), the Authority may only grant a licence if the following mandatory minimum capital requirement is met:

- €50,000, if the applicant company does not have power of attorney and does not trade for its own account;
- €125,000, if the applicant company has power of attorney;
- €730,000, if the applicant company engages in own-account trading for others; or
- €5 m, if the applicant engages in deposit-taking activities.

The initial capital must be freely available and must not result from borrowing. The KWG contains details on how the initial capital is calculated (mainly paid-up capital and reserves, less withdrawals by, and loans granted to, general partners, or less the total nominal amount of the cumulative preferential shares). The Federal Banking Supervisory Authority reserves the right to change the minimum capital requirement on an individual basis.

As an ongoing capital requirement, the KWG legislates that portfolio managers or other financial services institutions must have own funds amounting at least to one-quarter of their costs shown in the profit and loss account of the last set of annual accounts under general administrative expenses, depreciation of tangible and intangible fixed assets and value adjustments. If a set of annual accounts has not yet been drawn up, the figure is to be estimated by those contained in the current business plan.

In addition, financial services institutions are subject to own-funds requirements that take into account market risk positions. These additional requirements only apply to institutions which conduct trading for their own account, or which are authorized to obtain ownership or possession of funds or securities of customers.

The Investment Companies Act

The Investment Companies Act (KAGG), which is the decisive law for German investment companies in addition to the KWG, provides that the Banking Supervisory Authority may grant a financial institution the licence to carry out investment fund activities if the paid-in nominal capital is at least DM 5 m (€2.6 m). There is no variable component in the capital requirement for investment companies.

The Insurance Supervision Act

The capital requirements contained in the Insurance Supervision Act (VAG) only apply to asset managers that are insurance companies that continue to manage their own funds in-house. To ensure that their liabilities under the insurance contracts can permanently be met, the VAG requires insurance undertakings to establish free uncommitted own funds in an amount not less than the solvency margin. This margin depends on the total volume of business. One third of the margin is deemed to be the guarantee fund.

The Decree on the Capital Requirement of Insurance Companies (Kapitalausstattungs-Verordnung) of 16 April 1996 contains the provisions on the calculation of solvency margins. For life assurance companies, the solvency margin depends on the mathematical reserves and the risk capital. The Decree also lays down the minimum guarantee funds. For life assurance companies, the minimum guarantee fund is €800,000. These solvency requirements for the insurance business capture the capital requirements for the asset management part of insurance.

The Separation of Clients' Assets

Basic safe-custody rules are laid down in the Safe Custody Act (Depotgesetz) and apply to all non-private persons performing safe-custody activities. This Act specifies the legal responsibility of the custodian to ensure safe keeping and provides for punishment in case of breaches.

The Banking Act (KWG) classifies custodian services as a banking activity that correspondingly requires a licence from the Banking Supervisory Authority. Only in very rare cases is a custodian not a credit institution.

According to the Banking Act, financial services institutions that manage assets on a discretionary basis (portfolio managers) have to keep securities in a safe-custody account of the customer at a credit institution; otherwise, portfolio managers would require a licence to conduct safe-custody business and hence would be credit institutions themselves.

Strict safe-custody rules arise for investment companies according to the Investment Companies Act (KAGG). The KAGG requires that assets purchased with the funds paid in by investors have to be kept physically separate from the business assets and liabilities of the company managing the fund. They are held in safe custody and under the supervision of a depository bank (Depotbank). The depository bank can be part of the same group as the investment company.

In the case of investment companies, Depotbanks have the following authorities and responsibilities:

- they must act purely in the clients' interest;
- they must ensure that the KAGG and any other contractual obligations with clients are satisfied;
- they are empowered and required to take action against the investment companies in their own name on behalf of the clients;

- they must place and hold all assets held in custody in a blocked account; and
- they distribute the assets held in custody on default of the investment firm.

Still in the case of investment companies, the custodian controls and supervises asset allocation rules. The role extends to calculating the value of collective investment schemes, but there is no legal requirement to do so in individual schemes. If there is a mistake, then the custodian only pays for misvaluations. Other mistakes are the responsibility of the investment company.

Separate obligations apply to life assurance companies as laid down in the Insurance Supervision Act (VAG). Assets must be held physically separate and secured in such a way that they can only be accessed upon written approval of a trustee or a deputy of the trustee, who has been appointed by the supervisory board of the business and approved by the Insurance Supervisory Authority. At the end of the balance sheet, the trustee must certify that funds have been invested and kept in compliance with the applicable rules.

Disclosure

According to the Investment Companies Act, firms are required to submit reports on funds on a regular basis.

Enforcement

Under the Banking Act (KWG), the Banking Supervisory Authority is allowed to impose sanctions and fines in accordance with the provisions of the Administration Enforcement Act (Verwaltungsvollstreckungsgesetz) to punish breaches with administrative regulations and enforce compliance. The Act also contains details on the upper limits of the fines. Additional rights include dismissing the managing director or withdrawing the licence to pursue investment management business.

The Insurance Supervision Act grants similar enforcement rights to the Insurance Supervisory Authority.

Compensation

Prior to 1998, there was no specific investor compensation scheme to provide for monetary losses arising as a direct result of failure of investment firms handling securities transactions. However, a voluntary deposit protection or guarantee fund, managed by the Federal Association of German Banks, covered the deposits in private commercial banks. Payments were made on the default of deposit-holders to all non-banking institutions and private persons up to a limit of 30 per cent of the defaulting bank's equity capital per creditor.

In August 1998, the Deposit Guarantee and Investor Compensation Act came into force. It implements EC Directive 94/19 on deposit guarantee schemes and EC Directive 97/9 on investor compensation schemes into national law. Since then, all registered providers of financial services are legally obliged to join and financially contribute to the Compensatory Fund of Securities Trading Companies (Entschädigungseinrichtung der Wertpapierhandelsunternehmen, EdW). Investment companies are only required to join if they undertake third-party portfolio management. The scheme grants compensation if an affiliated company gets into financial difficulty and cannot repay or meet its obligations. It provides for minimum protection only. The amount of compensation granted is limited to 90 per cent of the value of deposits taken, up to a maximum of €20,000; and to 90 per cent of the liabilities from security transactions, again up to a maximum of €20,000 per investor and financial services institution. Excluded from compensation are insurance companies, capital investment companies, medium-sized and large companies, and state-owned companies.

Prior to commencing a commercial relationship, institutions are required to inform their non-institutional customers about the guarantee provisions, including the scope and amount of the guarantee, in a written and easily comprehensible form.

Complaints

Conduct-of-business rules require firms (in banking groups) to implement internal procedures to deal with complaints.

Authorization

The Banking Act and Investment Companies Acts

Any enterprise wishing to pursue financial services, including asset management activities, needs a written licence from the Federal Banking Supervisory Authority. In addition to satisfying the minimum capital requirements, conditions to be granted a licence include the following.

The institution must have trustworthy managers with the necessary professional qualifications.

Proprietors, legal representatives, or general partners of an enterprise holding a qualified participating interest must be trustworthy, and must satisfy the requirements regarding sound and prudent management of the institution.

The institution must be in a position to make the organizational arrangements necessary for the proper operation of the business.

If the institution is a subsidiary of another enterprise domiciled abroad, the parent must be effectively supervised in the state where it is registered or has its head office. The appropriate supervisory body must be prepared to cooperate satisfactorily with the Federal Banking Supervisory Authority.

The institution must file with the application a business plan that contains:

- projected financial accounts for the first three financial years;
- a detailed description of the planned operations;
- customer contracts, business management agreements, and safe-custody authorizations, where they have been drawn up;
- a description of the organizational structure; and
- a description of the planned internal monitoring procedures.

The Insurance Supervision Act

Licences to carry out insurance business are granted by the Insurance Supervisory Authority. When applying for a licence, the enterprise must file a detailed operating plan, which in addition to the minimum capital requirement outlined above, must contain:

- a description of the purpose and organization of the insurance undertaking;

- information about the classes of insurance to be provided;
- details on any proposed outsourcing of activities, such as portfolio management;
- estimates of expenses and the liquidity situation for the first three financial years; including a statement on how liabilities under insurance contracts and the requirements with respect to the financial resources are to be met;
- information about intended reinsurance;
- information necessary to judge the reliability and qualification of managers and directors;
- information on major participations held;
- information about close relations existing between the insurance undertaking and another natural or legal person; and
- information necessary to judge the reliability and qualification of the responsible actuary.

Supervision

The Banking Act grants the Banking Supervisory Authority (BAKred) several supervision rights including:

- upon request, supervised institutions must provide information about all business activities and present documentation;
- the BAKred may carry out audits and inspect business premises, even if there is no special reason for them;
- the BAKred may send representatives to shareholders' meetings or general meetings.

The regulator checks the asset allocation of investment firms every month or every three months. In addition, institutions must submit their monthly returns on a quarterly basis. They are also required to deposit the annual accounts with the BAKred within three months of the following financial year. The final audited accounts must be submitted immediately after the completion of the audit. Furthermore, institutions have to inform the BAKred immediately about important events, such as significant losses or changes in management.

Similar provisions are laid down in the Insurance Act. While the BAV may only inspect insurance companies every seven or eight years, firms need to inform the regulator about asset structure every three months and provide other information every year. The BAV also has the right to carry out random audits and business inspections, or to send representatives to meetings.

6A.3   IRELAND

The Regulatory Authorities

The Department of Finance is responsible for the development of legislation regarding the regulation of financial services. The principal regulatory body with responsibility for implementing legislation regarding the asset management industry is the Central Bank of Ireland (the Bank). All credit institutions,[3] investment managers, and investment intermediaries are authorized and supervised by the Bank. As the lead regulator for financial groups headquartered in Ireland, the Bank has the ultimate supervisory authority for all of a group's financial activities.

The Bank receives its statutory powers under the provisions of a number of Acts,[4] and legislation governing the operation of collective investment schemes. The Department of Enterprise, Trade and Employment devises legislation concerning the regulation of collective investment schemes, which are directly authorized and regulated by the Bank.

At the end of 1998, the Bank was responsible for the supervision of some 877 institutions. Of these, 742 were supervised under the Investment Intermediaries Act 1995, of which 175 were International Financial Services Centre companies. The number of banks supervised was 77. In addition, a total of 1,500 funds (including sub-funds) were authorized under collective investment scheme legislation, and the Bank supervised five professional bodies, three exchanges, and their member firms.

The Department of Enterprise, Trade and Employment is responsible for the authorization and supervision of insurance companies. Where

---

[3] The credit institutions supervised by the Bank include licensed banks, building societies, Trustee Savings Bank, ACC Bank, ICC Bank, and ICC Investment Bank.

[4] The Central Bank Acts, 1971–98, the Building Societies Act 1989, the Trustee Savings Bank Act 1989, the Investment Intermediaries Act 1995, the Stock Exchange Act 1995, the ACC Bank Act 1992, and the ICC Bank Act 1992.

the asset management function is carried out by an insurance company, it comes under the supervision of the Department. Conversely, where an insurance company establishes a subsidiary, which is not an insurance company itself, it is authorized and supervised by the Bank. Similarly, the Pensions Board has responsibility in relation to pension funds and the trustees of those funds. However, it is common practice for pension funds to have their assets managed by institutions that are primarily regulated elsewhere (for example, by the Bank or the Department).

The Investment Intermediaries Act 1995 provides the legislation necessary for the authorization and supervision of investment firms by the Bank. This Act was introduced in order to transpose the Investment Services Directive into the Irish law.[5]

The Capital Requirements

In accordance with the EU Directive on the Capital Adequacy of Investment Firms and Credit Institutions, the Central Bank of Ireland has devised rules for Irish investment firms. Capital is defined as own funds and financial resources. Firms are required to hold capital that is equal to or greater than the largest of the following:

- the firm's capital shall never be less than one-quarter of the fixed overheads in the proceeding year;[6] or

- firms must ensure that financial resources are sufficient to cover the sum of the capital requirements calculated in respect of position risk, underwriting, settlement, and counterparty risk, foreign-exchange risk, and large exposures for their trading book business; imposed in the Solvency Ratio Directive and imposed by the Bank to cover risks arising in connection with business outside the scope of the Capital Adequacy Directive and Solvency Ratio Directive.

[5] Although the provision of investment advice is a non-core activity within the Investment Services Directive, it is covered by the Investment Intermediaries Act, and investment advisers are subjected to a similar regulatory regime as other investment businesses.

[6] Fixed overheads include all expenses incurred by the firm with the following exceptions: exceptional and extraordinary items that have previously been agreed with the Bank; shared commissions paid, other than to officers and staff of the firm; profit shares, bonuses, etc.; losses arising on the translation of foreign currency balances; depreciation; and any other non-fixed expense that has been agreed with the Bank.

Firms that hold clients' money and/or financial instruments must hold an initial capital of €125,000 (IR£98,446). Firms that only receive and transmit orders from investors and are not authorized to hold clients' money or financial instruments, to deal for own account, or to underwrite issues on a firm commitment basis must have initial capital of €50,000 (IR£39,378). All other firms must have initial capital of €730,000 (IR£574,922). The Bank reserves the right to impose additional capital requirements on firms that are exposed to higher levels of operational risk.

The Separation of Clients' Assets

Section 52 of the Investment Intermediaries Act 1995 places requirements on authorized investment firms regarding the safekeeping of clients' funds and instruments. In general, an authorized firm must hold client money separate from its own money. Where an authorized firm holds money on behalf of a client, it must ensure that the money is held in a client account with a credit institution that is continually assessed. If an authorized firm deposits client's money with an institution that is part of the same group as the authorized firm, then:

- an ongoing risk assessment of that institution must be undertaken, ensuring that this assessment is as rigorous as that faced by any other institution that is not part of the group;
- the firm must inform the client in writing; and
- the identity of the institution concerned must be made known to the client.

Disclosure

Each new client must be given a copy of the firm's investment management agreement. The purpose of this agreement is to set out the basis, on which the firm's services are provided. The following information should be included in the investment management agreement:

- an outline of the services to be provided;
- an outline of the firm's understanding of the client's investment objectives and investment restrictions, if any;

- details of the firm's charges;
- an outline of the firm's policies in relation to conflicts of interest;
- details of the firm's policy in relation to the taking of principal positions;
- details of the firm's arrangements for custody of investments held for clients; and
- in the case of any discretionary client or any client for whom the firm borrows money or deals in derivatives, underwriting or stock lending, the terms shall include details of such services and the firm shall procure that the terms are signed by the client.

In addition, an investment manager must send a statement to a client at least once every six months. This statement must detail the value of the portfolio at the beginning and end of the period, its composition at the end, and, for a discretionary client, changes in its composition between those dates. Unless stated otherwise in the investment management agreement, the periodic information should include:

The contents and value of portfolio—the number of units of each asset in the portfolio on the date on which the statement is made up, the opening value of the portfolio, the value of each of the assets at the closing date, and the aggregate of their values at that date;

The basis of valuation—a statement explaining the calculation of the value of the portfolio at the closing date;

Details of any assets loaned or charged—details of assets that were on loan to a third party at the closing date, or assets that were charged to secure borrowings made on behalf of the portfolio;

Income received—the aggregate income received on behalf of the client, earned on all assets contained in the portfolio;

Interest paid—details of interest paid in respect of amounts borrowed on behalf of the portfolio;

Transaction details—particulars in respect of each transaction entered into by the manager in the assets of the portfolio during the account, and details of each payment made to the client and amount received from the client by the manager during that period;

Manager's remuneration—a statement of the fees and charges for the period, unless previously advised;

Manager's remuneration from third parties—a statement of any remuneration received by the manager from a third party, which is attributable to the transactions entered into by the manager for the portfolio; and

A statement of the difference between the value of the portfolio at the closing date and its opening value, paying particular attention to:

- the total amount of assets received from the client and added to the portfolio during the period of account;
- the aggregate of the value of assets transferred, or of amounts paid, to the client during the period of account;
- the aggregate of income received on behalf of the client during the period of account in respect of all the assets comprised in the portfolio;
- the aggregate of interest payments referred to above; and
- the aggregate realized and unrealized profits or gains and losses attributable to the assets comprised in the portfolio during the period of account.

If the portfolio contains open positions in derivatives, the following information should be included in the statement of periodic information:

- the name and address of the manager;
- the client's designation and account number;
- each payment made and amount received by the manager in respect of the account during the month;
- a statement of the resulting profit or loss to the client after deducting commission in respect of each transaction;
- a statement of the amount of the unrealized profit or loss attributable to each open position; and
- a statement of the aggregate of each of the following in the client's account: cash; collateral; unrealized profits attributable to open positions; and unrealized losses attributable to open positions.

Enforcement

Under the Investment Intermediaries Act 1995, the Central Bank of Ireland has the authority to enforce compliance with the regulations. The following actions may be taken by the Bank in the event of a violation of the regulations:

- at the time of authorization or any subsequent time, conditions may be imposed on a firm relating to advertising, acquiring transactions, or holding client money;

- an application for authorization from a firm may be denied;
- upon the issue of a Direction, a firm may be instructed to conduct, or discontinue an activity;
- authorization to conduct investment activities may be withdrawn;
- a second audit of the firm's accounts may be ordered;
- an application may be submitted to the court to remove an officer or employee from a firm;
- inspectors may be appointed to examine the activities of the firm;
- offences contained in the Act may be prosecuted. Convictions may result in fines (of £1000 or £1 m) and/or a term of imprisonment (of one or ten years); and
- a 'Determinations Committee' may be established with responsibility to impose fines and other enforcement measures. The establishment of this committee is waiting upon the mandatory ministerial decision, which had not been made at the time of writing.

Audit

Legislation stipulates that, in certain circumstances, external auditors of credit institutions are required to provide the Central Bank with information about the company. For example, the external auditor must notify the Bank if, during the course of an audit:

- matters arise that are likely to affect the solvency of the company;
- there are material deficiencies in the financial systems of control; or
- there are significant omissions or inaccuracies in returns to the Bank.

The Bank must be informed if the auditor intends to publish a qualified report. If the auditor wishes to resign their post, then the Bank must be notified. The Bank has the right to seek specific information from the auditors in relation to the affairs of the company.

Compensation

The Investor Compensation Company was established under the Investor Compensation Act 1998 with the aim of providing compensation to private clients of a failed investment firm.[7] This Act transposed the Investor Compensation Directive into law. According to this directive, all member states are required to have an investor compensation scheme for firms authorized in their own country to conduct certain types of investment business. This compensation scheme must guarantee a minimum level of protection for the private investor if an investment firm cannot compensate investors. These firms are entitled to carry out that same business in any other member state, without having to be authorized by that country's regulator. Individual member states may increase this level for their own compensation schemes.

The Investor Compensation Company is funded by contributions from member firms. Firms covered by the scheme include:

- investment firms regulated by the Central Bank;
- stockbrokers regulated by the Central Bank;
- insurance brokers, agents, and tied agents;
- banks and building societies licensed by the Central Bank which carry out investment services; and
- accountants certified by their professional bodies to conduct investment business.

The types of investment covered by the scheme include:

- public and private company shares;
- units in collective investment schemes;
- prize bonds;
- life and non-life insurance policies;
- tracker bonds; and
- futures and options.

Compensation is only payable where the firm is unable, due to its financial circumstances, to return a client's money or investments as determined either by the courts or the Central Bank. As set out in the Investor Compensation Directive, the maximum level of compensation payable is 90 per cent of the net loss, subject to a maximum payment of IR£15,751 (€20,000). Investors have five months from the time the investment firm is deemed to have failed to make a claim.

---

[7] Investors that suffer a decline in the value of investments as a result of poor advice, market movements, or inflation are not eligible to receive compensation.

Currently the Investor Compensation Company has made a provision of £640,000 in the accounts on the basis of claims, awaiting verification, from investors in Money Markets International Stockbrokers, a stock broker, which has gone into liquidation.

Complaints

Asset management companies are required to maintain a record of all written complaints received against them from their clients, including a record of their response and any action taken as a result of the complaint. An adequate procedure must be in place to ensure the effective handling of complaints. If a client is not satisfied with the company's response to a complaint, then the company should inform the complainant of their right to refer the matter to the Central Bank.

Authorization

Prior to authorization, an investment firm must satisfy the Bank that:

- the directors and managers of the company are persons of probity and competence;
- the firm has sufficient capital; and
- the requirements set out by the Bank are likely to be met.

In order to receive authorization for an investment business from the Bank, the following steps must be satisfied:

- the Bank must fully understand the nature of the activity and the risks involved;
- the suitability of shareholders must be assessed, including, where relevant, the ultimate and beneficial shareholders;
- the probity and competence of directors and senior management in relation to their proposed function must be examined. Where appropriate, it may be necessary to use detailed questionnaires and contacts with other supervisors and security checks;
- the applicant's financial standing must be assessed, with particular emphasis on the capacity to provide for the future capital needs of the business;

- it is necessary to establish that the entity can be supervised effectively with particular reference to the need for consolidated supervision of each financial group and ensuring that the business is controlled from Ireland; and
- compliance with legislative requirements and those of relevant EU directives must be ensured.

At the time of authorization, the Bank may impose further detailed requirements on the entity in accordance with the relevant legislation. Non-bank firms are subject to requirements that fall into the following categories:

- general reporting requirements;
- capital requirements;
- requirements in relation to the safekeeping of client assets;
- advertising requirements;
- conduct-of-business requirements; and
- guidelines in relation to anti-money laundering.

The Bank has issued a code of conduct for investment managers, which details general and specific principles to which the investment manager must adhere when conducting all transactions. The general principles state that an investment manager shall ensure that in all transactions, it:

- acts honestly and fairly in conducting its business activities in the best interests of its clients and the integrity of the market;
- acts with due skill, care, and diligence in the best interests of its clients and the integrity of the market;
- has and employs effectively the resources and procedures that are necessary for the proper performance of its business activities;
- seeks from its clients information regarding their financial situations, investment experience, and objectives as regards the services requested;
- makes adequate disclosure of relevant material information, including commissions, in its dealings with its clients;
- makes a reasonable effort to avoid conflicts of interests and, when they cannot be avoided, ensures that its clients are fairly treated;
- complies with all regulatory requirements applicable to the conduct of its business activities; and
- adheres to the code of conduct.

An investment firm must also ensure that any transaction it executes on behalf of a client or advice given to a client is suitable to the client. The firm must also ensure that it deals to the best advantage of its clients.

Supervision

Following authorization, a firm faces ongoing supervision, which depends on the type of institution and activities being conducted. The Bank may generally conduct both on- and off-site monitoring, which are common to all firms. Off-site monitoring includes regular collection and analysis of data; regular review meetings with management; and addressing issues as they arise.

The Bank receives returns from regulated firms or individuals on a monthly, quarterly, or six-monthly basis. Returns submitted to the Bank typically include profit and loss accounts and balance sheets, as well as detailed calculations in relation to the firm's capital position. Upon examination of this information, the Bank can check compliance with regulatory rules, and monitor any changes in the financial statements, or the pattern of income and expenditure. Furthermore, external auditors of regulated firms are required to notify the Bank in writing if they have any reason to believe that there are material inaccuracies in, or omissions from, any returns of a financial nature.

Review meetings take the form of discussions with senior management of supervised institutions and, on average, are held with each institution twice a year. These meetings provide a forum for discussion of issues such as:

- the financial performance of the institution;
- the impact of any organizational changes;
- agreeing remedial action to deal with any areas of prudential concern;
- the institution's future plans and projections; and
- a general discussion of the changing business and financial environment, and its impact on the institution.

On-site inspections involve the examination of the books and records of the supervised entity (and any subsidiary, if appropriate), and an assessment of its compliance with the Bank's supervisory requirements and with relevant legislative provisions. The frequency of such inspections depends on many considerations, including the structure of the supervised entity (locally incorporated or a branch), its quality of ownership, size, the activities of the institution, and the associated risks—including risks associated with investor protection, risks to the financial system, financial risks to the institution, and risks associated with poor internal controls.

The frequency of inspections can range from several in one year to once every two or three years. Inspections may be of a broad, general nature, seeking to examine most of the institution's main activities. Alternatively, they may focus on a specific activity or area, such as treasury operations, credit-control procedures, or compliance with client asset requirements. Following an inspection, a report is prepared and a letter is issued to the relevant entity, recommending remedial action where appropriate.

6A.4 ITALY

The Regulatory Authorities

According to the Consolidated Law on Financial Markets (Legislative Decree 58/1998), which came into force on 1 July 1998, supervision of financial intermediaries is divided between the Bank of Italy and Consob. The Bank of Italy is responsible for prudential supervision, information monitoring, and conducting on-site controls with the aim of limiting risks and ensuring the stability of intermediaries. Consob has a role in ensuring transparency and proper conduct.

An asset management company managing a fund will therefore be supervised by the Bank of Italy, while one managing assets on behalf of a private client or managed account is supervised by Consob. In practice, it is difficult to distinguish precisely between the role of Consob and the Bank of Italy in the regulation of asset management companies.

It is worth noting that the Consolidated Law allows asset management companies to engage jointly in the activities of management on a client-by-client basis as well as a collective basis.

The Capital Requirements

Capital adequacy requirements are determined by the Bank of Italy. The capital requirement imposed on asset management companies consists of two components: a fixed and a variable amount. The current legislation requires a single level of share capital of 2 billion lire (€1.03 m) to be met. Prior to the implementation of the legislation contained in the Consolidated Law, the amount of share capital set for asset management companies differed according to the type of funds managed. This change in legislation is a result of a change in the licensing arrangements. Asset management companies are now granted a single licence that allows them to establish and manage funds of any kind.

In addition to this fixed component, capital adequacy requirements are also a function of the value of the assets under management, and are equal to:

- 0.5 per cent of the value of assets in open-ended funds, SICAVs, and pension funds;
- 2 per cent for closed-ended funds; and
- an additional capital charge required in the case of pension funds that guarantee the repayment of principal.

In any event, the total capital requirement must be at least equal to 25 per cent of the company's fixed operating costs in the previous financial year. However, the proportion of OPEX for each company is determined by the Bank of Italy. In effect, the proportion may be higher or lower than 25 per cent, depending on the regulator's evaluation of the company's business plan and activities.

The Separation of Clients' Assets

The Bank of Italy has issued new rules to deal with the holding of clients' assets, in order to ensure that there is separation between the assets of individual customers, and between customers' assets and those of the intermediary. The regulations include:

- the separation of clients' assets from those of other clients and from those of the company. In effect, this means that clients' assets must be held outside the company, but may be held within the group to which the company belongs;

- the separate reporting of the assets of each customer;
- the prohibition of the use of clients' assets by intermediaries, unless authorized in writing by the customer; and
- the prompt deposit with a bank of sums of money received from customers.

Disclosure

The Bank of Italy and Consob may require the following information:

- the names of asset management companies' shareholders;
- the directors of companies and entities that hold capital in asset management companies to provide the names of their controllers; and
- trust companies that hold capital in asset management companies to provide the names and details of the beneficiaries.

Enforcement

In the event of serious administrative irregularities or violations of regulations, the administrative body of an asset management company may be replaced by a provisional administrator, appointed by the chairman of Consob, for a maximum of 60 days.

The Minister of the Treasury may issue a decree dissolving the management of an asset management company where:

- serious administrative irregularities or violations of laws, regulations, or bylaws governing its activity are found;
- serious capital losses are expected; and
- the dissolution has been the object of a reasoned request by the management, an extraordinary meeting of shareholders, or the provisional administrator appointed by the chairman of Consob.

Similarly, the Minister of the Treasury may issue a decree withdrawing authorization to continue business, and ordering compulsory liquidation of asset management companies.

Provision of investment services without authorization or a breach of regulations will result in imprisonment and a fine.

Audit

Authorized asset management companies, or their auditors, may be required to provide data and information to the Bank of Italy and Consob. Any irregularities discovered by the auditors during their examination of the company must be promptly reported to the Bank of Italy and Consob. In addition, firms engaged to audit the accounts of an asset management company are also required to provide an opinion on the investment fund's statement of operations. Auditors are not permitted to conduct examinations of companies without prior warning.

Compensation

The provision of investment services is dependent on the membership of a compensation scheme aimed at protecting investors. The organization and operation of the scheme is determined by the Minister of the Treasury following consultation with the Bank of Italy and Consob.

There are two separate compensation schemes. Banks have developed a scheme whereby their clients may claim for any losses. Asset management companies and security houses have developed a joint scheme, which has been in operation since 1991. However, in light of failures by security houses, there is currently a debate on whether a separate compensation scheme should be established for clients of asset management companies.

Complaints

There is no specific ombudsman to deal with complaints relating to asset management activity against firms regulated by Consob and the Bank of Italy. However, individual investors may complain to Consob, with the potential of taking the complaint before the courts.

Authorization

The provision of the service of collective asset management and management on a client-by-client basis is authorized by the Bank of Italy, after consultation with Consob. To receive authorization, the following conditions must be satisfied:

- the legal form adopted is that of a 'società per azioni';
- the registered office and the head office of the company are located in Italy;
- the paid-up capital is not less than that established on a general basis by the Bank of Italy;
- the persons performing administrative, managerial, or control functions must fulfil integrity and experience requirements set out by the Minister of the Treasury;
- the shareholders must fulfil integrity requirements set out by the Minister of the Treasury;
- the structure of the group of which the company is part is not prejudicial to the effective supervision of the company;
- any information required by the regulator is provided;
- a programme of initial operations and a description of the organizational structure have been submitted, together with the instrument of incorporations and bylaws; and
- the name of the company contains the words 'società di gestione del risparmio'.

Supervision

The Bank of Italy and Consob may conduct inspections of authorized persons. In supervising companies, Consob may assign a ranking to asset management companies, although the methodology used to develop this ranking is not publicized. On the basis of this, Consob will increase the frequency of visits to those companies that are deemed to be of higher risk. Inspections conducted by Consob or the Bank of Italy are not publicized.

6A.5 THE NETHERLANDS

The Regulatory Authorities

The Stichting Toezicht Effectenverkeer (STE) was established in 1988 as an independent organization charged with the supervision of securities trade in the Netherlands. Its creation provided for the separation of regulation from the government and from the industry itself. STE's objective is to ensure the proper functioning of the securities markets, to protect the position of investors, and to increase the transparency of the securities markets.

Two groups of institutions are regulated by the STE. The first consists of securities institutions that operate directly in one of the securities markets in the Netherlands. The second consists of securities institutions, known as 'off-exchange institutions', which do not trade directly on a securities market in the Netherlands. Off-exchange institutions refer to securities brokers and portfolio managers. Portfolio management is defined as the management or investment of securities owned by another party. Portfolio managers invest client monies subject to a prior contractual agreement, at their discretion and in the interests of the clients. They are not permitted to hold clients' money or securities. Collective investment schemes are regulated by the Dutch Central Bank (De Nederlandsche Bank). Insurance companies and pension funds that manage their own funds are regulated by the Insurance Chamber (Verzekeringskamer).

On 15 June 1992, the Supervision of Securities Trade Act (Wet toezicht effectenverkeer, Wte) transferred the responsibilities and powers of the finance minister to the STE. Under this Act, the STE is responsible for exercising its mandate, such as granting licences, reviewing stock exchange regulations, and investigating cases of insider trading. The Wte contained only framework regulations. Full regulations were detailed in the Decree on the Supervision of Securities Trade (Besluit toezicht effectenverkeer, Bte) and in the Further Regulation on the Supervision of Securities Trade, drafted by the STE. Furthermore, on 31 December 1995, the Wte was replaced by the Supervision of Securities Trade Act 1995 (Wte 1995). This new legislation, the aims of which are similar to those of the original Wte, was necessary in order to incorporate the Investor Services and Capital Adequacy Directives into domestic legislation.

The Capital Requirements

According to 'Further Regulations on the Supervision of the Securities Trade 1999', the amount of capital a portfolio manager is required to hold is made up of two components: equity capital and actual own funds. The former refers to:

- the issue and paid-up share capital, excluding cumulative preference shares, in the case of a company limited by shares or a private limited company;
- the individual paid-up capital contributions of the partners, in the case of a general partnership;
- the individual paid-up capital contributions of the managing partners, and the paid-up capital contributions of the limited partners, in the case of a limited partnership;
- the capital paid-up or contributed by the members, in the case of a cooperative; or
- in any other case, the positive difference between assets and liabilities.

The level of equity capital is at least equal to the following:
€35,000, if the portfolio manager receives orders from clients and transmits these orders to another company.
€50,000, if the portfolio manager:

- receives and transmits orders on behalf of clients in another state that is subject to the agreement regarding the European Economic Area;
- receives and executes orders on behalf of clients;
- offers to obtain receivables by opening accounts;
- operates as a local enterprise;
- carries out portfolio management, where portfolio management is defined as the management of clients' financial instruments or monies, including transmission or execution of orders.

€730,000, if the portfolio manager:

- trades on its own account;
- underwrites issues of securities;
- executes transactions in order to maintain a market in financial instruments.

These levels are similar to those set out in the Capital Adequacy Directive. However, the middle level of equity capital of €125,000 identified in the Capital Adequacy Directive has been excluded. The reason reported for this is that this level of capital was to be imposed on 'securities institutions' that held clients' monies. However, under the Dutch legislation, custody rules prohibit any 'securities institution' from holding clients' monies unless it is a credit institution.

The level of actual own funds is equal to the highest of at least 25 per cent of the fixed costs[8] of the institution in the preceding year, or the minimum of the sum of the capital adequacy requirements to cover:

- position risk;
- settlement, delivery, and counterparty risk;
- large exposures;
- foreign-exchange risk; and
- other risks.

The Separation of Clients' Assets

It is the duty of the portfolio manager to make necessary arrangements that will ensure that the clients' assets are protected. Legislation details custody rules for the firms according to their activities. Asset management companies that only act as a financial intermediary must ensure that the monies and securities of clients are held in one or more bank accounts in the client's name. For institutions that execute transactions or conduct securities operations, clients must hold their monies or assets in one or more accounts in their name with a financial institution that is involved in the settlement of transactions in accordance with the tripartite agreement in place between the asset manager, the client, and the institution itself. In the case of 'beleggersgiro',[9]

[8] Fixed costs include all costs except the variable costs of staff whose contract of employment cannot be determined immediately and without payment of compensation; the costs of staff whose contract of employment can be determined immediately and without payment of compensation; the variable costs relating to the securities services performed for the securities institution; depreciation; interest costs on subordinated loans; extraordinary costs of a non-recurring nature; and other variable costs that have been approved by the STE in writing.
[9] According to the Wte 1995, a 'beleggersgiro' refers to anyone acting in a professional or commercial capacity who offers others the opportunity to obtain financial assets in the form of securities by opening an account by means of which transactions in securities may be effected.

clients' accounts must be strictly separate from that of the institution. This strict separation is realized by placing accounts into a legally separate entity (the 'effectengiro') and imposing on it a number of conditions relating to securities depository institutions. In addition, alternative custody rules take effect in the case of cross-border securities transactions and custody outside the Netherlands.

To summarize, clients' monies must be held separately from the assets of the company, but not necessarily held in the custody of a third party, with the exception of a 'beleggersgiro', who must ensure that clients' assets are held with a separate legal entity.

Institutions that hold client monies are required to ensure that records are available to the client of the assets held in custody.

Disclosure

A portfolio manager is required to provide returns to the STE each quarter. The return will include company accounts, such as balance sheet, profit and loss account, the level of actual own funds, and large exposures. The company is also required to provide clients with a statement of their account every quarter.

Sufficient information must be disseminated to the clients in order to enable them to make an informed assessment of the institution. In particular, the following information must be provided to the client:

- the name, place of registered office, and place of business of the institution;
- a list of the services provided by the institution;
- details of the characteristics of the financial instruments to which the services relate, including the specific investment risk attached to the financial instruments;
- the types of costs that will be charged to the client and the calculation on which such costs are based;
- information about potential or existing conflicts of interest;
- details of any other institution that may be involved with the client; and
- information about the termination of the contract.

Enforcement

On 1 January 2000, the Wte 1995 was amended to include two instruments to be used for the enforcement purposes. As a result, the
STE may impose a fine in the case of a breach of regulations set out in
the Wte 1995, the Bte 1995, and Further Regulations on the Supervision
of Securities Trade 1999. In addition, the STE will have the power
to penalize institutions for continually failing to comply with
regulations.

Both measures will be imposed by order. The order imposing a fine
will detail the regulation that was breached, the amount to be paid, the
basis upon which the amount of the fine has been determined, and
the period within which this amount must be paid. The STE will notify
the institution of its intention to impose a fine in advance. In some
cases, the institution will be invited to put its case before the STE in
relation to the breach in question.

Institutions have the right to appeal and object to any fines, and
objections must be lodged with the STE. A decision on the objection
may be appealed against to the court in Rotterdam, after which there
is the option of appeal to the Industrial Appeals Court.

During 1999 the STE took steps to sanction institutions, as detailed
in Table 6A.1.

In total, there were 69 cases of enforcement conducted by the STE.
The measures most frequently used were reprimands, refusals to grant
licences, or withdrawals of licences and reports.

Furthermore, companies are required to record breaches of
regulations and provide a regular report to the STE on all breaches
combined.

Table 6A.1. The cases of supervisory measures

Supervisory measures	1999
Issues of reprimands	20
Refusals of licence applications/withdrawals of licences	17
Reports	26
Appointments of secret receivers	1
Public earnings	5

Source: STE, 'Annual Report 1999'.

Audit

External audit of portfolio managers is conducted on an annual basis. The auditor is appointed by the portfolio management company. Annual audited accounts must be submitted to the STE.

Compensation

On 26 September 1998 the Investor Compensation Scheme directive was implemented in the Netherlands. Consequently, two investor compensation schemes were initiated:

The Collective Guarantee Scheme of Credit Institutions for Repayable Funds and Portfolio Investments, which is administered by De Nederlandsche Bank, and provides compensation to investors and creditors in the event of a credit institution no longer being able to meet its commitments as a result of its financial position;

The Investor Compensation Scheme, which is administered by the STE, with the aim of providing compensation to investors, should a securities institution be unable to meet its commitments as a result of its financial position. A securities institution is defined as an institution that is required to hold a licence under Section 7, subsection 1 of the Wte 1995. Under the Investor Compensation Scheme, an investor can receive compensation, up to a maximum payment of €20,000, in the event that an institution is unable to return monies or securities owing to investors. Compensation can only be paid to non-professional investors.

Complaints

Each institution supervised by the STE must comply with the further regulations concerning the handling of complaints, which specify that complaints must be dealt with within a reasonable period of time. In most cases, the responsibility to ensure the suitable handling of complaints falls with the managers of the institution. The complaint, and the way in which it is handled, must be recorded in order to track the complaints process and for internal and external audit process. If a proposed solution fails to provide satisfaction to the complainant, then the company must inform the complainant of their right to notify the

STE of the matter. The STE may also be notified during the initial stages. Although the STE does not have the power to compensate the complainant, it can ensure that such a problem does not recur.

In addition, the Dutch Securities Institute has established a complaints committee to deal with complaints from private investors concerning firms regulated by the STE. The committee arbitrates on cases where the complainant fails to receive satisfaction from the firm.

Authorization

Section 7, subsection 1 of Wte 1995 states that it is prohibited to operate as a portfolio manager without a licence. A licensed institution must meet several legal requirements, including the following:

- management must consist of at least two people;
- management must prove themselves reliable and competent;
- conditions relating to a minimum of shareholders' equity and own resources;
- rules concerning accounting procedures; and
- requirements relating to information to be issued to investors.

The STE monitors compliance with these regulations.

Supervision

Portfolio managers are subject to continual assessment and monitoring by the STE. In particular, the adequacy of financial resources is investigated. Violations of regulations will result in the imposition of fines and penalties.

6A.6 THE UK

The Regulatory Authorities

Regulation of financial services in the UK is overseen by the Financial Services Authority (FSA), which was established in October 1987 as an independent non-governmental body to replace the Securities and Investment Board. The FSA is responsible for the supervision of banks under the Banking Act 1987, a duty transferred from the Bank of England, and from the date of implementation the regulation of investment business under the Financial Services and Markets Act 2000.

Frontline regulatory bodies, or self-regulating organisations (SROs), authorized, recognized, and supervised by the FSA are involved in the supervision of firms that provide financial services.[10] The Investment Management Regulatory Organisation (IMRO) is the SRO charged with the supervision of companies that:

- manage the investments of others;
- operate unit trusts and manage assets of those trusts;
- manage the investments of pension funds and investment trusts;
- provide investment advice to institutional or corporate clients; and
- act as a trustee of unit trusts.

In practice, this implies that the IMRO regulates firms involved in such activities in the following categories:

- fund managers;
- unit trust managers and trustees;
- banks;
- life offices and friendly societies;
- local authorities;
- trustees and in-house managers of pension funds;
- venture capital managers; and
- institutional investment advisers.

The implementation of the Financial Services and Markets Act 2000 has now established the FSA as the single regulator of financial services. Steps were taken before that date to transfer responsibility for financial services supervision to the FSA. Staff previously employed by the IMRO and other SROs were transferred to new contracts of employment with the FSA.

---

[10] Under the Financial Services Act 1986, the FSA must be satisfied that the rules of an SRO provide adequate protection to investors.

The Three-tier Regulation

The implementation of the Companies Act in 1989 led to a change in the regulatory framework implemented under the Financial Services Act 1986. The new approach introduced three tiers to the regulation of investment business:

- principles—introduced by the FSA to ensure particular standards for persons authorized to provide investment services;
- core rules—which relate to the conduct of business and financial resources;
- third-tier rules—which provide guidance from the SROs.

Principles

To conduct investment business of the type described above, a firm or person must receive authorization from the IMRO. The process of authorization requires firms to prove that they are, and will remain, fit and proper persons to undertake investment business. In judging whether a firm is behaving appropriately in carrying out its business, the IMRO examines whether the firm has observed the Principles as set out in the IMRO *Rulebook*. The ten principles require that a firm:

- maintain high standards of integrity;
- act with due skill, care, and diligence;
- maintain high standards of market conduct;
- obtain information about clients, such as investment objectives;
- supply to the client any information that will allow the client to make an informed decision;
- avoid conflict of interests;
- ensure that clients' assets are properly protected by segregation;
- maintain adequate financial resources;
- ensure that staff are properly trained and supervised; and
- cooperate with the regulator and inform the latter of any relevant issues.

In addition, internal systems, and controls must be installed to ensure compliance with the IMRO Rules. The financial condition of the firm must be reported to the regulator periodically. The firm must provide the regulator with any requested information and cooperate with any investigation by the IMRO. It must agree to be subject to the disciplinary system of the IMRO and pay its share of the costs of the IMRO.

The Capital Requirements

Regulatory financial requirements are contingent on the types of services offered by the firm. The financial resources requirement for an authorized UK investment firm consists of an own-funds requirement and a liquid capital requirement. The liquid capital requirement is equivalent to a total capital requirement. A firm must calculate its own funds and liquid capital in the manner set out in Table 6A.2.

Having calculated own funds, an Investment Services Directive firm's own-funds requirement is:

- €730,000, if the firm deals for its own account and/or underwrites issues; or

Table 6A.2. The calculation of own-funds requirement

Financial resources	Category
Tier 1	
Paid-up share capital (excluding preference shares)	A
Share premium account	
Audited reserves	
Non-cumulative preference shares	
Less: Investments in own shares	B
Intangible assets	
Material current-year losses	
Material holdings in credit and financial institutions	
Tier 1 capital = (A − B)	C
Plus: **Tier 2**	
Revaluation reserves	D
Fixed-term cumulative preference share capital	
Long-term qualifying subordinated loans	
Other cumulative preference share capital and debt capital	
Qualifying arrangements	
'Own funds' = (C + D)	E
Plus: **Tier 3**	
Net trading book profits	F
Short-term qualifying subordinated loans and excess Tier 2 capital	
Less: Illiquid assets	G
Add: Qualifying property	
Other allowable items	
'Liquid capital' = (E + F − G)	

Source: IMRO *Rulebook*.

- €125,000, if the firm holds clients' monies or assets, but does not deal for its own accounts or underwrite issues; or
- €50,000, for a firm that does not hold clients' monies or assets, or participate in dealing for its own account or underwriting issues.

The liquid capital requirement is the total capital requirement that is the sum of its:

- expenditure-based requirement;
- position risk requirement;
- counterparty risk requirement;
- foreign-exchange requirement; and
- other assets requirement.

The expenditure-based requirement is equal to a fraction of the annual audited expenditure of the firm.[11] The relevant fraction is determined by the activities of the firm. According to the '13-week' rule, the fraction is set at 13/52 or one-quarter of the annual audited expenditure if the firm is an investment manager or a custodian and the firm either:

- holds clients' monies or assets itself; or
- procures the appointment as custodian of its clients' monies or assets of an associate of the firm that is not an approved bank.

The lower fraction of 6/52 will be set as the expenditure-based requirement if the firm:

- is an authorized unit trust manager; or
- acts only as an authorized corporate director of a UK open-ended investment company; or
- is an investment manager, which includes the operator of an unregulated collective investment scheme in relation to which the firm carries on the activity of an investment manager.

Apart from the risk requirements calculated as part of a firm's capital requirements, an investment firm is also required to monitor its large exposures and ensure that exposure to counterparties does not exceed the limits, as set by the IMRO.

---

[11] Annual audited expenditure is the amount described as total expenditure in the most recent annual financial return.

The Separation of Clients' Assets

The IMRO has devised rules that apply to a firm, which is itself the custodian of a client's assets, or which has recommended another firm to provide this service. The primary purpose of the rules is to restrict the commingling of client and firm assets. The rules are as follows.

The client investments must be 'separately identifiable' from those belonging to the firm.

The investments must be properly registered in the client's name, the name of a nominee, or a custodian.

The client investments must not be released into the possession or control of a third party unless it has proper authority from the client to do so.

The appropriate internal controls and systems must be in place in order to ensure the protection of clients' investments.

The firm will be responsible for any acts of an own nominee in the event of clients' investments registered in the name of an own nominee.

A firm may employ, or recommend, the services of another to safeguard clients' assets, provided that the firm is satisfied that firm is suitable.

Proper records must be maintained of client investments which the firm has in its custody, or which are held in custody by another person.

A reconciliation must be performed at least twice in every calendar year by a firm that is the custodian, or which appoints another firm to be the custodian.

A firm must send clients a statement of their investments that are in the custody of the firm, or which are held by another firm.

Disclosure

An authorized investment firm is required to provide its private clients with its identity and business address, the identity and status with the firm of employees and other relevant agents with whom the customer has contact, and the identity of the firm's regulator.

Details of transactions must be reported to the regulator. The format of such reports is set out in the *Transaction Reporting Handbook*.

The report must contain details on the following aspects of the transaction:

- the identity of the relevant investment, and the quantity of units bought or sold;
- the date and time of the transaction;
- the price paid or received; and
- the identity of any other European investment firm which is a counterparty to the transaction.

Furthermore, clients must be notified of any sale or purchase that was conducted on their behalf. Such a report is known as a contract note.

As investment manager, a firm must send a report to the client stating the value of the portfolio or account at the beginning and end of the period, its composition at the end, and, in the case of a discretionary portfolio or account, changes in its composition between those dates. The periodic statement must include:

- details of the contents and value of the portfolio;
- the basis of valuation;
- details of any assets loaned or charged;
- details of income received;
- transaction details;
- details of the charges and remuneration;
- details of any movement in the value of the portfolio;
- any changes in the composition of discretionary managed portfolio; and
- benchmarks.

Enforcement

The IMRO may take a number of actions to enforce regulations, including the following.

A warning may be issued if the firm has failed to comply with a particular rule or if the management of the firm is no longer deemed fit and proper. In the event that a fine is to be imposed on the firm, previous warnings will be taken into account. Failure to refine conduct will result in disciplinary proceedings.

Powers of intervention allow the IMRO to place restriction or impose requirements on firms. For example, it may prohibit a firm from conducting business.

A summary fine will be imposed if a firm fails to supply the regulator with financial returns or a statement of representation.

An investigation of the firm may take place if the firm has failed to comply with regulations or it is no longer deemed fit and proper. The investigation team presents a report to the Enforcement Committee. Depending on the decision of the committee, the case may proceed to the Disciplinary Tribunal. The latter may decide to reprimand the firm, impose a fine, remedy the situation, or suspend or terminate membership or registration of the IMRO. Appeals against decisions of the Disciplinary Tribunal will be heard and determined by the Appeal Tribunal.

Audit

An investment management firm that is required to submit annual audited financial returns to the IMRO must appoint a properly qualified auditor to prepare such accounts. A firm must require its auditor to report to the IMRO, stating whether the audit has been conducted in accordance with auditing standards and whether, for example, in the auditor's opinion:

- the annual financial return together with the annual accounts are a reflection of the affairs of the firm; and
- the annual financial return has been properly prepared in accordance with the financial returns rules.

A second auditor may be appointed by the IMRO to examine and report to it on any financial statements prepared under the rules, or on any other information reported on, or verified by, the firm's auditor.

Compensation

A scheme was established by the FSA in the form of a separate company, under the Financial Services Act 1986, to provide compensation to private investors in the event of a firm being unable to meet its defined investment business liabilities.[12] The amount of compensation paid by the Investors Compensation Scheme is currently set at a maximum of £48,000. This is calculated as the full payment of the first £30,000 of the claim plus 90 per cent of the next £20,000. Investors who make a claim under the scheme are not charged. The funds used to pay compensation come from other authorized investment firms.

Table 6A.3 shows the total number of claims dealt with by the Investors Compensation Scheme on an annual basis throughout the period 1988–98. During the year until 31 March 2000 the Investors Compensation Scheme completed 7966 claims. This represents almost 31 per cent of the total number of decisions on claim applications since 1988.

Since the beginning of the scheme in August 1988 to date, compensation and interest payments have totalled £193 m (€271 m). Payments over the last year amounted to £51.6 m (€84.3 m) (Table 6A.4).

Table 6A.5 shows that, during the last year, 3762 investors received compensation from the scheme. This brings the total number of people who have received compensation from the scheme to 16,329 since 1988, which means that each investor received an average of over £11,800 compensation over the period.

Since August 1988, the Investors Compensation Scheme declared a total of 1321 firms in default. A firm can be declared 'in default' by the scheme if it fails to return money or investments owed to the private investors, or is unable to pay investors' losses. During 1999–2000, the scheme declared 346 firms in default following almost 1100 completed solvency investigations. This represents 45 per cent of the total number of firms declared in default since the beginning of the scheme (Table 6A.6).

Apart from 1996/7, the number of firms declared in default has been increasing—the largest increase was in 1998/9.

Of the total number of default investment firms, only ten were regulated by the IMRO. This is a very small proportion of the total number of firms regulated by the IMRO. This number may consist of asset managers as well as other financial firms that are regulated by the IMRO. The majority (1210) of firms in default were regulated by the FIMBRA; 60 by the Personal Investment Authority; 4 by the Securities and Investment Board; 22 by the SFA; and 15 by the IBRC.

---

[12] Investors who have received bad investment advice or poor investment management typically resolve problems with the firm using the complaints procedure that the firm is required to have in place. However, should the firm be unable to pay the investors' claims as a result of incorrect advice or poor service, the Investors Compensation Scheme will provide compensation to the investors.

Table 6A.3. The total claims completed, 1988–2000

	1988/90	1990/1	1991/2	1992/3	1993/4	1994/5	1995/6	1996/7	1997/8	1998/9	1999/2000
Completed claims	917	272	1869	2015	2662	999	1466	2251	2061	3480	7966
% of total claims since 1988	3.5	1.0	7.2	7.8	10.3	3.8	5.6	8.7	7.9	13.4	30.7

Note: This table reports the number of claims completed, which is not necessarily equal to the number of new claims received. For example, during 1999/2000 the Investors Compensation Scheme received 7400 new claims. This represents an increase on the previous year, when total new claims amounted to 5624.

Source: The Investors Compensation Scheme, '1999 Annual Report' and '2000 Annual Report'.

Table 6A.4. The compensation paid by the Investors Compensation Scheme, 1988–2000 (€m)

	1988/90	1990/1	1991/2	1992/3	1993/4	1994/5	1995/6	1996/7	1997/8	1998/9	1999/2000
Compensation paid	4.8	2.6	16.5	23.5	32.8	19.6	31.4	15.2	15.6	24.8	84.3

Source: The Investors Compensation Scheme, '1999 Annual Report' and '2000 Annual Report'.

Table 6A.5. The number of investors compensated, 1989–2000

	1989/90	1990/1	1991/2	1992/3	1993/4	1994/5	1995/6	1996/7	1997/8	1998/9	1999/2000
Investors compensated	971	231	1598	1723	2271	909	1524	914	973	1507	3762

Source: The Investors Compensation Scheme, '1999 Annual Report' and '2000 Annual Report'.

Table 6A.6. The number of investment firms in default, 1988–2000

	1988/90	1990/1	1991/2	1992/3	1993/4	1994/5	1995/6	1996/7	1997/8	1998/9	1999/2000
Failed firms	7	11	35	38	39	52	71	46	81	346	595

Source: The Investors Compensation Scheme, '2000 Annual Report'.

Table 6A.7. The IMRO-regulated firms declared in default

Name of firm	Declared in default	Number of investors paid	Compensation paid (£ '000)
Allied Equity Ltd	1988–90	54	271
Herrington Financial Services Ltd	1991–2	244	2988
DBRN Ltd	1995–6	3	39
Independent Property Securities Ltd	1995–6	2	124
Lancaster Hilton Investments plc	1995–6	2	23
Wessex Asset Management	1996–7	1	2
A P Black Ltd	1997–8	9	287
Adams & Neville Asset Management Ltd	1999–2000	2	64
Total		317	3798

Source: The Investors Compensation Scheme, '2000 Annual Report'.

Table 6A.7 provides information on the amount of compensation and the number of investors compensated for eight IMRO-regulated firms declared in default by the Investors Compensation Scheme.

In only one of these eight cases, the amount of compensation paid exceeds the maximum of £48,000, as set by the Scheme. The average compensation payment for investors in the above eight companies amounted to £11,981. This is broadly consistent with the average size of claims paid since the Scheme began. It is worth noting that no compensation claims were paid to investors of the other two IMRO-regulated firms declared in default by the Scheme.

Complaints

According to the IMRO Rules, regulated firms are required to have a written complaints procedure. The minimum provisions that this procedure must contain are also set out in the IMRO *Rulebook* as follows.

Any complaint must be considered by an Officer or employee of suitable seniority who was not personally involved in the case. Where this is not possible, the case must be considered by an Officer or employee of the firm or an appointed representative. A substantive reply must be sent promptly.

If within one month of the substantive reply being sent to the complainant, the firm has not heard anything from the complainant, to the effect that they are not satisfied, then the case can be considered settled.

If the complaint has not been settled within two months of it being received, the firm must give notice to the IMRO of the details of the complaint and of the action taken in response to it. The complainant should be informed that the IMRO has been notified.

If the first substantive reply to the complainant fails to offer a reasonable settlement, then the complainant must be notified of their right to complain directly to the Investment Ombudsman and a copy of the Informal Guide to the Investment Ombudsman service must be enclosed.

Having notified the IMRO of a complaint, the firm must also notify it if the complaint is settled and the terms of settlement.

A full record of each significant complaint, and of the action taken in response to it, must be kept by the firm for three years after the date of the last response.

The Investment Ombudsman Scheme

The Investment Ombudsman has been appointed to deal with complaints relating to investment business against firms regulated by the IMRO. The Ombudsman investigates such complaints independently, with a view to recommending to the parties a settlement that is considered fair and reasonable. In appropriate cases, an adjudication may be arranged. Claims for financial loss are normally limited to a maximum of £100,000, and claims for distress and inconvenience to a maximum of £750.

Reasons for complaints are given in Table 6A.8. The number of new complaints received during the period from 1997 to 2000 increased by 45 per cent. The principal cause for complaint seems to be poor administration, followed by failure to carry out instructions. Complaints arising from poor administration have increased by 96 per cent since 1997. These problems are almost invariably as a result of human error.

Details of payments awarded by the Investment Ombudsman are reported in Table 6A.9.

The total number of awards given during 1999–2000 is greater than in the previous year. The average award given during 1999 was approximately £557, while the average award in 2000 was approximately £50 lower, at £527. This suggests that the increase in the number of awards is larger than the increase in compensation, thereby resulting in a decline in the average size of the award.

Table 6A.8. An analysis of the basis for new complaints

	1997–8	1998–9	1999–2000
Poor administration	173	273	339
Failure to carry out instructions	110	118	58
Inadequate explanations	39	53	49
Customer agreements	54	30	29
Performance	37	30	20
Unsuitable advice/product	27	27	18
Misleading documentation	25	24	17
Inadequate documentation	20	18	8
Fees/charges	19	16	5
Conflicts of evidence	17	15	5
Churning	3	7	3
Best execution	5	3	3
Inadequate knowledge of customer	4	3	3
Advertising	3	3	2
Conflicts of interest	—	—	2
Other	46	52	28
Total	582	672	589
New complaints received	299	395	433

Note: The total number of complaints reported in this table exceeds the number of complaints received in each year because a complaint may have a number of different causes.

Source: IMRO, 'Report & Accounts 1998–9' and 'Report & Accounts 1999–2000'.

Table 6A.9. The size of awards, 1999 and 2000

Size of awards	Year ended 31 March	
	1999	2000
£100 or less	100	94
£101–500	56	69
£501–1000	12	21
£1001–5000	11	21
£5001–10,000	1	1
£10,001–20,000	3	1
Over £20,000	0	0
Total number of awards	183	207
Highest award made during year	£16,000	£14,415
Total of all awards made during year	£101,999	£109,209

Source: The Investment Ombudsman, 'Annual Report 1999/2000'.

Supervision

The supervision of investment firms incorporates the following steps.

Authorized firms are continually monitored. This involves assessing the adequacy of financial resources and internal systems and controls.

Dealings with investors are examined to ensure that there is disclosure of information and that investors are protected.

Arrangements are made for handling complaints against firms and the resolution of disputes.

Penalties are imposed on those firms that have breached regulatory rules. The range of penalties can vary, from firms providing compensation to investors in the case of bad advice, to the withdrawal of the IMRO authorization. According to the IMRO's 'Report & Accounts 1999–2000', seven fines were imposed on firms during 1999–2000—three less than the previous year, as shown in Table 6A.10. The number of firms that received fines and registrations is a small percentage of the 1160 firms regulated by the IMRO.

The number of cases of enforcement action declined by 14 per cent over the period from 1994 to 1999/2000. The number of cases of disciplinary action reached a peak of 77 in 1995/6. However, it is worth noting that 80 per cent of these cases resulted in no public action.

Table **6A.10**. The disciplinary tribunals/enforcement committee from 1994

	1994/5	1995/6	1996/7	1997/8	1998/9	1999/2000
No public action taken[1]	29	60	46	32	24	22
Reprimand issued	1	0	1	1	1	1
Fine imposed	7	15	16	11	10	7
Authorization terminated[2]	0	2	1	0	0	2
Total number of cases completed in year	37	77	64	44	35	32

Notes:
[1] Includes warning or no action.
[2] Firms and individuals.

Source: IMRO, 'Report & Accounts 1998–9'.

6A.7   **THE USA**[13]

The Regulatory Authorities

To be regulated as an investment adviser, generally a firm or person must satisfy three requirements: the firm or person must engage in the business of providing advice, making recommendations, issuing reports, or furnishing analyses on securities, directly or through publications; and receive compensation. The following groups are not considered as investment advisers:

- a bank, or bank holding company as defined in the Bank Holding Company Act 1956, which is not an investment company (that is, a US domestic bank);
- any broker or dealer for whom the provision of advice is incidental to the conduct of their business, and who therefore receives no additional compensation;
- any lawyer, accountant, engineer, or teacher whose provision of advice is incidental to the practice of their profession;
- the publisher of any bona fide newspaper, news magazine, or business, or financial publication of general and regular circulation;
- government securities dealers; or
- any other persons identified by the SEC who cannot be classified as an investment adviser according to the definition.

The regulation of investment advisers is governed by the Investment Advisers Act 1940. Investment advisers can be regulated at a state or federal level, a split that occurred in 1996 when the Congress passed the National Securities Markets Improvement Act, dividing regulatory jurisdiction over investment advisers between the SEC[14] and the states. In general, advisers with \$25 m or more assets under management or which provide advice to investment company clients are permitted to register with the SEC. Smaller advisers register under the state law with the state securities authorities.

There is some overlap between federal regulation, as applied to the SEC-registered advisers, and that applied to state-registered advisers.

---

[13] There follows here a brief discussion of the regulatory framework in the USA. It is discussed more extensively in the next chapter.

[14] The Division of Investment Management, within the SEC, is charged with the regulation of investment advisers.

Although, the latter are governed primarily by the state law, several provisions of the Investment Advisers Act and Commission Rules apply to such advisers. For example, they are required to comply with federal regulations that prohibit fraudulent behaviour.

The Capital Requirements

The SEC does not impose a regulatory capital charge on the investment advisers it regulates,[15] although some state securities authorities do place capital requirements on advisers. For example, in California, an investment adviser that has power of attorney over, or custody of, clients' assets is required to do the following.

Ensure that the total aggregate indebtedness does not exceed 500 per cent of its tangible net capital or permit its current aggregate indebtedness to exceed its current net capital; and

Maintain tangible net capital of not less than:

- $25,000; or
- $5000, if the investment adviser is charged with the power of attorney from any investment advisory client to execute transactions and not having custody of the client's securities or funds; or
- $1000, if the investment adviser does not have the power of attorney or custody of client's assets, and it receives fees for periodic publications or other investment advisory services.

The Separation of Clients' Assets

Under the Investment Advisers Act 1940, advisers are permitted to hold clients' securities and funds. An adviser will be deemed to have custody if it directly or indirectly holds client funds or securities, has any authority to obtain possession of them, or has the ability to appropriate them. However, such advisers are subject to additional requirements. An SEC-registered adviser with 'custody' must provide the following information to clients.

[15] However, it is worth noting that investment advisers are required to disclose their financial position in the registration form, Form ADV.

Securities held on behalf of a client must be segregated, clearly marked as the funds of the client, and held in a place free from risk of destruction or loss.

Clients' funds in the custody of the investment adviser must be deposited in one or more bank accounts that contain only clients' funds. Such account, or accounts, must be maintained in the name of the investment adviser as an agent or trustee for such clients. A separate record of each account containing clients' funds must be maintained and details regarding the composition of these accounts must be sent to the relevant client.

Having accepted custody or possession of funds from a client, the investment adviser must immediately notify the client in writing of the details concerning how such securities and funds will be held and any changes to this information.

An itemized statement must be sent to each client at least every three months. This statement must show the funds and securities in the custody of the adviser at the end of the period and any transactions during this period.

All such funds and securities of clients will be examined and verified by an independent accountant at least once during each calendar year and without prior notice to the investment adviser. Following the examination, the accountant's report will subsequently be filed with the SEC.

Disclosure

Under the Investment Advisers Act 1940, every adviser is required to send to each prospective client a written disclosure statement. This 'brochure' must describe the adviser's business practices and educational and business background. Existing clients must also receive a copy of this brochure every year. The information included in the brochure is the same as that contained in Part II of Form ADV. To comply with the brochure rule, an investment adviser may deliver Part II of Form ADV, or another document containing at least the information disclosed in Part II of Form ADV.

Advisers are not required to deliver a brochure to investment company clients or clients for whom they provide only impersonal services for less than $200. An adviser entering into a contract for impersonal advisory services for $200 or more need only offer to deliver the brochure.

The Division of Investment Management requires that an investment adviser must disclose to clients all material information regarding its compensation, such as if the adviser's fee is higher than that typically charged by other advisers for similar services. An investment adviser must disclose all potential conflicts of interest between the adviser and its clients, even if the adviser believes that a conflict has not affected and will not affect the adviser's recommendations to its clients. This obligation to disclose conflicts of interest includes the obligation to disclose any benefits the adviser may receive from third parties as a result of recommendations to clients.

An SEC-registered investment adviser that has custody of clients' funds is required to disclose promptly to the clients and prospective clients any financial conditions of the adviser that are reasonably likely to impair the ability of the adviser to meet contractual commitments to clients. The rule also requires advisers to disclose promptly to clients legal or disciplinary events that are material to an evaluation of the adviser's integrity or ability to meet its commitments to clients.

Enforcement

The Division of Enforcement is responsible for enforcing the federal securities laws. As part of this charge, the Division conducts investigations into possible violations of federal securities laws and recommends appropriate remedies for consideration by the SEC. Furthermore, the SEC's civil suits are prosecuted by the Division in the federal courts, as well as its administrative proceedings.

In civil suits, the SEC seeks injunctions to prohibit future violations. If a person is found to have violated such an injunction, they will be subject to fines or imprisonment for contempt. Frequently, the SEC seeks civil money penalties and the disgorgement of illegal profits. The courts may also bar or suspend individuals from acting as corporate officers, directors, or in other capacities in the industry, such as employees or advisers.

Administrative proceedings, brought by the SEC, are heard by administrative law judges and the SEC itself. With respect to regulated entities, such as investment advisers, and their employees, the SEC may instigate administrative proceedings to revoke or suspend registration, or to impose bars or suspensions from employment. In proceedings against regulated persons, the SEC is authorized to order the payment of civil penalties as well as disgorgement.

Table 6A.11. The enforcement actions initiated, 1995–9

	1995	1996	1997	1998	1999	Total
Civil injunctive actions	171	180	189	214	198	952
Administrative proceedings	291	239	285	248	298	1361
Contempt proceedings	23	32	14	15	29	113
Reports of investigation	1	2	1	0	0	4
Total	486	453	489	477	525	2430

Source: SEC, 'Annual Report 1999'.

Table 6A.12. The enforcement cases initiated by the SEC against investment advisers and investment companies, 1999

	Civil actions		Administrative proceedings		Total	
	Number	% of total	Number	% of total	Number	% of total
Investment advisers	7	3.1	34	11.4	41	7.8
Investment companies	0	0.0	3	1.0	3	0.6
Sub-total	7	3.1	37	12.4	44	8.4
Total enforcement cases	227	100.0	298	100.0	525	100.0

Source: SEC, 'Annual Report 1999'.

Table 6A.11 shows the enforcement actions that were initiated over the period 1995–9.

The SEC initiated 2430 enforcement actions from 1995 to 1999, over half of which took the form of administrative proceedings (SEC 2000, 2001). The total number of enforcement actions has increased by 8 per cent over this period.

Table 6A.12 reports the number of enforcement cases that were brought against investment advisers and investment companies during 1999.

According to Table 6A.12, of the 525 enforcement cases initiated by the SEC during the fiscal year 1999, only 8.4 per cent were against the investment advisers and investment companies. In fact, 7.8 per cent of enforcement cases were initiated against investment advisers, while only 0.6 per cent of the total number of enforcement cases were brought against investment companies. Administrative proceedings involving investment advisers account for 11.4 per cent of the total number of administrative proceedings. This is the common type of enforcement action brought against investment advisers.

Audit

The Office of Compliance and Examinations is responsible for the examination programme at the SEC. Inspections and examinations are authorized under the Securities Exchange Act 1934, the Investment Company Act 1940, and the Investment Advisers Act 1940. Investment advisers are subject to such inspections.

During 1998, the Office completed 1280 inspections of investment advisers. This implies an average inspection frequency of once every five years. The non-investment company assets managed by the advisers inspected totalled $1.7 trillion. About 78 investment advisers were inspected for cause.

Serious violations were uncovered in 52 of the examinations, and these cases were referred to the Division of Enforcement. The most common violations resulting in referrals involved fraud, failure to comply with the 'Brochure Rule' on disclosure, and conflicts of interest.

Authorization

To register with the SEC as an investment adviser, a firm must file a registration form, Form ADV, and keep it updated by filing periodic amendments, including an annual amendment on Schedule I to Form ADV. Part I includes information about the adviser and persons associated with the adviser. Part II requires disclosure of the background and business practices of the investment adviser. A decision regarding the application is considered within 45 days. The SEC may grant the registration or begin proceedings to deny it if the applicant is not eligible or has committed prohibited acts.

In addition, registration requires firms to comply with the 'Brochure Rule'; maintain accurate and current books and records; and be subject to inspection and examination by the SEC staff.

Best execution

As a fiduciary, an investment adviser has a duty to seek to obtain 'best execution' of clients' transactions. This implies that an adviser must execute transactions in a manner to ensure that the clients' total proceeds or cost in each transaction are the most favourable under the circumstances. In assessing whether this standard is met, an adviser should consider the full range and quality of a broker's services when placing brokerage, including, among others, execution capability, commission rate, financial responsibility, responsiveness to the adviser, and the value of any research services provided.

7

The Regulation of Investment
Management Services in the USA

This chapter provides further details on the regulatory rules and requirements for investment advisers and investment management companies in the USA. Regulation of advisers relates to registration, capital requirements, the handling of client money, and disclosure. Regulation of investment management companies relates to the form of oversight by the SEC, capital requirements, disclosure, custody rules for client assets, and the need for bonding of particular individuals against fraud and theft. The chapter then describes the common enforcement of both groups by the SEC, including the incidence of, and scope for, prosecution.

7.1 THE INVESTMENT ADVISERS

7.1.1 The Definition of Investment Advisers

In the USA, investment advisers provide guidance on individual and pooled investments. The Investment Advisers Act 1940 defines an investment adviser as:

any person or firm that: (1) for compensation; (2) is engaged in the business of; (3) providing advice, making recommendations, issuing reports, or furnishing analyses on securities, either directly or through publications.

A person or firm must satisfy the three elements to be regulated under the Investment Advisers Act 1940. The SEC's Division of

Investment Management interprets these elements broadly. For example, compensation is construed as the receipt of any economic benefit. A fee for advisory services need not be separate from other fees charged. 'Being engaged' in this type of business depends on whether the person is viewed as an investment adviser; whether the person receives compensation for providing investment advice; and the frequency and specificity of the advice provided.[1] The SEC has identified the following as areas of advice:

- market trends;
- the selection and retention of other advisers;
- the advantages of investing in some as against other securities;
- providing a selective list of securities; and
- asset allocation advice.

The following institutions are excluded from the definition of investment adviser.

Banks and bank holding companies not engaged in the provision of investment advisory services are not included in the definition. However, under the Gramm—Leach—Bliley Act 1999, banks and bank holding companies acting as an investment adviser to a registered investment company are included in the definition. If such services are performed through a 'separately identifiable department', and not the bank itself, this department will be deemed to be the investment adviser. Savings and loans institutions, federal savings banks, foreign banks, and credit unions are included in the definition of investment adviser.

Lawyers, accountants, engineers, and teachers if they provide advisory services, which are solely incidental to their professions.[2]

Brokers and dealers if their performance of advisory services is solely incidental to the conduct of their business, and they do not receive any special compensation for this advice.

Publishers of bona fide newspapers, news magazines, and business or financial publications of general and regular circulation.

[1] The SEC staff considers a person as acting as an adviser 'if he advertises as an investment adviser or financial planner, uses letterhead indicating activity as an investment adviser or, maintains a telephone listing or otherwise lets it be known that he will accept new advisory clients'.

[2] Factors used to assess whether advice is incidental to a profession include whether the professional is viewed as an investment adviser; whether the advice is reasonably related to the professional services provided; and whether the charge for advisory services is based on the same factors that determine the professional's usual charge.

Persons and firms whose advice, analyses, or reports are related only to securities that are direct obligations of, or obligations guaranteed by, the USA, or by certain US government-sponsored corporations designated by the Secretary of the Treasury.

7.1.2   Registration

Unless exempt, a person or firm satisfying all three of the elements described above is required to register as an investment adviser with the SEC.[3] To complete this procedure, an applicant must file with the SEC. This filing requests information on the following.

The name and form of organization, the name of the state or other authority under which the adviser is organized; the location of the principal office and branch offices, details (education and past and present business affiliations) of the partners, officers, directors, and persons performing similar functions, or, if such an investment adviser is an individual, of such individual, and the number of employees.

The means of conducting business, such as the manner of supplying advice and rendering analyses.

A balance sheet certified by an independent accountant and other financial statements if the applicant has custody of client assets, or requires payment of more than $500 in fees per client and six or more months in advance.

The control exercised by the investment adviser over clients' funds and accounts.

The form of compensation.

Whether the investment adviser or associated person received any disqualification, which would be the basis for denial, suspension, or revocation of registration.

The disclosure of any regulatory and civil judicial action taken against the investment adviser.

A decision to grant the application will be made by the SEC within 45 days of its receipt. Conversely, the Commission may begin proceedings, which may continue for 120 days, to determine whether the registration

---

[3] Although employees of advisory firms may be classified as investment advisers according to the definition, the SEC generally does not require these individuals to register as investment advisers. Thus, the registration of the advisory firm also covers its employees and other persons under its control.

should be denied. Failure to reach a decision to grant or deny the application may lead the SEC to extend the period for consideration of the application for a further 90 days.

An application to register may be denied if the investment adviser has committed prohibited acts, or is prohibited from registering with the Commission.

Following an amendment to the Investment Advisers Act contained in the National Securities Markets Improvement Act in 1996, responsibility for the regulation of investment advisers was divided between state and federal authorities. Thus, unless an adviser is qualified and permitted to register with the SEC, it must register with state regulatory authorities. An adviser is permitted to register with the SEC if it:

- manages assets of $25 m or more;
- advises a registered investment company;
- maintains its principal office and place of business in the State of Wyoming (because this state does not regulate advisers) or outside the USA; or
- has been exempted by the SEC from the disqualification to register with the SEC.

While an unregistered investment adviser is not subject to the record-keeping rules outlined in the Investment Advisers Act 1940, it is subject to the anti-fraud provisions contained in the Act.

In addition, entities not required to register with the SEC and with fewer than 15 clients in the preceding 12 months must not present themselves to the public as an investment adviser.

An investment adviser may withdraw its registration by filing a Form ADV-W (Notice of Withdrawal from Registration) with the SEC. Upon finding that an investment adviser has ceased to operate or is no longer eligible to remain registered with the SEC, the SEC will seek to cancel the adviser's registration. The SEC will also cancel registration if it is found that an investment adviser has failed to update the Form ADV.

Interestingly, although investment advisers are required to report education qualifications to clients and potential clients as part of the Brochure Rule (see Section 7.1.5), the Investment Advisers Act 1940 does not regulate the level or type of educational requirements. However, certain employees of the adviser may have to pass securities examinations in the states in which they have a principal place of business.

The following entities are not required to register with the SEC:

- investment advisers whose clients are resident in the same state as their main business operations ('intrastate' advisers);
- an investment adviser whose clients consist solely of insurance companies;
- an investment adviser who counselled no more than 15 clients during the preceding 12 months; and
- any investment adviser that is a charitable organization.

7.1.3   The Capital Requirements

Federal regulation of investment advisers does not require an adviser to maintain any minimum net capital, and there is no bonding requirement.

State authorities, however, may impose capital requirements on registered investment advisers, provided that the state does not require:

an investment adviser to maintain a higher minimum net capital or to post any bond in addition to any that is required under the laws of the State *in which it maintains its principal place of business*, if the investment adviser:

(a) is registered or licensed in the State in which it maintains its principal place of business; and

(b) is in compliance with the applicable net capital or bonding requirements of the State in which it maintains its principal place of business.

Thus, a number of state authorities require investment advisers to satisfy capital requirements. In Minnesota, for example, state-registered investment advisers are required to hold a surety bond of $25,000 if the adviser has custody of, or discretionary power over, clients' assets, and have a minimum capital of $100,000. Investment advisers registered with the Arkansas authorities are required to hold capital of $12,500. Investment advisers with custody of clients' assets or power of attorney, registered with Californian state authorities, are required to maintain total aggregate indebtedness below 500 per cent of its tangible net capital or current aggregate indebtedness below current net capital. In addition, the following requirements are placed on the investment adviser.

The investment adviser shall at all times have and maintain tangible net capital of not less than $25,000.

If the investment adviser has any power of attorney from any investment advisory client to execute transactions and does not have regular, or periodic custody, or possession of any of its investment advisory clients' securities or funds, except the receipt of prepaid subscriptions for periodic publications, or other investment advisory services, it shall at all times have and maintain tangible net capital of not less than $5,000.

If the investment adviser receives fees for periodic publications or other investment advisory services paid six months or more in advance of the services, and it does not have the power of authority, or does not otherwise have regular or periodic custody, or possession of any of its investment advisory clients' securities or funds, it shall at all times have and maintain tangible net capital of not less than $1000.

7.1.4 The Separation of Clients' Assets

Investment advisers are required to state in their registration application to the SEC whether they hold the clients' assets and securities. An adviser will be deemed to have custody if it directly or indirectly holds the client funds or securities, has any authority to obtain possession of them, or has the ability to appropriate them. Under the Rule 206(4)-2, an investment adviser in possession of clients' assets must ensure the following.

Each client's securities are segregated, marked as to the identity of the client, and held in safekeeping.

The clients' funds are held in bank accounts, containing only clients' funds, which are in the name of the investment adviser as agent or trustee for such clients, and the investment adviser maintains a separate record for each such account, which shows the name and address of the bank where such account is held, the dates and amounts of deposits in and withdrawals from such account, and the exact amount of each client's beneficial interest in such account.

Having accepted custody, the investment adviser must notify the client of the location and manner in which the assets are held, and of any change in these details.

Once every three months, the client is supplied with a statement detailing the funds held by the investment adviser for the client, and all debits, credits, and transactions in such client's account during such period.

The funds and securities of clients must be verified annually by an independent public accountant, at a time chosen by the accountant and unknown to the investment adviser. The accountant should then send the details of the examination to the SEC.

If the client is an investment company, the investment adviser must comply with the regulations regarding custody as set out in Section 2.6 of the Investment Company Act 1940.

7.1.5   Disclosure

Disclosure obligations of investment advisers are set out in Rule 204-3 of the Investment Advisers Act 1940, otherwise known as the Brochure Rule. This rule requires registered investment advisers to:

deliver to each prospective advisory client a written disclosure statement, or 'brochure', describing the adviser's business practices and education and business background.

The brochure must include at least the information contained in Part II of Form ADV. The SEC has recently proposed amendments to this rule concerning the format of the brochure supplied to clients. The amendments suggest that the brochure should be 'a narrative document, written in plain English, providing information about the advisory firm, its business practices, and its disciplinary history'. Supplementary information would include disciplinary information about advisory personnel.

An adviser may provide the brochure to the client at least 48 hours before the commencement of a (written or verbal) contract with the client; or at the beginning of the contract, provided that the client is permitted to terminate the contract without incurring a penalty within five working days of its initiation. In addition, investment advisers are required to offer to provide a brochure to existing clients on an annual basis without charge. Advisers whose clients consist of investment companies, or who provide impersonal advisory services for less than $200, are not required to deliver a brochure. An adviser entering into a contract to provide impersonal advisory services for $200 or more need only offer to deliver a brochure.

In addition to the brochure rule, investment advisers who have discretionary control over clients' funds or require advance payment of advisory fees are also obliged to disclose 'any financial conditions of the adviser that are reasonably likely to impair the ability of the adviser to meet contractual commitments to clients', and 'legal and disciplinary events that are material to an evaluation of the adviser's integrity or ability to meet its commitments to clients'. Further, investment advisers are required to inform clients of fees and (existing and potential) conflicts of interest.

7.1.6 Fraud

Investment advisers are fiduciaries. As such, they owe their clients particular duties and must comply with minimum standards of behaviour. Most important are the duties of care and loyalty (discussed further in Section 7.3.5). Therefore, in acting on behalf of a client, an investment adviser is obliged to act in the best interest of the client and eliminate conflicts of interest. The extent of these duties depends on a number of factors such as:

- the expertise of investment advisers;
- their control over their client's assets and investment decisions; and
- the degree of client reliance on the advisers.

As a consequence of this fiduciary duty, anti-fraud regulations in the Investment Advisers Act 1940 deal with fraud in the offer and provision of investment advice, including discretionary advice by fiduciaries, as well as with fraud in the offer and sale of securities included in the Securities Act of 1933 and the Securities Exchange Act of 1934.

  Fraud under the Investment Advisers Act 1940 may involve failure to disclose required information to clients and prospective clients. In order to prevent fraud, the regulations state that:

it shall be unlawful for any investment adviser by use of the mails or any means of instrumentality of interstate commerce, directly or indirectly—

(1) to employ any device, scheme, or artifice to defraud any client or prospective client;

(2) to engage in any transaction, practice, or course of business, which operates as a fraud or deceit upon any client or prospective client;

(3) acting as principal for his own account, knowingly to sell any security to or purchase any security from a client, or acting as broker for a person other than such client, knowingly to effect any sale or purchase of any security for the account of such client, without disclosing to such client in writing before the

completion of such transaction the capacity in which he is acting and obtaining the consent of the client to such transaction. The prohibitions of this paragraph shall not apply to any transaction with a customer of a broker or dealer if such broker or dealer is not acting as an investment adviser in relation to such transaction.

(4) to engage in any act, practice, or course of business which is fraudulent, deceptive, or manipulative. The Commission shall for the purposes of this paragraph (4) by rules and regulations define, and prescribe means reasonably designed to prevent such acts, practices, and courses of business as are fraudulent, deceptive, or manipulative.

Such behaviour represents a breach of fiduciary duty owed to clients by advisers, which may be resolved through disclosure and sometimes only by express consent. An adviser's duties to clients differ from those owed to prospective clients.

7.2   THE INVESTMENT COMPANIES

7.2.1   Definition

An investment company is an issuer of securities that is primarily engaged in the business of investing in securities. Alternatively an investment company is defined as a company engaged in holding and trading in securities where at least 40 per cent of its assets are invested in investment securities. Thus, intent or asset composition may establish an issuer as an investment company. The formal definition of an investment company in the Investment Company Act 1940 is:

Investment company means any issuer which—

(A) is or holds itself out as being engaged primarily, or proposes to engage primarily, in the business of investing, reinvesting, or trading in securities;

(B) is engaged or proposes to engage in the business of issuing face-amount certificates of the instalment type, or has been engaged in such business and has any such certificate outstanding; or

(C) is engaged or proposes to engage in the business of investing, reinvesting, owning, holding, or trading in securities, and owns or proposes to acquire investment securities having a value exceeding 40 per cent of the value of such issuer's total assets (exclusive of Government securities and cash items) on an unconsolidated basis.

The following institutions are excluded from the definition of investment companies:

- domestic banks, savings and loan institutions, insurance companies, broker-dealers, and some employee stock bonus, pension, or profit-sharing trusts; and
- domestic funds that are maintained by a bank 'exclusively for the collective investment and reinvestment of moneys contributed to the account by the bank in its capacity as a trustee, executor, administrator, or guardian'.

The 1940 Act divides investment companies into three classes.

A 'face-amount certificate company' issues face-amount certificates of the instalment type.

A 'unit investment trust':

- is organized under a trust indenture, contract of custodianship or agency, or similar instrument,
- does not have a board of directors, and
- issues only redeemable securities, each of which represents an undivided interest in a unit of specified securities, but does not include a voting trust.

The term 'management company' is used to define investment companies that cannot be classified as a face-amount certificate company or a unit investment trust.

Management companies are classified as open- or closed-end companies. An open-end investment company (mutual fund) continually offers new shares and is obligated to redeem the shares they issue at their approximate net asset value at any time. Mutual funds include equity funds, bond and income funds, short-term municipal bond funds, and money market funds. Unlike open-end investment companies, the shareholders of closed-end investment companies do not have the option to redeem shares at their net asset value. Open- and closed-end companies can be further divided according to the level of diversification. According to Section 5(b)(1) of the Investment Company Act 1940:

'Diversified company' means a management company which meets the following requirements: At least 75 per centum of the value of its total assets is represented by cash and cash items (including receivables), Government securities, securities of other investment companies, and other securities for the purposes of this calculation limited in respect of any one issuer to an amount not greater in value than 5 per centum of the value of the total assets of such management company and to not more than 10 per centum of the outstanding voting securities of such issuer.

Investment advice may be offered to investment companies internally and externally. Internal advisory services may be provided by an investment company's trustees, officers, directors, and employees, or the advisory services may be outsourced and offered externally by an investment adviser, as detailed in a contract. Typically, open-end investment companies are managed externally. In fact, discussions suggest that approximately 80 per cent of the mutual funds are managed externally. External management usually allows advisers to organize a number of investment companies with different investment policies. A group of such companies is referred to as a fund complex. The internally managed investment company may also organize many investment companies, and they own the adviser.

By providing smaller investors an opportunity to invest in securities markets, investment companies present a number of advantages, such as diversification, access to professional investment advice, and an opportunity to participate in international markets.

7.2.2   The Structure of a Mutual Fund

Figure 7.1 shows the typical structure of a mutual fund.

Through their voting rights, mutual fund shareholders elect directors and approve the terms of the investment advisory contracts and any change in a fund's 'fundamental' investment policies. A mutual fund is governed by a board of directors that has responsibility for the management of the fund's business matters. Legally, the board of directors is seen as having a fiduciary duty (see Section 7.3.5), which means that a director must be adequately informed about matters that come before the board and conform to the duty of loyalty, including avoidance of conflicts of interest. Recent amendments to federal regulations require that at least a majority of the fund's board of directors must be independent of the fund's adviser or principal underwriter. Current figures suggest that at least 50 per cent of the directors of most mutual funds in the USA are disinterested directors.

An investment adviser to a mutual fund is responsible for selecting portfolio investments that satisfy the investment policy and objectives of a mutual fund. The investment adviser places orders with

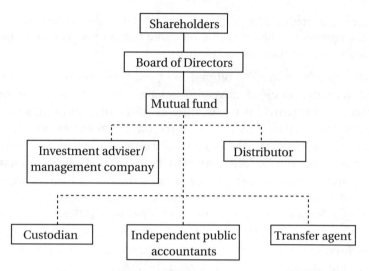

Fig. 7.1. The structure of a mutual fund

Source: ICI (2000).

broker-dealers and is responsible for obtaining the best overall execution of these orders. The duties of an investment adviser are detailed in the 1940 Act, which imposes fiduciary duties on the adviser, and in the contract with the investment company, which also describes the annual fee received by the investment adviser. This fee is typically expressed as a percentage of the fund's average net assets. Administrative services may be provided by an affiliate of the fund (for example, the investment adviser), or by an unaffiliated third party. These services include supervising the performance of other companies that provide services to the fund, and ensuring that the fund's operations comply with the legislation.

New shares in a mutual fund are continually offered to the public at a price based on the current value of fund assets plus any sales charges. Usually, these shares are distributed through the principal underwriters, which are subject to the same regulations as broker-dealers and the National Association of Securities Dealers' (NASD) rules governing mutual fund sales practices. A qualified bank is the most common type of custodian used by mutual funds to hold their portfolio securities. The SEC requires mutual fund custodians to segregate mutual fund portfolio securities from other bank assets. The functions of a transfer agent relate to the maintenance of records. Thus, their duties include maintaining records of shareholder accounts, the calculation and distribution of dividends, and the preparation and mailing of shareholder account statements, federal income tax information, and other share-holder notices.

7.2.3   Registration

An investment company must submit a 'notification of registration' to the SEC. It must subsequently file 'a registration statement' with the Commission, which must contain the following information.

A statement outlining the types of activities the investment company intends to perform, such as operating as an open- or closed-end company, borrowing money, and issuing securities.

All investment policies, which may be amended only with the shareholder approval.

All other policies, which are deemed part of the fundamental policy.

The name and address of each affiliated person of the registrant; the details of all other companies where each such person is an officer, director, or partner; a brief statement of the business experience for the preceding five years of each officer and director of the registrant.

All information that would be required to register under the Securities Act 1933 and the Securities Exchange Act 1934.

In addition, the Commission may request the following information.

Copies of the most recent registration statement filed by the registrant under the Securities Act 1933, or, in the absence of such a statement, copies of a registration statement filed under the Securities Exchange Act 1934.

Copies of any reports filed under the Securities Exchange Act 1934.

If the registrant is a unit investment trust whose assets consist mainly of securities issued by another registered investment company, it is not necessary for the registrant to re-submit information on the issuer that is already contained in the latter's registration statement.

If a company fails to complete the registration process as outlined, the SEC will notify the company and set a date by which time the company may correct or re-submit its registration statement. If the problem is not corrected within this time period, the SEC has the power to suspend or revoke such registration.

The Commission will terminate the registration of an investment company if it is found that the company has ceased to operate as an investment company.

In addition to registering the company, an investment company must register its securities in compliance with the regulations set out in the Securities Act 1933.

7.2.4 Regulation

The SEC regulates investment companies under the Investment Company Act 1940, which requires investment companies to register with the SEC and meet operating standards; the Securities Act 1933, which relates to disclosure of information; the Securities Exchange Act 1934, which details anti-fraud rules concerning the purchase and sale of fund shares; and the Investment Advisers Act 1940 and the Investment Company Act 1940, which regulate investment advisers to investment companies. This regulatory framework is designed to minimize the risks to investors arising from the following:

- failure to safeguard a company's assets;
- incorrectly valued assets;
- managerial discretion that is not in the best interests of investors; and
- fraud by management.

The regulatory framework encapsulated in the Investment Company Act 1940 aims to:

- ensure the continuation of the company's existing investment policy;
- maintain truth and accuracy of information divulged by the investment company to the public;
- ensure correct pricing of securities for sale or redemption;
- control the use of fund assets to promote distribution;
- ensure that fees paid to investment advisers are reasonable;
- provide for the safekeeping of assets;
- assure integrity of management, and, in its absence, provide protection to investors;
- require independent checks on management; and
- restrict the leveraging of investment company assets.

Investment advisers to investment companies are also regulated by this Act, although an individual may be defined as an adviser under the

Investment Advisers Act 1940, but not under the Investment Company Act, and vice versa. The Investment Company Act 1940 is mainly concerned with the regulation of external advisers to investment companies that act as independent contracts, subject to fiduciary duties. According to the Investment Company Act 1940, an investment adviser to an investment company is defined as:

(A) any person (other than a bona fide officer, director, trustee, member of an advisory board, or employee of such company, as such) who pursuant to contract with such company regularly furnishes advice to such company with respect to the desirability of investing in, purchasing or selling securities or other property, or is empowered to determine what securities or other property shall be purchased or sold by such company, and

(B) any other person who pursuant to contract with a person described in clause (A) regularly performs substantially all of the duties undertaken by such person described in clause (A); but does not include

(i) a person whose advice is furnished solely through uniform publications distributed to subscribers thereto;

(ii) a person who furnishes only statistical and other factual information, advice regarding economic factors and trends, or advice as to occasional transactions in specific securities, but without generally furnishing advice or making recommendations regarding the purchase or sale of securities;

(iii) a company furnishing such services at cost to one or more investment companies, insurance companies, or other financial institutions;

(iv) any person the character and amount of whose compensation for such services must be approved by a court; or

(v) such other persons as the Commission may by rules and regulations or order determine not to be within the intent of this definition.

While there is not a standard format for the contract between investment advisers and investment companies, the Investment Company Act 1940 does list the following areas, which are required to be covered by the contract:

- the compensation to be paid under the contract;
- the period of validity of the contract may continue for more than two years only if approved annually by the majority of the board of directors and shareholders;
- the details of contract termination, which may occur at any time, without the payment of a penalty, and is decided by the board of directors of such registered company, or by vote of a majority of the

outstanding voting securities of such company on not more than sixty days' written notice to the investment adviser; and

- the automatic termination of the contract in the event of its assignment.

The terms of the contract between an investment adviser and investment company must be approved by the vote of a majority of directors, as well as independent directors.

Violations of the Investment Company Act 1940 carry criminal and administrative sanctions.

7.2.5   **The Capital Requirements**

Although investment companies are not subject to explicit capital requirements, regulations have developed relating to the minimum amount of initial capital held and their capital structure. Prior to the regulatory framework promulgated under the Investment Company Act 1940, it was relatively easy for a sponsor to establish and in turn abandon an investment company, at the expense of investors. In order to prevent such 'fly-by-night' operators establishing an investment company and to protect investors, the Investment Company Act 1940 details a number of requirements that must be satisfied before a registered investment company can invite the public to join. A registered investment company is not permitted to make a public offering of securities unless the company has:

- a net worth of at least $100,000; or
- previously made a public offering of its securities, and at the time of such offering had a net worth of at least $100,000.

Although there is no legal restriction on the maximum size of an investment company, 'any substantial further increase in size' may be investigated by the SEC in order to ensure that investors are not adversely affected by this change.

The Investment Company Act 1940 contains restrictions on the capital structures of investment companies. This regulatory action was necessary in order to prevent management companies from borrowing heavily with insufficient assets and reserves. A registered closed-end company is not permitted to issue any class of senior security,[4] or to sell any such security of which it is the issuer, unless if such a class of senior security represents an indebtedness:

- the security has an asset coverage of at least 300 per cent immediately following the issuance or sale;
- the senior security has an asset coverage of at least 300 per cent after deducting the amount of the dividend;

  and provision is made either:

- that if the class of senior securities has an asset coverage of less than 100 per cent on the last day of business for 12 consecutive months, the holders of such securities are entitled to elect at least a majority of the members of the board of directors of the registered management company until the asset coverage exceeds 110 per cent on the last business day for three consecutive months; or

- that an event of default will be declared if the asset coverage of such class of senior securities is less than 100 per cent on the last business day for 24 consecutive calendar months.

If such a class of senior security is a stock then:

- the security must have an asset coverage of at least 200 per cent immediately following the issuance or sale;
- the announcement of any dividend is prohibited unless the senior security has asset coverage of at least 200 per cent after deducting the amount of the dividend;
- the holders of senior securities have the right to elect at least two directors at all times, and, subject to the prior rights, if any, of the holders, of any other class of senior securities outstanding, to elect a majority of the directors if at any time dividends on such class of securities shall be unpaid in an amount equal to two full years' dividends on such securities, and to continue to be so represented until all dividends in arrears shall have been paid or otherwise provided for;
- provision is made requiring approval by the vote of a majority of such securities, voting as a class, of any plan of reorganization adversely affecting such securities or of any action requiring a vote of security holders; and

[4] A senior security is defined as 'any bond, debenture, note, or similar obligation or instrument constituting a security and evidencing indebtedness, and any stock of a class having priority over any other class as to distribution of assets or payment of dividends.'

- such class of stock shall have complete priority over any other class as to the distribution of assets and payments of dividends, which dividends shall be cumulative.

A registered open-end investment company is not permitted:

to issue any class of senior security or to sell a senior security of which it is the issuer, except that any such registered company shall be permitted to borrow from any bank: *Provided*, that immediately after any such borrowing there is an asset coverage of at least 300 per cent for all borrowings of such registered company: *And provided further*, that in the event that such asset coverage shall at any time fall below 300 per cent such registered company shall, within three days thereafter (not including Sundays and holidays) or such longer period as the Commission may prescribe by rules and regulations, reduce the amount of its borrowings to an extent that the asset coverage of such borrowings shall be at least 300 per cent.

7.2.6   Disclosure

Investment companies are required to prepare prospectuses that contain information on the policies, objectives, risks, and expenses of the fund, and must be delivered to the investor before, or accompanying, delivery of the security or the confirmation of purchase. These prospectuses must also be submitted to the SEC for examination. The Commission's staff examines the content of the registration statement covering the issued securities to ensure compliance with disclosure regulations.

In addition, investment companies must give 'truthful and non-misleading' reports to the SEC and their shareholders twice a year. These reports and other financial statements must be verified by independent public auditors. The advertising materials of an investment company are also subject to regulations.

Any material that is submitted to the SEC may be made available to the public, unless the Commission finds that 'public disclosure is neither necessary nor appropriate in the public interest or for the protection of investors.' If this documentation has not been publicly disclosed, it is illegal for any individual employed by the SEC to reveal this information to 'any person other than an official or employee of the United States or of a State'.

7.2.7 Custody Rules

Mutual funds and closed-end funds are required to keep their assets in the custody of a qualified US bank, or, subject to SEC rules, with a broker-dealer that is a member of a national securities exchange. A central depository may be used for an investment company's portfolio securities. Unit investment trusts are also required to place their assets in the custody of qualified US banks. Foreign custodians that satisfy certain regulations may hold foreign securities.

An investment company with self-custody must place assets with a qualified bank. Independent public auditors must verify these assets at least three times during each fiscal year. Two of these times must be chosen by the accountant, without prior notice to the company.

7.2.8 Audit

The regulations described in the Investment Company Act 1940 require an investment company to retain accounts, books, and other documents, which relate its financial position for a period specified by the SEC. These records will be subject to 'reasonable periodic, special, and other examinations by the Commission' at any time and intermittently. The Commission also has the authority to require investment companies to prepare these accounts in a uniform manner. Each financial statement that is submitted to the SEC must be certified by an independent public accountant, who has been elected by a majority of the board of directors who are not interested persons of the registered investment company.

7.2.9 Fraud

A person convicted of a crime involving securities is automatically barred from working for investment companies, or any other entity connected with the companies, such as their investment advisers, for a period of ten years.

7.2.10 **Insurance**

Under the regulations contained in the Investment Company Act 1940, the SEC has the power to require:

any officer or employee of a registered management investment company who may singly, or jointly with others, have access to securities or funds of any registered company, either directly or through authority to draw upon such funds or to direct generally the disposition of such securities (unless the officer or employee has such access solely through his position as an officer or employee of a bank) be bonded by a reputable fidelity insurance company against larceny and embezzlement in such reasonable minimum amounts as the Commission may prescribe.

A lack of capacity and development in the commercial insurance market during the 1980s led to the formation of the ICI Mutual Insurance Company, a captive insurance provider that concentrates exclusively on the provision of insurance services to the investment management industry.

As part of its range of products, ICI Mutual offers a fidelity blanket bond to protect against losses incurred as a result of employee theft, third-party fraud and various other types of event. This type of insurance product is required under the Investment Company Act 1940. In addition, ICI Mutual provides Directors and Officers (D&O) and Errors and Omissions (E&O) bonds. The D&O/E&O policy protects directors and officers against losses from lawsuits, regulatory investigations, and other claims made against them for their negligent acts, errors, omissions, or other 'wrongful acts'. This policy also protects each insured company against losses from lawsuits, regulatory investigations, and other claims made against the company itself for 'wrongful acts' committed by the company or by persons for whose 'wrongful acts' the company is legally responsible (including employees acting within the scope of their employment).

ICI Mutual has partially solved the potential moral hazard problem in insuring directors and officers of investment companies by only writing insurance for companies that meet certain underwriting criteria. In submitting an application form for ICI Mutual, a company must disclose information on internal control guidelines, trade policy, brokers, the number of employees working in the compliance department, (internal and external) audit department, details regarding the directors and their background, and SEC/NASD inspections. Furthermore, the

SEC must be notified of claims by investment companies on insurance policies.

7.3 COMMON REGULATIONS FOR INVESTMENT ADVISERS AND INVESTMENT COMPANIES

7.3.1 Enforcement

The SEC's Division of Enforcement undertakes investigations into the possible violations of the federal securities laws. Two types of legal action can be taken. Civil suits allow the Commission to obtain an injunction, which prohibits future violations. Contravening an injunction may lead to fines or imprisonment for contempt for the offender. The Commission also seeks civil money penalties and the disgorgement of illegal profits. In civil actions, the federal courts also have the authority to prevent or suspend individuals from acting as corporate officers or directors.

Following authorization by the SEC, the Division of Enforcement may also undertake administrative proceedings, which are heard by administrative law judges and the SEC. These actions may result in the revocation or suspension of registration, or the imposition of bars or suspensions from employment. Moreover, in proceedings against regulated persons, the Commission has the power to order the payment of civil penalties as well as disgorgement.

Table 7.1 shows the enforcement actions that were initiated over the period 1995–2000.

The SEC initiated 2933 enforcement actions between 1995 and 2000, over half of which took the form of administrative proceedings (SEC 2000, 2001). The total number of enforcement actions has increased by more than 3 per cent over this period. The Division of Enforcement was successful in obtaining orders requiring violators of securities law to disgorge illegal profits of approximately $445 m and to pay civil penalties of more than $43 m.

Table 7.2 reports the number of enforcement cases that were brought against investment advisers and companies during 2000.

According to Table 7.2, of the 503 enforcement cases initiated by the SEC during the fiscal year 2000, only 8.8 per cent were against the

Table 7.1. The enforcement actions initiated, 1995–2000

	1995	1996	1997	1998	1999	2000	Total
Civil injunctive actions	171	180	189	214	198	223	1175
Administrative proceedings	291	239	285	248	298	244	1605
Contempt proceedings	23	32	14	15	29	36	149
Reports of investigation	1	2	1	0	0	0	4
Total	486	453	489	477	525	503	2933

Source: SEC (2000, 2001).

Table 7.2. The enforcement cases initiated by the SEC against investment advisers and investment companies, 2000

	Civil actions		Administrative proceedings		Total	
	Number	% of total	Number	% of total	Number	% of total
Investment advisers	13	5.0	27	11.1	40	8.0
Investment companies	1	0.4	3	1.2	4	0.8
Sub-total	14	5.4	30	12.3	44	8.8
Total cases	259	100.0	244	100.0	503	100.0

Source: SEC (2001).

investment advisers and investment companies. In fact, 8 per cent of enforcement cases were initiated against investment advisers, while only 0.8 per cent of the total number of enforcement cases were brought against investment companies. Administrative proceedings involving investment advisers account for 11.1 per cent of the total number of administrative proceedings. This is the most common type of enforcement action brought against investment advisers.

7.3.2 Audit/Compliance

The Office of Compliance Inspections and Examinations is responsible for ensuring 'compliance with securities laws, to detect violations of the law, and to keep the Commission informed of developments in the regulated community'. Under the Securities Act 1934, the Investment Company Act 1940, and the Investment Advisers Act 1940, the Office is authorized to undertake examinations and inspections of registered self-regulatory organizations, broker-dealers, transfer agents, clearing agencies, investment companies, and investment advisers. Upon detection of a violation of the relevant legislation, the Office issues a deficiency letter, stating the problems that need to be addressed. It continues to monitor the case until compliance is achieved. Serious violations that cannot be dealt with using this method are referred to the Division of Enforcement.

The SEC Annual Report 2000 reports that the Office of Compliance Inspections and Examinations inspected 263 investment company complexes and 1458 investment advisers (SEC 2000). Under the Government Performance and Results Act, the Office of Compliance Inspections and Examinations aims to inspect the 1080 investment companies and the 6700 registered investment advisers once every five years. The investment companies inspected control $1.7 trillion assets in 2603 portfolios. About 35 cases were conducted on a 'for cause' basis, implying that the SEC initiated the action because it believed that a problem existed. Violations or deficiencies were identified in 213 inspections, resulting in a deficiency letter to the registrant. These letters concerned problems relating to registration and SEC filings, internal control procedures, boards of directors' monitoring, conflicts of interest, and books and records. Serious violations in 18 cases warranted further investigation by the Division of Enforcement. These infringements included fraud, the role of the fund's board of directors, conflicts of interests, and record keeping.

The 1458 investment advisers inspected by the Office managed non-investment company assets amounting to $2.8 trillion. About 75 cases were inspected 'for cause'. The Office sent 1318 deficiency letters relating to breaches concerning Form ADV, books and records, custody, conflicts of interests, and internal controls. In 54 cases, serious violations involved fraud, Form ADV or brochure disclosure or delivery, record keeping, conflicts of interest, and performance advertising.

7.3.3 Compensation

Through civil action or administrative proceedings, the SEC may seek civil monetary penalties, or the return of illegal profits. However, unlike the Investor Compensation Scheme in the UK, there is no formal process for individual investors to apply for compensation. Discussions suggest that mutual funds tend to rectify pricing errors by compensating investors. For situations when this is not possible, the investment companies have recourse to insurance (Section 7.2.10).

7.3.4 **Complaints**

The SEC created the Office of Investor Education and Assistance specifically to serve individual investors, ensuring that the SEC is aware of the problems encountered by such investors. Upon receipt of a complaint, the case may be referred to the Division of Enforcement for investigation. A copy of the complaint will be sent to the company concerned, which will be asked to report to the client and the SEC. If the complaint is not resolved following these actions, the SEC is unable to mediate and the investor may take legal action.

7.3.5 **The Fiduciary Duty**

Investment advisers and directors of investment companies are fiduciaries. The definition of fiduciary involves the following components:

- fiduciaries offer services, and, in doing so, are entrusted with power or property from another party (the 'entrustor');
- in assigning power or property to fiduciaries, the entrustor is exposed to risk that the fiduciaries will use the power or assets entrusted for a use other than for the benefit of the entrustor; and
- fiduciaries provide no mechanism to mitigate the risk of such misappropriation.

In this light, the legislation contained in the 1940s' Acts provides the necessary protection to investors, and thereby strengthens advisers' and directors' trustworthiness.

The two most important duties of a fiduciary are those of care and loyalty. The basis for the latter is that the adviser acts for the benefit of their client. The duty of loyalty obligates advisers to place their clients' interests above their own, and not to favour one client over another. Since the information between an adviser and their client is asymmetric, in the sense that the former is unable to perfectly observe the skill and care exercised by the latter, fiduciaries also have a duty of care.

For directors of investment companies, the duty of loyalty ensures that fiduciaries do not benefit from power or property entrusted to them. The duty of care obligates directors not to be negligent in providing services, and to perform to the standard (or level of expertise) that they purport to possess. According to the business judgement rule, a director's decision cannot be reviewed by a court if the decision was reached:

- after obtaining relevant information;
- after deliberation taking account of this information and other considerations; and
- in 'good faith'—without conflicts of interest.

By satisfying these elements, a director may not be subjected to scrutiny based on the duty of care. In addition, directors are required to pay attention to:

- the management's performance of the daily operations of the corporation and their relation to corporate objectives;
- the 'danger areas' arising from recent corporate events, or the nature of the corporation's business;
- the unique important occasions, such as the sale of the corporate business; and
- other items requiring attention as specified in the legislation.

Under the Investment Company Act 1940, the board of directors is also responsible for the approval of the following:

- the advisory contract, including evaluation of advisers' fees and profits;
- the underwriting contract;
- the contract for the custody of assets;
- bonding requirements of investment companies; and
- purchases during underwriting by affiliates.

As discussed in Section 7.1.6, the 1940s' Acts not only deal with fraud concerning the offering and sale of securities, as in the Securities Act 1933 and the Securities Exchange Act 1934 (based on contract law), but also fraud in the provision of investment advice. Consequently, these Acts take account of fiduciary law. Other differences also exist between the contract and fiduciary law. For example, under the contract law, information relating to the interests of another party may be disclosed only after being requested. In contrast, advisers' duty to disclose to existing and potential clients is far greater.

7.4 **CONCLUSIONS**

The previous chapter provided an overview of the US regulation in the context of European rules. The regulation of investment advisers and companies in the USA focuses on the prevention of fraud. In the case of investment advisers, there are few capital requirements, at least at the federal level, and there is no specific compensation scheme. Instead, regulation emphasizes disclosure of information, auditing, insurance, the segregation of clients' assets, and enforcement through the courts.

8

The Basel Committee's Proposals on a Capital Charge for Operational Risk

8.1 INTRODUCTION

In 1988 the Basel Committee on Banking Supervision introduced a Capital Accord, designed to reduce the systemic risk associated with banking, and, thus, the potential loss to depositors arising from a bank's failure (Basel Committee 1988). The 1988 Accord required banks to hold capital equal to at least 8 per cent of a basket of assets measured in different ways according to their levels of risk. Capital is divided into two tiers: 'Tier 1' being shareholders' equity and retained earnings; and 'Tier 2' being additional internal and external resources available to the bank. The bank must hold at least half of its measured capital in 'Tier 1' form. Initially, these proposals were implemented by banks in the G10 countries, but were subsequently adopted by more than 100 countries worldwide. The European Commission imposed the requirements contained in the 1988 Accord on Member States through its Directive on the Capital Adequacy of Investment Firms and Credit Institutions.

The main driving force behind the introduction of the 1988 Accord was a concern that the level of capital in the world's banking system had become dangerously low following persistent erosion through competition. In terms of ensuring an adequate amount of capital in the system and a level playing field, the 1988 Accord may be hailed as a success. However, the Accord did not take account of risk-mitigation techniques and created distortions, as banks were encouraged to remove high-quality assets from their balance sheets, thereby reducing the value of bank loan portfolios. In light of these adverse effects, the

Basel Committee published proposals for a new capital adequacy framework in June 1999, which were subsequently revised in January 2001 (Basel Committee 1999*b*, 2001*a*).

The 1988 Basel Accord is the basis for the current legislation imposed on the EU Member States regarding the capital adequacy of investment firms, credit institutions, and internationally active banks. As the 2001 consultation package published by the Basel Committee suggests, as the financial services industry became more complex, the European Commission realized that the broad-brush approach of the 1988 Accord was no longer appropriate. Consequently, it began in 1998 to consult on an alternative structure for the regulation of the financial services industry.

The EU Member States that are also full members of the Basel Committee are Belgium, France, Germany, Italy, Luxembourg, the Netherlands, Spain, Sweden, and the UK. The European Commission itself participates as an observer. The joint membership of the EU and the Basel Committee for nine countries means that the European Commission has a role in devising 'global best practice standards for prudential soundness' and ensuring an international level playing field for institutions. Furthermore, as observer, the Commission is in a position to relate recent developments to non-Basel EU states. Consequently, the legislation adopted in the EU concerning the regulation of financial institutions has closely mirrored that formulated by the Basel Committee.

8.2 THE NEW ACCORD

It is hardly surprising that, given the increasing intricacies of the financial system, the proposals published by the Basel Committee in 2001 are significantly more detailed than those introduced more than a decade earlier. The approach adopted in the new Accord relies on 'three pillars': minimum capital requirements, supervisory review process, and market discipline through disclosure. Unlike the one-size-fits-all, broad-brush structure inherent in the 1988 Accord, the new Accord is designed to provide a menu of approaches: greater flexibility, risk sensitivity, and incentives to improve risk management. While the first pillar concerning capital adequacy retains the current definition of capital and the overall minimum requirement of 8 per cent of capital to risk-weighted assets, it also explicitly includes a capital charge for operational risk. In spite of this and other modifications to the measurement of credit risk, the Committee aims 'to neither raise nor lower the aggregate regulatory capital, inclusive of operational risk, for internationally active banks using the standardized approach'. Further, the revised Accord is to be applied on a consolidated basis—that is, up to holding company level—ensuring that all risks within the whole banking group are captured.

Under the second pillar, supervisors are required to ensure that each bank has 'sound internal processes' in place to certify the adequacy of its capital based on a thorough evaluation of its risk. The objective of the third pillar is to improve market discipline through increased disclosure by banks. The Committee argues that 'effective disclosure is essential to ensure that market participants can better understand banks' risk profiles and the adequacy of their capital positions.' Disclosure requirements are proposed in a number of areas, including, for example, in the process of calculating capital adequacy and risk-assessment methods.

At the time that our report was going to press, the Basel Committee had received over 250 comments following the consultation period on the new Accord, which ended in May 2001. The Committee also published a working paper on the regulatory treatment of operational risk in September 2001 (Basel Committee 2001c) and a paper outlining potential modifications to the Committee's proposals in November (Basel Committee 2001d). The Committee's proposals will be revised and released for a further consultation period in 2002, with implementation in 2005.

8.3 THE IMPLICATIONS OF THE BASEL PROPOSALS

The Basel Committee's proposals have been met with criticism from some parts of the financial community, not merely because of their complexity. In particular, the asset management industry is concerned that, following the European Commission's adoption of these rules, the industry will face a new capital charge for operational risk. The following areas address the appropriateness of imposing a capital requirement for operational risk on asset managers.

8.3.1 **The Operational and Systemic Risks**

As discussed in Chapter 11, the economic rationale for imposing capital requirements on financial institutions is to ensure stability of the financial system and to provide a capital buffer for depositors in the event of a systemic failure. Interestingly, however, the Risk Management Group (RMG) of the Basel Committee has stated that the definition of operational risk does not include systemic risk. This then begs the question as to why a capital requirement for a non-systemic risk, like operational risk, is to be levied on institutions when other forms of protection may be more effective in protecting investors in the absence of systemic risk. For example, a significant proportion of the respondents to our survey had indemnity, employee fidelity and fraud insurance, and used an external custodian. Moreover, our sample of asset managers ranked insurance, internal profits, and parent-firm guarantees as the predominant method used to finance losses, compared to capital.

8.3.2 **The Differences Between Asset Managers and Banks**

As the European Commission's Second Consultative Document on Review of Regulatory Capital for Credit Institutions and Investment Firms stated, the European Commission intends to impose a capital requirement for operational risk, similar to that described under the Basel proposals, on credit institutions and investment firms up to the level of the financial holding company. While it may be argued that the harmonizing requirements for banks, investment firms, and other financial institutions reduces regulatory arbitrage, there are a number of problems in imposing the Basel proposals, which were aimed chiefly at banks, on credit institutions, and investment firms.

There are several important differences between banks and asset managers. For instance, the imposition of a capital requirement on banks to mitigate credit risk may be justified if it provides protection to depositors. As discussed in Chapter 11, contagion is less prevalent in asset management. Therefore, the justification for an operational risk capital charge (which, as the RMG states, is unrelated to systemic risk) in asset management is less obvious, especially when firms adopt other forms of investor protection, such as insurance or external custody. These differences mean that the Basel proposals, which were primarily designed for internationally active banks, may not be suitable for asset managers.

In particular, the Basel Committee has set the proportion of economic capital allocated to operational risk at 12 per cent (previously 20 per cent) on the basis of responses from a quantitative impact survey. However, as will be seen in Chapter 9, the ratio of operational loss to economic capital may be significantly lower for asset managers (see, for example, Table 9.13). Indeed, the European Commission has recognized that because the figure of 12 per cent was calculated on the basis of a sample consisting mainly of banks, it may not accurately reflect the ratio of operational risk to economic capital for investment firms. Therefore, the Commission has requested views from investment firms on the economic capital they allocate to operational risk.[1] Gross income, used in the Basic Indicator and Standardized Approaches to capture a firm's exposure to operational risk, may not be a good indicator of a firm's exposure to operational risk in the asset management industry. Moreover, there may not be an obvious linear relationship between gross income and operational losses as proposed in the Basel consultation papers. Until more data on the frequency and size of operational losses becomes available, these problems will remain unresolved.

Table 8.1 compares the current and proposed capital requirements for the sample of firms that responded to our survey. The results of this hypothetical example were obtained by assuming that, under the January proposals, the beta factors are equal to 0.1 per cent, and, under the October proposals, 0.06 per cent (due to a reduction in the proportion of economic capital allocated to operational risk from 20 to 12 per cent). Furthermore, the business line weighting assigned to asset management is 10 per cent (the midpoint of the range 8–12 per cent suggested in the January proposals).

According to Table 8.1, the levels of capital requirements for operational risk calculated under the Standardized Approach are lower when calculated under the October proposals when compared with the January proposals. Furthermore, compared with the current capital requirement, the aggregate level of capital is always higher under the Standardized Approach. However, this result does not continue to hold in certain size ranges.

---

[1] The Commission has stated that a decision on the imposition of an operational risk charge to investment firms will be taken following consideration of responses received on a questionnaire (aiming to assess the impact of new proposals), and the outcome of a one-day meeting to be held with the industry.

Table 8.1. The impact of the Basel proposals—a hypothetical example

Size (assets under management, €m)	Assets under management (average, €m)	Current capital requirements (€m)	Proposed capital charge for operational risk (€m)[1]	
			Beta = 0.1% (January)	Beta = 0.06% (October)
< 12,000	3094.6	4.2	3.1	1.9
> 12,000 and < 40,000	24,771.9	14.3	24.8	14.9
> 40,000 and < 80,500	64,932.9	18.0	64.9	39.0
> 80,500	164,898.3	102.0	164.9	98.9

Note:
[1] Since our survey does not provide data on gross income which was proposed as an indicator in the October RMG Working Paper, these results have been calculated using assets under management as the indicator for the asset management business line, as set out in the January consultative package.

The overall impact of the additional capital charge for operational risk on asset managers is uncertain. The Basel proposals on credit and operational risks have been calibrated to ensure that the overall level of capital in the (banking) industry remains unchanged. However, asset managers are not affected by the changes in credit-risk charge, and therefore the overall impact of the new capital requirement for operational risk on their regulatory capital is unclear. If the additional capital charge for operational risk leads to an increase in the overall level of actual capital, the costs of increasing the level of this regulatory requirement are likely to be passed on to investors.

8.4 THE PROPOSED CAPITAL CHARGE FOR OPERATIONAL RISK

8.4.1 The Definition of Operational Risk

The January 2001 consultative package contained the following definition of operational risk: 'the risk of direct or indirect loss resulting from inadequate or failed internal processes, people and systems or from external events.' This definition includes legal risk, but excludes strategic or reputational risk. Thus, the Committee originally intended that the capital buffer for operational risk should shield institutions from both direct and indirect losses arising from such risk. Hence, the calculation of the loss arising from an operational failure should include the costs to rectify operational risk problems, payments to third parties, and write-downs. Other types of loss or event, such as near misses, potentially undisclosed losses or contingent losses, may also be included. The costs of improvement in controls, preventative action, quality insurance, and investment in new systems would not be included.

The Committee recognizes that, in some instances, distinctions between losses and costs may be difficult and is therefore 'seeking comment on how better to specify the loss types for inclusion in a more refined definition of operational risk'. Furthermore, while in theory a capital charge for operational risk should provide for the unexpected, as well as expected, losses, accounting procedures may make this difficult in practice.

The Potential Modifications to the Definition of Operational Risk

Comments received on the definition of operational risk described in the January consultative package expressed concern about the distinction between the direct and indirect losses. Strategic and reputational risks are not included in this definition, and, furthermore, the capital charge is not intended to cover all indirect losses or opportunity costs. Consequently, in the 'Working Paper on the Regulatory Treatment of Operational Risk', the Risk Management Group (RMG) of the Basel Committee proposes to remove the reference to direct and indirect losses from the original definition of operational risk (Risk Management Group 2001).

The RMG hopes that, by defining the types of loss events that should be recorded in the internal loss data, clearer guidance can be given on the relevant losses for regulatory capital purposes. Thus, the revised definition states that operational risk is 'the risk of loss resulting from inadequate or failed internal processes, people and systems, or from external events'. This causal-based definition attributes the occurrence of an operational loss to four main reasons: people, processes, systems, and external factors. While this definition is useful in the management of operational risk, it is less helpful in the quantification of operational loss, and in ensuring consistency in the collection of loss data across banks, which both require definitions that are readily measurable and comparable. Interestingly, the working paper states that 'the RMG confirms that this definition does not include systemic risk.'

8.4.2 **The Approaches and Calculation**

As discussed in Chapter 6, investment firms operating in the EU Member States are usually subject to a minimum capital charge based on expenditure. The European Commission's 'Second Consultative Document on Review of Regulatory Capital for Credit Institutions and Investment Firms' maintains that:

this expenditure-based requirement was introduced to allow investment firms to withstand a short-term drop in their activities, and functions as a backstop ratio, i.e. investment firms should meet the higher of this expenditure-based requirement and the risk based requirement for credit risk and market risks. (European Commission 2001)

However, the role of this expenditure-based requirement has not yet been clarified. The European Commission recognizes that the introduction of an explicit capital requirement based on risks is likely to reduce the importance of the current expenditure-based requirement. Therefore, it proposes to revise the role and calibration of the current requirement considering the new risk-based requirements.

To allow for differences in the development of internal controls and the collection of data on operational losses, in its January 2001 consultation document, the Basel Committee has detailed three methods to calculate the capital charge for operational risk—the Basic Indicator Approach, the Standardized Approach, and the Internal Measurement Approach (Basel Committee 2001*b*). The Committee envisages these approaches as 'a continuum of increasing sophistication and risk sensitivity'. It is envisaged that as operational risk-management techniques develop, banks move along this spectrum to more advanced approaches and benefit from a lower level of capital requirement. A bank may adopt a particular means of calculating its capital requirements only if it satisfies specified qualifying criteria. If a bank has satisfied the criteria for a particular approach, it should be allowed to use that approach, even if it had previously been using a simpler method. Moreover, a bank is not permitted to revert to simpler methods once it has qualified for a more advanced approach. Internationally active banks and banks with significant operational risk are expected to use a more sophisticated approach within the overall framework. On the basis of data provided by a small sample of banks, the Committee has concluded that operational risk accounts for an average of 20 per cent of economic capital. In the absence of data for a larger sample, this figure of 20 per cent has been used in the calculation of the capital charge for operational risk.

The characteristics of the three approaches are now discussed in detail. These approaches are summarized in Table 8A.1.

The Basic Indicator Approach

The simplest method, the Basic Indicator Approach, assigns operational risk capital using a single indicator to capture an institution's overall exposure to operational risk. The indicator proposed is gross income, which is measured as the sum of net interest income and net non-interest income, reflecting the income before the deduction of operational losses. The capital charge is then calculated by multiplying this indicator by a fixed percentage, α. On the basis of the finding that a sample of banks allocate 20 per cent of their economic capital to operational risks, α has been provisionally set at 30 per cent. However, in its January 2001 consultation paper (Basel Committee 2001b), the Committee acknowledged that this figure may increase in order to provide banks with incentives to progress to more sophisticated approaches. Furthermore, the Committee admitted that this calibration of α might need to be revised since it was calculated using data from a sample of internationally active banks, whereas it is anticipated that the Basic Indicator Approach will be adopted by smaller, domestic, banks.

The simplicity of the Basic Indicator Approach means that it can be applied by any bank. Therefore, there are no qualifying criteria per se, although banks adopting this method must comply with the Committee guidance on operational risk sound practices (Basel Committee 2001e).

The Standardized Approach

The Standardized Approach classifies a bank's business into a number of 'standardized' business lines. These lines are similar to those developed to ensure consistency in the collation of data on operational losses. For each business line, a broad indicator is specified to capture the size or volume of a bank's activity in this area. The indicator is intended to serve as a rough proxy for the amount of operational risk within each of these business lines. Table 8.2 reports the business units, business lines, and size/volume indicators adopted for the Standardized Approach.

Table 8.2. The business units, business lines, and size/volume indicators in the Standardized Approach

Business units	Business lines[1]	Indicator[2]
Investment banking	Corporate finance	Gross income
	Trading and sales	Gross income[3]
Banking	Retail banking	Annual average assets
	Commercial banking	Annual average assets
	Payment and settlement	Annual settlement throughput
Others	Retail brokerage	Gross income
	Asset management	Total funds under management

Notes:
[1] A business line for agency services (custody, corporate agency, and corporate trust) is intended to be included in the final proposal. An insurance business line may also be incorporated in both the Standardized and Internal Measurement Approaches, where insurance is included in a consolidated group for capital purposes.
[2] The indicator is the data for that business line. For example, for corporate finance, it is gross income for that business line, not the whole bank.
[3] An alternative may be value at risk.

Source: Basel Committee on Banking Supervision (2001*b*).

For each business line, the capital charge is calculated by multiplying a bank's financial indicator by a 'beta' factor. The beta factor captures the relationship between the industry's operational risk loss experience for a given business line and the broad financial indicator representing the bank's activity in that business line, which satisfies regulatory standards. Thus, for the asset management business line, the capital charge is equal to the product of the beta factor for asset management and total funds under management. The total capital charge for the institution is calculated as the sum of the capital charges for each business line. A bank with more highly developed internal controls in some business lines will be allowed to calibrate the operational risk capital charge using the more advanced Internal Measurement Approach for these business lines and the Standardized Approach for the remaining business lines.

In addition to satisfying the requirements set out in 'Operational Risk Sound Practices', in order to be eligible for the Standardized Approach, banks must meet the criteria relating to risk management and control, and measurement and validation. Effective risk management and control must be achieved through:

- an independent risk control and audit function, efficient use of risk-reporting systems, an involved board of directors and senior management, and appropriate documentation of risk-management systems;

- an autonomous operational risk-management and control process; and
- regular reviews of the operational risk-management process and measurement methodology by the internal audit group.

For appropriate measurement and validation, banks must:

- have appropriate risk-reporting systems;
- begin to systematically track relevant operational risk data for each business line in the firm; and
- develop specific, documented criteria for allocating current business lines and activities into the standardized framework.

The Internal Measurement Approach

The Internal Measurement Approach advocates the use of banks' own internal data on operational losses, while limiting the supervisor's role to that of imposing 'quantitative and qualitative standards to ensure the integrity of the measurement approach, data quality, and the adequacy of the internal control environment'. Under the Internal Measurement Approach, the capital charge for operational risk is calculated using the following steps.

A bank's activities are categorized according to the same types of business lines used in the Standardized Approach. Operational risk in each business line is then further divided into 'non-overlapping and comprehensive' loss types (a description of loss event types is contained in Table 8A.2).

The supervisor stipulates an exposure indicator (EI) for each business line/loss-type combination to capture the size of exposure to, or amount of operational risk in each business line.

Using their internal loss data, banks estimate the probability of loss event (PE) and the loss given that event (LGE). The product of EI, PE, and LGE is then used to calculate the expected loss (EL) for each business line/loss-type combination.

The supervisor specifies a factor (the 'gamma term') for each business line/loss type combination. The overall charge for a particular bank is the sum of all the resulting products.

Banks must submit each of the individual components of the expected loss variable to the supervisors.

Thus, in this approach, business lines, risk types, and exposure indicators are standardized by supervisors and individual banks are able to use the internal loss data. The regulator sets the gamma term of the Internal Measurement Approach on the basis of an industry-wide loss distribution. However, the risk profile of individual banks may differ from that of the industry-wide loss distribution. To take account of the differences between individual banks and the industry, a risk profile index has been proposed to reflect the ratio of unexpected losses to expected losses of the bank's distribution compared to that of the industry-wide distribution. The risk profile index of the industry loss distribution is equal to one. If a bank experiences a long tail of the distribution (that is, a positive frequency of large losses), its risk profile index will be greater than one. Similarly, a bank with a smaller tail of the distribution will have a risk profile index less than one.

To use the Internal Measurement Approach, any bank must first satisfy the requirements of the Standardized Approach, and must meet the following requirements for effective risk management and control.

The accuracy of loss data, and confidence in the results of calculations using that data (including PE and LGE), have to be established through 'use tests'. Banks must use the collected data and the resulting measures for risk reporting, management reporting, internal capital allocation purposes, risk analysis, etc. Banks that do not fully integrate an internal measurement methodology into their daily activities and major business decisions should not qualify for this approach.

Also the following requirements are needed for measurement and validation.

Banks must develop sound internal loss reporting practices, supported by an infrastructure of loss database systems that are consistent with the scope of operational losses defined by the supervisors and the banking industry.

Banks must have an operational risk-measurement methodology, knowledgeable staff, and an appropriate systems infrastructure capable of identifying and collecting comprehensive operational risk loss data necessary to create a loss database and to calculate appropriate PEs and LGEs. Systems should be able to gather data from all appropriate sub-systems and geographic locations. Missing data from various systems, groups, or locations should be explicitly identified and tracked.

Banks need an operational risk loss database extending back for a number of years (to be set by the Committee) for significant business lines. Additionally, banks must develop specific criteria for assigning loss data to a particular business line and risk types.

Banks must have in place a sound process to identify in a consistent manner over time the events used to construct a loss database and to be able to identify, which historical loss experiences are appropriate for the institution and are representative of their current and future business activities. This entails developing and defining loss data criteria in terms of the type of loss data and the severity of the loss data that goes beyond the general supervisory definition and specifications.

Banks must develop rigorous conditions, under which internal loss data would be supplemented with external data, as well as a process of ensuring the relevance of this data for their business environment. Sound practices need to be identified surrounding the methodology and process of scaling public external loss data or pooled internal loss data from other sources. These conditions and practices should be revisited on a regular basis, must be clearly documented, and should be subject to independent review.

The sources of external data must be reviewed regularly to ensure the accuracy and applicability of the loss data. Banks must review and understand the assumptions used in the collection and assignment of loss events and resultant loss statistics.

Banks must regularly conduct validation of their loss rates, risk indicators, and size estimations in order to ensure the proper inputs to the regulatory capital charge. Banks must adhere to rigorous processes in estimating parameters such as EI, PE, and LGE.

As part of the validation process, scenario analysis, and stress testing would help banks in their ability to gauge whether the operational environment is accurately reflected in data aggregation and parameter estimates. A process would need to be developed to identify and incorporate plausible historically large or significant events into assessments of operational risk exposure, which may fall outside the observation period. These processes should be clearly documented and be specific enough for independent review and verification. Such analysis would also assist in gauging the appropriateness of certain judgements or over-rides in the data-collection process.

Bank management should incorporate experience and judgement into an analysis of the loss data and the resulting PEs and LGEs. Banks have to identify clearly the exceptional situations under which judgement or over-rides may be used, to what extent they are to be used, and who is authorized to make such decisions. The conditions under which these over-rides may be made and detailed records of changes should be clearly documented and subject to independent review.

The supervisors will need to examine the data collection, measurement, and validation process, and to assess the appropriateness of the operational risk control environment of the institution.

The Loss Distribution Approach

The Basel Committee also proposes a fourth method—the Loss Distribution Approach. However, the Committee acknowledges that internal measurement of operational risks and losses by banks is not sufficiently developed and therefore, this approach will not be available for regulatory capital purposes when the New Basel Capital Accord is introduced. Under the Loss Distribution Approach, a bank estimates two probability distribution functions for each business line (and risk type)—one on single-event impact and the other on event frequency for the next (one) year—using its internal data. Based on the two estimated distributions, the bank then computes the probability distributions, and calculates the probability distribution function of the cumulative operational loss. The capital charge is based on the simple sum of the value at risk for each business line (and risk type).

The Potential Modifications to the Measurement of Operational Risk

In the January proposals, the Committee based its calculations of the capital charge for operational risk on the finding that a sample of internationally active banks allocate 20 per cent of their economic capital for operational loss. The comments received on this proposal suggested that this 20 per cent figure overstates the amount of regulatory capital necessary to provide adequate coverage of banks' operational risk exposures. Respondents also criticized the sample used to calculate this 20 per cent figure, arguing that it was too small and not representative. Furthermore, this figure would lead to an increase in the general level of capital requirements, which is contrary to the Committee's stated objective to retain the overall level of capital constant for the industry as a whole.

In light of these comments and the data reported as part of the Quantitative Impact Survey, the Committee acknowledges that the figure of 20 per cent should be reduced to 12 per cent. It argues that this reduction is justified because it is consistent with the operational risks faced by banks, and partly reflects the use of insurance in mitigating these risks.

This change in the proportion of regulatory capital allocated to operational risk has implications for the calculation of the capital charge in both the Basic Indicator and Standardized Approaches. Thus, the RMG proposes that the alpha term under the Basic Indicator

Approach be reduced from 30 to 17–20 per cent, and the beta term under the Standardized Approach should fall within a similar range.

While the Basic Indicator and Standardized Approaches will continue to be the first two options available to calculate the capital charge for operational risk, the RMG has extended the 'most risk-sensitive' approaches available. Thus, the Advanced Measurement Approaches (AMAs), which incorporate the Committee-defined Internal Measurement Approach detailed in the January consultation paper (Basel Committee 2001a), allow banks to use internally generated risk estimates in the calculation of the operational risk capital requirement, subject to qualitative and quantitative criteria.

The main motivation behind the introduction of AMAs is the recognition by the Committee that the area of operational risk measurement and loss data gathering are being developed, and therefore, a methodology such as the Internal Measurement Approach would restrict banks and inhibit innovation of alternative methods. The regulatory capital requirement for operational risk under the AMA would be based on an estimate of operational risk derived from a bank's internal risk-measurement system. As stated previously, this risk estimate, which will be lower than that estimated under the simpler approaches, would be subject to a floor based on the capital charge for operational risk calculated under the Standardized Approach. The RMG proposes that the floor be set at 75 per cent of the capital requirement under the Standardized Approach, which implies a capital level of 9 per cent of minimum regulatory capital under the AMA (this topic is discussed further in Section 8.5.1).

To qualify to use the AMA, a bank must satisfy the following (qualitative and quantitative) criteria.

The bank's supervisory authority or authorities must approve of the use of the AMA. To give this approval, the supervisory authority must be satisfied with the bank's risk-management system and its implementation; staff resources; and that the bank's AMA is based on a rigorous analysis of internal and external data.

Supervisory authorities have the power to conduct an initial examination of a bank's AMA prior to its use for supervisory capital purposes.

The bank must have an independent operational risk-management function that is responsible for the design and implementation of the bank's operational risk-management system.

The board of directors and senior management must be actively involved in the operational risk-management process.

The bank's internal operational risk-measurement system must be closely integrated into the day-to-day risk-management process of the bank.

There must be regular reporting of operational risk exposures and loss experience to business unit management, senior management, and to the board of directors. In addition, the bank must track its internal loss experience.

The bank must undertake a regular programme of scenario analysis, particularly with regard to very infrequent but severe events that could cause substantial losses.

The bank must have a procedure in operation to ensure compliance with a documented set of internal policies, controls, and procedures concerning the operational risk-measurement system.

The operational risk-management processes and measurement systems must be regularly reviewed by an internal and/or external auditor. The operational risk-measurement system must be certified by external auditors and/or supervisory authorities.

The capital charge will equal the greater of the risk measure generated by the bank's internal operational risk-measurement system or a floor equal to 75 per cent of the Standardized Approach capital charge for operational risk.

The bank must be able to demonstrate that the risk measure used for regulatory capital charge purposes reflects a holding period of one year and a confidence level of 99.9 per cent.

The internal risk-measurement system must capture the impact of infrequent, but potentially severe, and operational risk events.

Any internal operational risk-measurement system used for regulatory capital purposes must be supported by loss database systems. The bank must have an appropriate system in place to identify and collect operational risk loss data necessary for this loss database.

The bank must develop specific criteria to assign loss data to particular business lines and risk types.

Internal loss data must be modified following a change in the size of the bank's operations (for example, after merger/divestiture, acquisition/sale of a business line).

The bank must establish procedures for the use of external data as a supplement to its internal loss data.

The bank must periodically review its methodologies and data inputs.

The bank must identify clearly those exceptional situations, in which judgement over-rides may be used, to what extent they are used, and who is authorized to make such decisions.

Internally generated operational risk measures used for regulatory capital purposes must be based on a minimum historical observation period of five years, although this may vary for some business lines.

The bank must regularly conduct validation of any parameters (for example, loss rates, risk indicators, or scale indicators) used in its internal loss-measurement systems in order to ensure that the inputs to the regulatory capital charge are reliable.

The bank will be permitted to recognize empirical correlations in operational risk losses across business lines and event types, subject to 'sound' systems for measuring these correlations.

Risk-mitigating activities (for example, insurance) will be taken into account in the calculation of the capital charge for operational risk.

Qualitative adjustments or scorecards must be used to allocate and adjust operational risk capital and to recognize possible improvement or deterioration in the firm's operational risk exposure and/or control environment, subject to standards that address the structure, comprehensiveness, and rigour of the adjustment.

The RMG has slightly amended the Standardized Approach to the calculation of the capital charge for operational risk. Instead of using the indicators specific to each business line, as reported in Table 8.2, the RMG suggests that, 'at the present time', like the Basic Indicator Approach, gross income be used as the indicator in all business lines 'for the sake of simplicity, comparability, reduction of arbitrage possibilities and, most significantly, a lack of evidence of greater risk sensitivity of other indicators'.

8.5 OTHER ISSUES

8.5.1 The 'Floor' Concept

The Basel Committee envisages that, as banks move to more advanced calibration techniques, the consequent improvements in internal controls and risk management will be reflected in a lower capital charge. However, the Committee will limit the reduction in capital held when a bank moves from a Standardized Approach to an Internal Measurement Approach by setting a floor below which the required capital cannot fall. The Committee will review the need for the existence and level of the floor two years after the implementation of the New Basel Capital Accord.

There are two proposed techniques for setting the level of the floor:

- to take a fixed percentage of the capital charge under the Standardized Approach and to specify that the charge calculated under the Internal Measurement Approach cannot fall below this level (at least for a period of time); and
- to set the minimum levels for elements of the expected loss calculation based on industry-wide loss data and distributions.

The Potential Modifications to the Floor

The RMG proposes that the floor imposed on the measurement of capital charges under the AMA will initially be stringent to reflect 'the fact that the internal methods used to quantify operational risk are still in the early stages of implementation and that the AMA, do not, as yet, contain detailed criteria for the specific quantification methods likely to be used by banks'. The Committee proposes to set the floor using the first, simplified method above, and recommends that it is equal to 75 per cent of the Standardized Approach capital charge. It is intended that, once implemented, this floor be reviewed every two years. Eventually, this floor may be lowered or even eliminated for more detailed approaches.

8.5.2 Outsourcing

The Committee recognizes that outsourcing by banks is increasing. Where outsourcing is conducted between banks, it is the entity that bears the ultimate responsibility for the operational loss that should hold the capital.

Risk Mitigation: Insurance

By encouraging better risk management, the Committee is eager to support risk-mitigation techniques in so far as they reduce, rather than transfer, risk. Following discussions with the industry, the Committee has recognized that firms were using, or considering using, insurance policies (bankers' blanket bonds and professional liability insurance) to mitigate operational risk. Insurance can be used to externalize the risk of potentially 'low-frequency, high-severity' losses, such as errors and omissions (including processing losses, physical loss of securities, and fraud). The Committee agrees that, in principle, such mitigation should be reflected in the capital requirement for operational risk. However, it believes that the market for insurance of operational risk is still developing. Moreover, banks that use insurance should recognize that they might, in fact, be replacing operational risk with a counterparty risk. There are also other questions relating to liquidity (that is, the speed of payment and coverage of insurance products), loss adjustment and voidability, limits in the product range, the inclusion of insurance payouts in internal loss data, and moral hazard.

The Proposed Modifications to Inclusion of Insurance

Responses to the January consultation paper highlighted the use of insurance contracts, such as bankers' blanket bonds, to protect against operational losses from events such as fraud and employee theft, and new insurance products intended to provide coverage of some of the emerging forms of operational risk. Consequently, respondents argued that, in spite of the Committee's arguments against insurance (such as, a less developed market and an increase in counterparty risk), the role of insurance in mitigating operational risk should be considered in the calculation of the capital charge for operational risk.

The RMG also recommends that 'robust and comprehensive' insurance against operational risks should only be acknowledged for banks using the AMA. Furthermore, the impact of insurance risk mitigation on the capital requirement will be limited by the imposition of the floor, which will be set at 75 per cent of the standardized capital charge. The Committee argues that this restriction recognizes that 'insurance may provide less than perfect coverage of operational risks, due to factors such as delays in payment or legal challenges of contractual terms' and that 'the remaining capital charge provides an adequate cushion for residual risk.'

The RMG intends to develop criteria which an insurance policy must satisfy in order to ensure that the contract provides sufficient coverage of operational losses. These criteria would cover the following areas:

- the timeliness of payment following operational failures;
- the certainty of coverage (that is, contingencies in the terms of the contract that might mean that certain losses would not be covered);
- the length of contract and policy renewal;

- standards for insurance companies issuing the policies (for example, minimum acceptable credit or claims payment ratings, use of, and policies surrounding, reinsurance, or regulatory oversight).

8.6 THE CAPITAL ADEQUACY LEGISLATION IN THE EUROPEAN COMMUNITY

8.6.1 The Current European Commission Proposals

On 5 February 2001, less than a month after the publication of the Basel proposals, the European Commission launched its second consultation document on a new capital adequacy framework for banks, investment firms, and credit institutions (European Commission 2001). Although not as voluminous as the Basel consultative package, the European Commission proposals generally 'overlap' with the recommendations set out by the Basel Committee. However, there are some differences. First, unlike the Basel process, the Commission's process is legislative. Second, the scope of the Commission's proposals is wider than those of Basel, since the former applies to all banks, investment firms, and credit institutions. Further differences may arise as the Commission's recommendations are 'fine-tuned' to take account of the structures of the European financial industries.

The General European Commission Proposals

The components of the European Commission's proposed approach to the regulation of financial institutions are minimum capital requirements, a supervisory review process, and market discipline. As with the Basel recommendations, the European Commission proposes to revise capital requirements to ensure that they accurately reflect the risks run by banks and investment firms, and simultaneously ensure no deterioration in the overall levels. The European Commission's consultation paper outlines two strategies to determine capital charges that are more reflective of the credit risk of financial transactions. These strategies reflect an approach based on the institutions' internal credit-assessment systems and a revision of the standardized credit risk-weighting scheme. The Commission's consultation paper also proposes the introduction of a capital charge for operational risk.

The objectives of the supervisory review process are to ensure that institutions have adequate capital to support their risks, and to encourage the development and use of better risk-management techniques in monitoring and managing these risks. The role of market discipline is to contribute to greater financial soundness and stability, while maintaining a level competitive playing field and recognizing the sensitivity of certain information.

In general, it is anticipated that the proposed approach will:

- be more sensitive to the different needs of industry participants;
- make capital charges more reflective of underlying economic risk;
- encourage enhanced risk-mitigation standards;
- provide a framework to support a comprehensive assessment of the risks to which banks and investment firms are exposed.

In order to prevent repetition of the comments received by the Basel Committee, the Commission designed a questionnaire for specific comments on its consultation paper. The consultation period ended on 31 May 2001. Initially, the European Commission proposals were expected to be implemented in 2004, consistent with the Financial Services Action Plan for a fully integrated market in financial services by 2005. However, in light of the extensive comments received, the Commission welcomed the Basel Committee's decision to extend the time-table for revision to allow an additional round of consultation in 2002, and implementation in 2005.

The European Commission Proposals on Operational Risk

Again, the European Commission's proposals on a capital charge for operational risk parallel those initially specified by the Basel Committee in its January consultation package. In the Commission's February consultation paper (European Commission 2001), operational risk is defined as 'the risk of direct or indirect loss resulting from inadequate or failed internal processes, people and systems or from external events'. It envisages three approaches that may be used to measure operational risk. The Standardized Approach will be the method that is most commonly applied. Banks, investment firms, and credit institutions, which satisfy stringent risk-management standards similar to those outlined by the Basel Committee, may use the Internal Measurement Approach. The Basic Indicator Approach, the simplest method, may be adopted by smaller institutions with limited activities and a low risk profile.

The Commission also concurs with the Basel Committee's estimate that '20 per cent of current capital requirements should be used as a benchmark for developing minimum capital requirements for operational risk'.

In 2001, the Commission compiled a questionnaire in order to assess the impact of an additional capital charge on investment firms. The deadline for completion of this questionnaire was extended from 31 July 2001 to 1 October 2001. Furthermore, the Commission has indicated that 'a decision on the possible application of an operational risk charge to investment firms will be taken in the light of the responses received and of the outcome of a one-day meeting, which will be held with the industry.'

Interestingly, the Commission has not yet commented on the potential modifications to the Basel Committee's proposals, including the amendment of the definition of operational risk, the lowering of the 20 per cent benchmark figure, and the introduction of the broader AMAs, which incorporate the Internal Measurement Approach.

8.7 CONCLUSIONS

The new Basel proposals have widespread implications for the imposition of capital requirements on asset management firms for operational risks. A number of different approaches involving progressively greater degrees of sophistication have been proposed, ranging from the Basic Indicator Approach, through the Standardized Approach to the Internal Measurement and Loss Distribution Approaches. The original proposals would have had far-reaching implications for the amounts of capital that asset management firms are required to hold. As it is, the modified proposals have less severe overall consequences for the asset management business as a whole, but a significant effect on certain classes of firms. In the European context, the importance of the Basel proposals stems from the fact that the European Commission is likely to adopt whatever finally emerges from Basel. The critical question that this therefore raises is whether the Basel proposals are appropriate for operational risks, in particular in the context of asset management firms.

Appendix

Table 8A.1. Summary of three approaches to calculate operational risk capital charge

Approach	Formula	Details
Basic Indicator Approach	$\alpha * \text{Indicator}$	• Uses a single indicator as a proxy for an institution's overall operational risk exposure • Gross income is proposed as the indicator • α is set by the Committee • α is initially set at 30%, revised downwards to 17–20%
Standardized Approach	$\Sigma \beta_{\text{BL}} * \text{Indicator}_{\text{BL}}$	• A bank's activities are divided into a number of standardized business units and business lines • Within each business line, regulators specify an indicator to reflect the size or volume of a bank's activity in this area • The beta factor serves as a rough proxy for the relationship between the industry's operational risk loss experience for a given business line and the broad financial indicator representing the bank's activity in that business line • The beta factor must satisfy supervisory standards • Originally, the proposed indicator for the asset management business line was total funds under management. More recent publications by the RMG, however, use gross income • More risk sensitive than the Basic Indicator Approach
Internal Measurement Approach	$\Sigma\Sigma\gamma * \text{EI} * \text{PE} * \text{LGE}$	• A bank's activities are categorized into a number of business lines • A broad set of operational loss types is defined and applied across business lines

Table 8A.1. (Continued)

Approach	Formula	Details
		• Within each business line/loss type combination, the supervisor specifies an exposure indicator, which is a proxy for the size (or amount of risk) of each business line's operational risk exposure • For each business line/loss type combination, banks measure the probability of loss event (PE) and loss given that event (LGE) using internal loss data • Expected loss is calculated as the product of EI, PE, LGE. These components must be validated by the supervisor • The supervisor sets the gamma term for each business line/loss type combination • The capital charge is then calculated as the sum of the product of the gamma term and the expected loss for each business line/loss type combination

Source: Basel Committee on Banking Supervision (2001*b*).

Table 8A.2. Detailed loss event-type classification

Event-type category	Definition	Categories	Activity examples
Internal fraud	Losses due to acts of a type intended to defraud, misappropriate property, or circumvent regulations, the law, or company policy, excluding diversity/discrimination events, which involve at least one internal party	Unauthorized activity	Transactions not reported (intentional) Transaction type unauthorized (with monetary loss) Mismarking of position (intentional)
		Theft and fraud	Fraud/credit fraud/worthless deposits Theft/extortion/embezzlement/robbery Misappropriation of assets Malicious destruction of assets Forgery Smuggling Account takeover/impersonation/etc. Tax non-compliance/evasion (wilful) Bribes/kickbacks Insider trading (not on firm's account)
External fraud	Losses due to acts of a type intended to defraud, misappropriate property, or circumvent the law, by a third party	Theft and fraud	Theft/robbery Forgery Hacking damage
		Systems security	Theft of information (with monetary loss)
Employment practices and workplace safety	Losses arising from acts inconsistent with employment, health or safety laws or agreements, from payment of personal injury claims, or from diversity/discrimination events	Employee relations	Compensation, benefit, termination issues Employee health and safety rules events Workers' compensation
		Diversity and discrimination	All discrimination types

Table 8A.2. (Continued)

Event-type category	Definition	Categories	Activity examples
Clients, products, and business practices	Losses arising from an unintentional or negligent failure to meet a professional obligation to specific clients (including fiduciary and suitability requirements), or from the nature or design of a product	Suitability, disclosure, and fiduciary	Fiduciary breaches/guideline violations Suitability/disclosure issues Retail consumer disclosure violations Breach of privacy Aggressive sales Account churning Misuse of confidential information Lender liability
		Improper business or market practices	Antitrust Improper trade/market practices Market manipulation Insider trading (on firm's account) Unlicensed activity Money laundering
		Product flaws	Product defects (unauthorized, etc.) Model errors
		Selection, sponsorship, and exposure	Failure to investigate client per guidelines Exceeding client exposure limits
		Advisory activities	Disputes over performance of advisory activities
Damage to physical assets	Losses arising from loss or damage to physical assets from natural disaster or other events	Disasters and other events	Natural disaster losses Human losses from external sources (terrorism, vandalism)

Table 8A.2. (Continued)

Event-type category	Definition	Categories	Activity examples
Business disruption and system failures	Losses arising from disruption of business or system failures	Systems	Hardware Software Telecommunications Utility outage/disruptions
Execution, delivery, and process management	Losses from failed transaction processing or process management, from relations with trade counterparties and vendors	Transaction capture, execution, and maintenance	Miscommunication Data entry, maintenance, or loading error Missed deadline or responsibility Model/system misoperation Accounting error/entity attribution error Other task performance Delivery failure Collateral management failure Reference data maintenance
		Monitoring and reporting	Failed mandatory reporting obligation Inaccurate external reports (loss incurred)
		Customer intake and documentation	Client permissions/disclaimers missing Legal documents missing/incomplete
		Customer/client account management	Unapproved access given to accounts Incorrect client records (loss incurred) Negligent loss or damage of client assets
		Trade counterparties	Non-client counterparty misperformance Miscellaneous non-client counterparty disputes
		Vendors and suppliers	Outsourcing Vendor disputes

Source: Risk Management Group of the Basel Committee (2001).

9

Survey of European Asset Managers

This chapter focuses on the results of a survey that was devised to obtain information on the types and frequency of operational risks faced by asset management companies in seven European countries. It is estimated that the companies in the sample have more than €5 trillion of assets under management globally.

The chapter is structured as follows:

- Section 9.1 details the functions of the asset management company;
- Section 9.2 sets out the methodology used in devising the survey;
- Section 9.3 describes the sample;
- Section 9.4 explores the distribution of assets under management for the companies in the sample;
- Section 9.5 describes the activities of the companies in the sample;
- Section 9.6 examines the operational risks and losses in discretionary asset management;
- Section 9.7 provides a summary of the responses on the forms of protection against operational losses and risks; and
- Section 9.8 summarizes the main results of the survey.

The sample of firms that responded to the survey are first described in terms of the location of main operations, the type of institution, and size, which is measured by assets under management, employment, and transactions. The type of services offered and activities conducted by the firms are then analysed. Third, the size of losses as a result of operational risks is examined. Finally, the forms of protection implemented to mitigate the impact of operational risks are reported.

A copy of the questionnaire sent to asset managers is provided in the appendix to this chapter.

9.1 THE FUNCTIONS OF THE ASSET MANAGEMENT INDUSTRY

Figure 9.1 provides a simplified description of the various activities in asset management.[1] This is helpful in order to understand the analysis of operational risks provided in subsequent sections. Activities related to a unit trust management are not explicitly noted since they are outside the scope of this study.

9.2 METHODOLOGY

The sample was selected on the basis of the countries under consideration in this book including France, Germany, Ireland, Italy, the Netherlands, and the UK, with the focus on companies that provided discretionary asset management services. Companies were asked to complete the questionnaire for their domestic operations only. Contacts were made with asset management associations (namely AFG–ASFFI, Assogestioni, EAMA, FMA, IAIM, Inverco) and with a large number of contacts in asset management companies. Trade associations in these countries provided a large proportion of the sample, and additional companies were identified from other sources. To obtain a representative sample, asset managers of various sizes were included. Responses were typically received from either heads of risk, compliance officers, finance directors, or, occasionally, the managing director of the asset management business. Survey responses were treated in the strictest confidence and confidentiality statements were signed. Great care has been taken in presenting the analysis of the responses to the questions to ensure that no firm-specific information has been divulged.

During the initial stages of the study, a pilot questionnaire was sent to ten companies. Interviews were conducted with these firms with the

---

[1] The diagram, provided by British Invisibles, was originally produced by PriceWaterhouseCoopers (PWC).

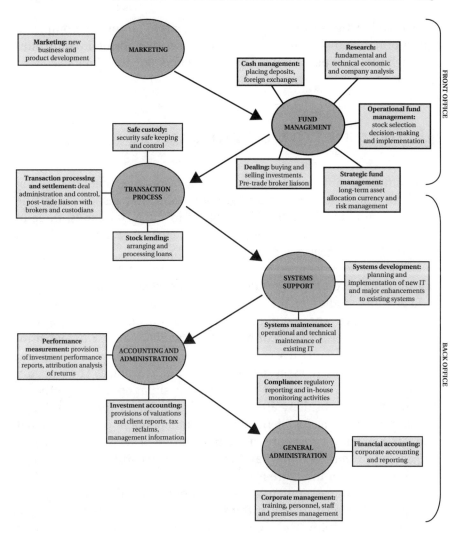

Fig. 9.1. The functions of the asset management industry
Source: British Invisibles, PWC.

purpose of improving and revising the structure of the questionnaire. Subsequently a revised questionnaire was sent to 83 companies in seven European countries (France, Germany, Ireland, Italy, the Netherlands, Spain, and the UK). About 29 replies were received from this mailing, in addition to the 10 already received. Thus the total number of completed questionnaires received was 39. The overall response rate was 42 per cent.

The following sections provide an analysis from 39 completed questionnaires that were received from asset management companies throughout Europe. Results usually relate to the financial year of 1999.

9.3 DESCRIPTION OF THE SAMPLE

The sample comprises asset management companies that are based in six European countries. Of the 39 companies that responded to the questionnaire, two have their head office in the Netherlands, three in Germany, four in Ireland, seven in Italy, eight in France, and 15 in the UK. No responses were received from Spain.

Of those that responded to the questionnaire, 34 are subsidiaries of a group, and five are independent, stand-alone companies.

Regulatory bodies of the asset management companies and their parent firms are reported in the appendix at the end of this chapter.

Firms were classified according to the activity of their parent firm, which was divided into five categories: banking, insurance, banking and insurance combined, asset management, and brokerage. The category 'asset management' is used to define the situation where both the parent and the subsidiary are asset managers. The difference between an asset manager as just defined and an independent company is that the latter is not a subsidiary of a parent group. The 34 subsidiaries of larger groups in the sample have been divided according to the activity of the parent firm in Figure 9.2.

Over half of the asset management companies are owned by banking groups, and approximately a third of companies are subsidiaries of insurance companies. The remainder are owned by asset management companies, bank and insurance service providers, or brokers.

Figure 9.3 shows the ownership of the asset management companies in the sample divided according to the location of head office.

Over 70 per cent of Italian firms in this sample are owned by banks. A similar proportion of firms operating in Ireland and Germany are also subsidiaries of the banking groups. The sample of firms in France consists of almost equal proportions of independent companies and subsidiaries of insurance companies. There is an approximately equal split of ownership of the UK companies between the banks and insurance companies. The results are broadly consistent with the observation from the aggregate industry statistics in Chapter 4 that

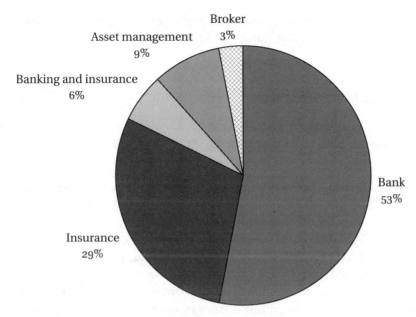

Fig. 9.2. The activity of parent firm

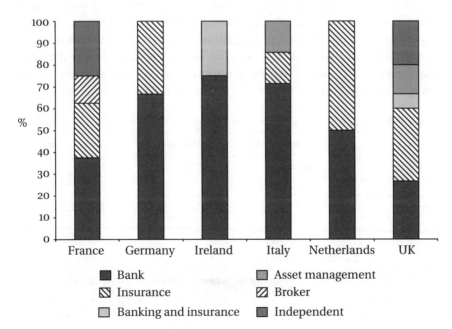

Fig. 9.3. The ownership of asset management companies by country

there is a more significant ownership of asset management companies by banks in Continental Europe than in the UK.

9.4 SIZE

The Assets Under Management

All 37 companies provided aggregate figures on assets under management. Table 9.1 shows the distribution of the firms in the sample that provided data on total assets under management.

Total *domestic* assets under management for the 37 companies amounted to €2255 billion. It is estimated that, *globally*, these companies manage over €5 trillion of assets. However, only 33 companies supplied detailed information on the division of total assets under management into pooled funds (that is, assets held through collective investment schemes) and mandates, as shown in Table 9.2. Pooled schemes include unit trusts, open-ended investment companies, and closed-ended funds.

Most asset managers engage in both management of pooled funds and discretionary mandates. Assets under management divided according to the above classification amount to €1873 billion. In aggregate, collective schemes account for 28 per cent of assets under management, while 63 per cent of the assets under management in the sample are mandates. Under the 'Other' category, companies have

Table 9.1. The distribution of sample by domestic assets under management

€ bn	Number of firms	Median (€ bn)	Mean (€ bn)
<12	10	0.5	3.1
>12 and <40	9	26.4	26.1
>40 and <80.5	9	61.1	63.4
>80.5	9	126.9	157.7

Table 9.2. The distribution of assets under management (€ billion)

Type of vehicle	Number of responses	Median	Total	%
Pooled	32	9.1	524.7	28
Mandates	28	20.6	1181.6	63.1
Other	10	4.2	166.3	8.9

reported the US defined-contribution pension plans (known as '401(k) funds'), real estate funds, direct investments in equities, institutional funds, charities, and a fund for the parent firm.

There may be some overlap between the different categories of funds—for example, some pension funds may also be investing in collective investment schemes.

Figure 9.4 shows the breakdown of assets under management for the firms in the sample according to parent activity.

For all categories of institutions, the majority of assets under management are in the form of mandates. Banking groups have a relatively higher proportion of assets held through pooled investments.

Figure 9.5 shows the breakdown of assets under management according to country.

The companies in the sample that operate in France, Ireland, and Italy have invested over half of the assets under management in pooled investments. This is a reflection of the relative importance of collective investment schemes in these countries. Mandates accounted for approximately 45 per cent of assets under management of the French companies and considerably less for the Italian companies.

Mandates are the largest category of assets under management reported by the UK companies. This reflects the UK industry as a whole,

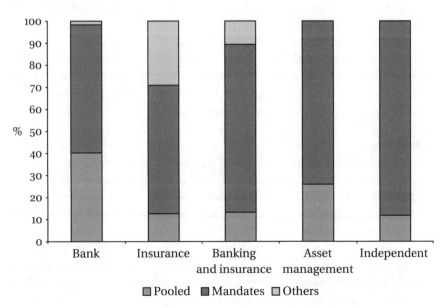

Fig. 9.4. The assets under management by institution and vehicle (%)

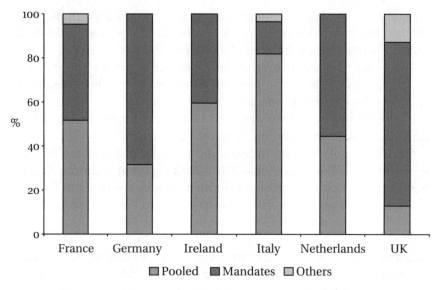

Fig. 9.5. The assets under management by country and vehicle (%)

where pension and insurance company funds together account for over 80 per cent of assets under management. The above results are consistent with the observations drawn from aggregate statistics in Chapter 4 of a comparatively more significant mutual fund business in Continental Europe than in the UK.

The second part of this question asked firms to provide information on the percentage of assets that were managed according to type of client. Eighteen companies provided the amount of assets managed on behalf of institutional and private clients. Institutional clients accounted for 76 per cent of assets managed, and private clients (including retail and mutual funds) for 23 per cent (see Figure 9.6). This result is consistent with the noticeable shift in the client base of asset management companies. Asset management was originally established to provide a service to private clients. However, this focus has shifted from private to institutional clients, such as pension funds or insurance companies.

The reduction in the proportion of assets managed on behalf of private clients is consistent with a trend in the UK. The British Invisibles report on fund management states that individual share ownership has declined from over 50 per cent in 1965 to nearly 17 per cent of total share ownership in 1998 (British Invisibles 2000).

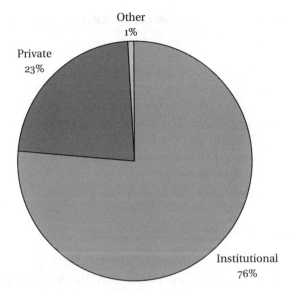

Fig. 9.6. The distribution of clients

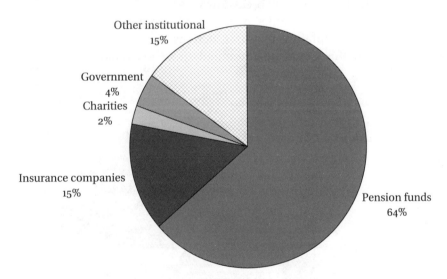

Fig. 9.7. The disaggregation of institutional clients

Furthermore, 16 companies provided a disaggregation of institutional clients into pension funds, insurance companies, government, charities, and other institutional clients. This breakdown is in Figure 9.7.

Pension funds are the single largest category of institutional client, accounting for 64 per cent of assets under management. Insurance companies and other institutional clients (such as banks) are jointly the second-largest category.

Thirty-one companies provided details of the division of assets under management into the percentage actively or passively managed. Passive management implies that assets track a particular index of the stock market, whereas active management involves strategic investment on behalf of the asset manager. The median percentage of assets that are actively managed is 100 per cent for all types of clients. The mean percentage of assets actively managed ranged from 85 to 100 per cent (depending on the type of client).

Transactions

The transactions were broken down into the following categories: equities, bonds, money market instruments, options and futures, and other. Figure 9.8 shows this breakdown.

Furthermore, 32 companies provided this detailed disaggregation of transactions. The total value of transactions reported by the firms that responded to this question amounted to €6809 billion. The 'other'

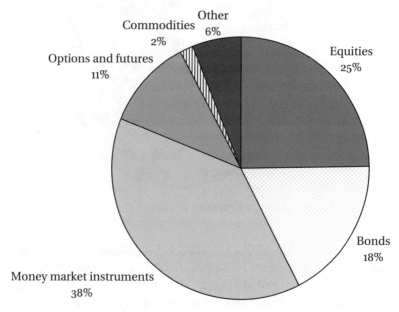

Fig. 9.8. The breakdown of transactions, by value

category largely consisted of transactions in foreign exchange or property. The figure for bonds includes both corporate and government bonds.

A further breakdown of transactions of equities and bonds into 'domestic', 'other Euro', 'emerging markets', and 'Other' was provided by a number of companies. For equities, the breakdown of transactions for 21 companies is shown in Figure 9.9.

The value of transactions in equities covered by this breakdown amounts to €717 billion. The 'Other' category accounts for almost half of transactions, most of which are conducted with the USA and Japan. Domestic transactions account for about one-third of the total transactions in equities. The smallest category is emerging markets, which accounts for only 5 per cent of the total value of transactions.

The breakdown of (government and corporate) bonds for 19 companies is shown in Figure 9.10.

The value of transactions covered by this breakdown is €786 billion. The breakdown of transactions in bonds reflects a similar pattern to the breakdown of equities. Similarly, the 'Other' category accounts for over 45 per cent of the total value of transactions, most of which are conducted with the USA and Japan. Transactions with emerging markets account for 1 per cent of the total value of reported transactions.

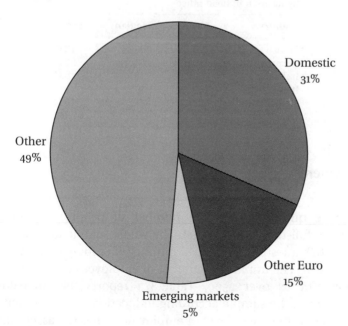

Fig. 9.9. The breakdown of equity transactions

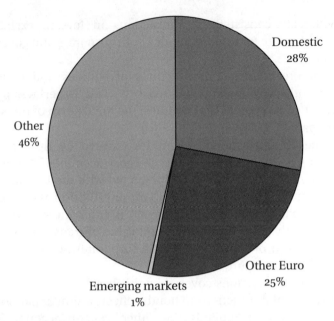

Fig. 9.10. The breakdown of transactions in bonds

Table 9.3. The number of employees in the sample by location of head office

Country	Mean	Median	Total
France	224	150	1795
Germany	210	200	631
Ireland	159	146	637
Italy	110	80	769
Netherlands	521	521	1042
UK	758	421	11,363

Employment

Firms were questioned on the number of people they employed (in terms of full-time equivalents). The whole sample of 39 companies replied to this question. The mean number of employees is 416 and the median is 220. The minimum number of employees is less than 10 and the maximum is over 2500. Table 9.3 reports the breakdown of employment in the sample according to location of head office.

According to the mean level of employment, the UK asset managers employ the largest number of workers.

Table 9.4. OPEX, working capital and fixed costs (€m)

	Number of responses	Mean	Median
OPEX	35	117.3	42.3
Working capital	27	61.1	22.9
Fixed costs[1]	31	22.8	15.7

Note:
[1] OPEX may include fixed costs.

Costs

Firms were asked to report their annual OPEX, working capital, and fixed costs for the last 12 months. These expenditures and costs are reported in Table 9.4.

9.5 ACTIVITIES

Stock Lending

All firms were asked whether they lend stock. All the firms in the sample responded to this question, and 18 companies replied that they lent stock. Of these, 15 companies provided detailed information on the amount available for lending. The mean amount available for lending was €10.2 billion and the median was €3.4 billion. The mean percentage of stock lent to assets under management was 14.5 per cent and the median was 9.2 per cent. The minimum percentage was 0.003 per cent and the maximum was 40.8 per cent. The common mechanism in place to safeguard stock lending is collateral. Two Italian companies replied that the regulator placed a limit on the amount of stock lending. Another company responded that, although it did not lend stock itself, there may be such arrangements between the client and the custodian.

The Guaranteed Products

Firms were asked whether they manage funds that include an implicit or explicit guarantee of return (for example, principal protection or equity return). All firms in the sample replied to this question, with 12 responding that they offer products that carry a guarantee. Of these, five are located in France, two in Italy, two in the UK, and one each in the Netherlands, Germany, and Ireland. According to the statistics produced by FEFSI, the number of guaranteed funds operating in France is 691, with assets worth €33.5 billion, compared to 11 funds, which provide a guarantee in the UK, with assets of €1.2 billion. One company replied that it did offer a guaranteed product, but that at the time of completing the questionnaire, this product had no investors. Guarantees mentioned include:

- a pension fund with a minimum guaranteed return of 1.5 per cent (currently unsubscribed);
- a guarantee of a maximum loss of 5 per cent per quarter; and
- various guaranteed funds.

Ten firms provided detailed information on the value of funds with a guarantee. The mean size of these funds is €2.4 billion and the median is €833 m. The mean ratio of the assets of the guaranteed funds to the total assets under management is 2.9 per cent and the median ratio is 1.07 per cent.

Of the 12 firms that offer guaranteed products, seven replied that they had hedged against the risks involved in providing guaranteed products. Only two companies provided information on the cost of hedging. The average cost of hedging for these companies is €15.75 m. A number of companies replied that hedging was not necessary because structured products included implicit hedging.

Services

Firms were asked to detail the percentage of clients (by value) that receive advice-only, execution-only, or discretionary services. Thirty-one companies replied to this question. The mean and median number of clients is reported in Table 9.5.

The majority of client accounts receive discretionary services from firms. In order to identify country-specific patterns, Table 9.6 reports the services provided to clients according to the location of head office.

Asset managers in Italy and Germany provide advice to a higher proportion of their clients.

Table 9.5. The services provided to clients

	Mean (%)	Median (%)
Advice-only[1]	6.6	0
Execution-only	3.3	0
Discretionary services	90.1	100

Note:
[1] These figures include a firm that provides both advice and execution for 5% of clients.

Table 9.6. The services provided to clients by country (%)

	Advice-only		Execution-only		Discretionary services	
	Mean	Median	Mean	Median	Mean	Median
France	1.2	0	0	0	98.8	100
Germany	24.8	7.5	0	0	75.2	92.5
Ireland	0.3	0	0.3	0	99.3	100
Italy	25	0	0	0	75	100
Netherlands	0	0	0	0	100	100
UK	1.7	0.2	7.2	0	91.1	99.5

Table 9.7. The services provided to clients by institution (%)

	Advice-only		Execution-only		Discretionary services	
	Mean	Median	Mean	Median	Mean	Median
Bank	8.0	0	0.1	0	91.8	100
Insurance	8.0	0	0	0	92.0	100
Banking and insurance	0	0	0	0	100	100
Asset management	0	0	50	50	50	50
Independent	5.1	5	0	0	94.9	95

Similarly, Table 9.7 reports the type of services received by clients according to the activity of the parent firm.

The company that is classified as a broker did not reply to this question. All institutions provide almost all of their clients with discretionary services.

The Internal and External Transactions

Firms were asked to divide the value of transactions (for example, transactions conducted with a broker) into those conducted within the parent group and outside the group. Thirty-three companies replied to this question, and Table 9.8 reports the results.

Most transactions are conducted with institutions outside the group. This question has been analysed further according to the institution and country for asset management companies. Table 9.9 examines the breakdown of transactions for the categories of institutions identified in this sample.

The split between the internal and external transactions has also been disaggregated according to country in Table 9.10.

Table 9.10 shows that there is considerable variation across countries, with the percentage of transactions carried out within the same group as the asset manager being larger in Italy compared to the UK. This is

Table 9.8. The internal and external transactions (%)

	Mean	Median
Within parent group	14.8	1
Outside group	85.2	99

Table 9.9. The breakdown of internal and external transactions according to the institution (%)

	Number of responses	Within group		Outside group	
		Mean	Median	Mean	Median
Banking	14	28.0	11	72.0	89
Insurance	10	0.7	0	99.3	100
Banking and insurance	1	1	1	99	99
Asset management	2	1.5	1.5	98	98
Broker	1	87	87	13	13
Independent	5	0	0	100	100

Table 9.10. The breakdown of internal and external transactions according to the country (%)

	Number of responses	Inside group		Outside group	
		Mean	Median	Mean	Median
France	6	18.6	0.8	81.4	99.2
Germany	2	25	25	75	75
Ireland	3	6.2	6	93.8	94
Italy	7	37.9	52.1	62.1	47.9
Netherlands	1	0	0	100	100
UK	14	3.1	0.5	96.9	99.5

not surprising, given the result from the previous table that banks are more likely to conduct transactions within their group, and that over 70 per cent of the Italian firms in the sample are subsidiaries of banks.

9.6 THE OPERATIONAL RISKS AND LOSSES

Risks

Firms were asked to rank a list of operational risks according to size and frequency of possible loss. Figures 9.11 and 9.12 show the ranking assigned to operational risks in terms of size of possible loss and frequency, with a value of 1 assigned to risks that had the smallest financial impact and were least likely to occur.

The list of risks described in the figures was drawn on the basis of a series of pre-survey interviews. Pre-survey interviewees were asked what risks were considered to be part of the operation of an asset management business. The list of risks identified is as follows.

Breach of client guidelines—this refers to a violation of the guidelines as set out by the client in their contract with the asset management company. For example, a client may specifically request that their portfolio does not contain any tobacco companies' stocks. Inadvertently purchasing tobacco stocks for this client would therefore contravene the client's guidelines. In order to reverse the transaction, the asset management company must sell the shares. In the meantime,

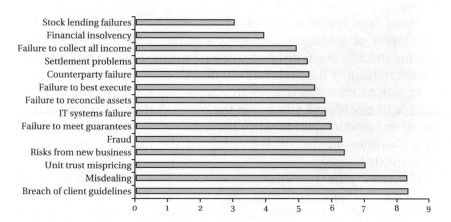

Fig. 9.11. The impact of operational risks

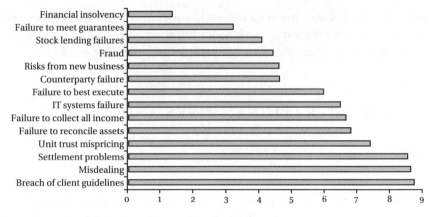

Fig. 9.12. The frequency of operational risks

the price of the share could have fallen, which could result in a loss for the asset manager.

Misdealing—this refers to generally unintentional errors, for example in issuing orders to brokers.

Risks arising in the process of taking over new business—operational failures may occur when a client mandate has been acquired from another asset management company. The previous asset manager may not have maintained current records, which implies that there may be discrepancies between what is reported and what is actually held in the client's account. This is a particular problem for businesses that are growing and are therefore taking on a relatively high proportion of new clients.

Fraud—this occurs as a result of dishonest behaviour conducted by employees or managers. Segregation of duties reduces the level of control that any one individual may have over a single transaction, and therefore reduces the probability of fraud.

Failure to meet guarantees—this arises when an asset manager is unable to provide the client with the return that was guaranteed on a particular product. This problem has a potentially large impact if there is a downturn in the stock market and the risks are unhedged or imperfectly hedged.

IT systems failure—this occurs as a result of a breakdown in the computer system. Installing back-ups to take over from the primary system may reduce any subsequent loss from a failure of the IT system.

Failure to reconcile assets under custodianship and internal records—this may arise when an asset manager is unable to reconcile the assets according to its own internal records with those according to the reports from the custodian. In order to minimize the probability of such a failure occurring, asset managers may conduct daily reconciliations of clients' accounts.

Failure to best execute—this refers to a failure to obtain the best price for a client.

Counterparty failure—this arises when a third party to an asset manager, such as a broker, becomes insolvent. The risk of counterparty failure is particularly high in dealing with financial intermediaries in emerging markets.

Settlement problems—these may occur, for example, when the asset management company has already paid the cost of purchasing stocks, but the broker, for some reason, is unable to deliver the stocks. This problem can be limited to some extent by implementation of a delivery-versus-payment system, which means that an asset management company will only pay the cost of the transaction upon receipt of the stocks.

Failure to collect all income—an example of this type of risk occurs in the event of a corporate action failure. For example, a client may hold stock in company A, which is being taken over by company B. Failure to complete the relevant documentation before a specified deadline may result in failure to transfer stock in company A into stock in company B. This could lead to losses, for example, in cases of depreciation of stock value.

Stock lending failure—this arises when the party that borrowed the stock is unable to repay the amount and collateral is insufficient to cover the total value of the stock lent.

In the process of gathering a list of risks, two risks were included in the survey that are not within the scope of this analysis: unit trust mispricing and financial insolvency. Unit trust mispricing is an important risk and is included to the extent that the sample of asset managers are also managing assets held through collective investment schemes, such as unit trusts. Financial insolvency is not an operational risk per se, but is included with a view to establishing whether insolvency is likely to occur.

Figure 9.11 shows the average ranking of each of the risks in terms of the potential financial impact these operational failures may have on the asset manager. A ranking of 8.4 was assigned to the operational risk with the largest potential financial loss—that is, breach of client guidelines.

The results from Figure 9.11 are as follows:

- misdealing and breach of client guidelines were cited by almost all respondents as the two operational failures which could be associated with the largest possible loss;
- the risk of operational failures arising from new business acquisition, which can result from the lack of information about the new business or client, was also ranked as having a potentially high financial impact;
- losses arising from fraud could also be associated with large financial impact; and
- stock lending failures were the operational failure with the lowest possible loss.

Figure 9.12 ranks operational risks according to the frequency of occurrence.

Firms have ranked financial insolvency as the risk least likely to occur. Breach of client guidelines and misdealing were ranked as most likely to occur. The pattern of results from the analysis of frequency of operational risks is to a large extent consistent with the pattern identified for the ranking of operational risks according to size of possible loss. Settlement problems arise frequently, but their financial impact is small.

Losses

Firms were asked to provide detailed information on the level of losses resulting from the operational risks listed above. Twenty-two firms responded to this question.

Table 9.11 records reported losses for a sample of 22 asset managers that responded to the specific question on losses and their detailed causes. For example, of the sample of 22 asset managers, 13 (that is, 59 per cent) reported losses arising from misdealing. The largest loss reported amounted to €7.2 m.

The next-largest loss borne by an asset manager was €3 m, arising from a breach of client guidelines. A company that responded to the questionnaire reported that, as a result of a breach of client guidelines, it had incurred a loss of €0.75 m (its largest loss from all the operational risks listed above). The situation that resulted in this loss arose from

Table 9.11. The reported losses for sample of 22 asset managers (€m)

	Number reporting losses	Largest loss (€m)	Mean total loss (€m)	Total losses (€m)
Misdealing	13	7.2	0.88	11.48
Breach of client guidelines	10	3	0.59	5.87
Failure to collect all income (including corporate action failures)	6	2.6	0.90	5.37
Settlement problems	8	0.2	0.13	1.00
Unit trust mispricing	7	0.3	0.08	0.58
Failure to reconcile assets under custodianship and internal records	2	0.1	0.2	0.4
IT system failure	2	0.1	0.14	0.28
Risks arising in the process of taking over new business	1	0.2	0.2	0.2
Failure to meet guarantees	1	—	0.1	0.1
Counterparty failure	1	—	0.1	0.1
Fraud	1	0.03	0.03	0.03
Stock lending failures	0	—	—	—
Financial insolvency	0	—	—	—
Failure to best execute	0	—	—	—

excessive cash being held for a period of time in the account, instead of being paid into the funds. The asset manager failed to invest two cash payments received from the client, and the subsequent loss as a result of this error was calculated on the basis of the opportunity cost of lost earnings (that is, the estimated earnings that the client could have made if cash had been paid into the funds).

The largest loss as a result of failure to collect all income was identified as €2.6 m. This resulted from a corporate action failure in which the asset manager missed the deadline. In addition, a loss of €1.2 m was identified, again as a result of corporate action failures. In this particular instance, shares were held in a company that was going through a takeover bid. The asset management firm failed to complete the paperwork and, as a result, was left with a minority holding in the company. By the time this error was detected, the market had moved by 2–3 per cent, which resulted in a loss of €1.2 m.

Settlement failures, although they may occur frequently, lead to low operational losses. This is consistent with the results reported in Figures 9.11 and 9.12. No firms reported losses as a result of failure to best execute, stock lending failures, or financial insolvency.

In some cases, firms listed risks other than those specifically mentioned. These other risks and their losses are reported in Table 9.12.

Table 9.12. The losses resulting from other risks

	Number reporting losses	Largest loss (€m)	Total losses (€m)
Foreign-exchange dealings	1	0.8	0.9
In specie transfer failures	2	0.14	0.792
Cash movement	1	—	0.07
Inaccurate reporting	1	0.04	0.046
Client service	1	—	0.04
Human error from manual activities	1	0.019	0.04
Order capture	1	—	0.03
Asset allocation	1	—	0.02
Client claims from mutual funds	1	0.003	0.007
Fund management	1	—	0.001
Portfolio valuation	1	—	0.001

Table 9.13. The ratios of losses to scaling factors

	Largest loss (€m)	OPEX (%)	Assets under management (%)	Transactions (%)	Actual capital (%)
Misdealing	7.20	17.021	0.00941	0.0027	37.500
Breach of client guidelines	3.00	7.500	0.00566	0.0011	4.412
Failure to collect all income (including corporate action failures)	2.60	0.139	0.00112	0.0043	0.163
Unit trust mispricing	0.30	0.283	0.00049	n/a	0.291
Risks arising in the process of taking over new business	0.20	0.087	0.00037	0.0002	0.100
Settlement problems	0.20	0.011	0.00009	0.0003	0.013
Failure to reconcile assets under custodianship and internal records	0.10	0.005	0.00004	0.0002	0.006
IT systems failure	0.10	0.044	0.00018	0.0001	0.050
Fraud	0.03	0.018	0.00003	n/a	0.012

Total losses for the 22 asset managers amounted to €27.2 m for the particular year analysed in the survey. On average, this corresponds to annual losses of approximately €1.3 m per asset manager.

The largest loss as a result of each risk identified in Table 9.11 is reported in Table 9.13 as a proportion of that particular firm's OPEX, domestic assets under management, and other scaling factors.

Table 9.13 shows that the largest reported loss (€7.2 m), which resulted from a misdealing error, corresponds to 17 per cent of annual OPEX. Using OPEX as a scaling factor allows a comparison to be drawn with the capital requirement rule typically used in the European countries represented in this sample. Therefore, in the case of this particular asset manager, capital equivalent to 25 per cent of annual expenditures would have been sufficient to fund the operational loss that arose from misdealing. The second-largest loss resulting from a breach of client guidelines amounts to 7.5 per cent of OPEX. Thus, during the period covered by the survey, no asset management company reported a loss that was in excess of reported OPEX.

In addition, the ratio of the largest loss to assets under management and transactions suggests that the losses reported account for only a very small proportion of each company's business, even in the case of the largest loss. The maximum loss as a proportion of total assets under management is 0.0094 per cent.

The final two columns of Table 9.13 show the largest losses as a proportion of actual capital held and regulatory capital. The firm that reported a loss of €7.2 m holds capital in excess of that amount. According to Table 9.13, this loss amounts to 37.5 per cent of the capital held by that company. As for the loss arising from the breach of client guidelines, this amounts to 4 per cent of capital held. The remaining losses each account for less than 1 per cent of each company's capital.

From interviews held with some of the largest companies responding to the questionnaire, it was widely thought that losses from misdealing could amount to, say, €20 m in one particular year. For example, a mistake on a transaction of €100 m could amount to a significant loss if there was a significant deterioration in the value of the stock involved in the transaction.

A Simulation of the Impact of Losses

To establish the financial impact of such loss, a straightforward simulation was run on average figures from four large asset managers in the sample. Total assets under management for these firms amount to €729.5 billion. Table 9.14 reports the result of a simulation that examines hypothetical losses ranging from €7.2 m to €100 m as a proportion of the variables used above. Figures for OPEX, assets under management, transactions, actual capital, and capital requirements have been calculated as the average of four large firms that participated in the survey.

According to this table, a loss of €100 m amounts to 16 per cent of average OPEX for the four large firms. A capital requirement based on the 25 per cent-expenditure rule would be sufficient to finance this loss.

Table 9.14. The financial impact of potential largest loss for the four large asset managers

Loss (€m)	OPEX (%)	Assets under management (%)	Transactions (%)	Actual capital (%)	Regulatory capital (%)
7.2	1.19	0.004	0.002	1.2	3.8
20	3.3	0.011	0.005	3.2	10.6
40	6.6	0.022	0.010	6.4	21.2
60	9.9	0.033	0.015	9.6	31.8
80	13.2	0.044	0.020	12.8	42.4
100	16.5	0.055	0.025	16.0	53.0

Furthermore, the losses shown in Table 9.14 represent less than 0.06 per cent of assets under management and transactions. Firms hold capital far in excess of the amount of the loss. Therefore, the loss of €100 m represents only 16 per cent of actual capital. Current regulatory capital requirements would have been sufficient to cover losses of the magnitude reported above.

The Total Losses for the Sample

As an alternative to providing detailed information on the level of losses, which may be either too time-consuming to provide or too confidential, firms were asked whether there were losses over the last 12 months, and to provide details of the losses in ranges. In addition to the 22 companies that provided detailed information on losses, 15 companies replied that there had been losses over the last 12 months. Table 9.15 provides information on the range of values for these losses.

Therefore, an estimate of the total losses for 37 companies is approximately €40 m.

This question only asks firms to report data on losses for the previous 12 months. However, as a further check of the robustness of the results, nine companies were asked during interviews to report their largest loss over the last ten years. The losses ranged from €0.2 m to €7.2 m. Table 9.16 reports these losses and their causes.

It is widely accepted that the last ten years have been a bull market and therefore the losses presented in this analysis may not be a perfect indication of the largest losses that may occur during a bear market.

Companies were asked whether there was a provision for losses in their company accounts. Eighteen companies replied to this question, and only nine responded that they had made internal provision for losses in their accounts. The maximum was €3 m. The median

Table 9.15. The range of losses

Range	Number of responses
<€100,000	6
€100,000–€500,000	2
€500,000–€1 m	3
>€1 m	4

Table 9.16. The largest loss for the nine asset managers over the last 10 years

Size of loss (€m)	Number of companies	Type of loss
0–0.75	2	Breach of client guidelines Misdealing
0.75–1	1	Breach of client guidelines
0.5–2	1	Failure to reconcile assets under custodianship and internal records
1–2	1	Undisclosed
2–3	2	Fraud of third party Corporate action failure
3.5–4	1	Undisclosed
5–10	1	Misdealing

provision was €1.2 m and the mean was €1.5 m. This is consistent with the data on losses reported in Table 9.11.

Complaints

Companies were asked to report the number of complaints that resulted from the operational risks listed above, and 17 companies responded. However, one firm that had experienced 22 complaints was unable to provide a detailed breakdown (Table 9.17).

9.7 THE FORMS OF PROTECTION

Capital

Firms were asked to report the level of actual capital held and regulatory capital. Table 9.18 reports the mean and median levels of capital and regulatory capital.

Table 9.17. The reported complaints

	Mean number of (non-zero) complaints	Total number of complaints
Misdealing	6	18
Failure to best execute	—	—
Settlement problems	1	1
Counterparty failure	—	—
Breach of client guidelines	10.25	41
Fraud	—	—
IT systems failure	31	62
Failure to meet guarantees	—	—
Unit trust mispricing	2.3	7
Failure to reconcile assets under custodianship and internal records	1	1
Failure to collect all income (including corporate action failures)	1	1
Stock lending failures	—	—
Financial insolvency	—	—
Risks arising in the process of taking over new business	2	2
Other		
Foreign-exchange dealing, business processes, fees	34	34
Outsourced retail administration	20	20
Clients' claims in mutual funds	3	3
In specie transfer failures	10	10
Inaccurate reporting	26	26
Fee billing error	3	3
Uninvested cash	4	4
Poor service to clients	20	20

Table 9.18. The actual and regulatory capital

Company	Capital requirements (€m)	Actual capital (€m)	Ratio of actual capital to regulatory capital
Mean	32.8	119.0	5.7
Median	7.2	20.2	2.7

Table 9.18 shows that firms hold capital in excess of regulatory requirements. When interviewed, respondents stated that the reason for holding capital in excess of regulatory capital requirements was not related to the risks faced by the business. For example, a number of firms stated that their capital was high as a result of merger and acquisition activity. A large proportion of firms had not conducted research into the calculation of the level of capital as a result of operational risks.

Eight companies from the entire sample replied that they had capital at risk as a result of taking own positions. The mean value of capital at risk for these firms is €47 m. The median is €9.5 m.

Furthermore, 17 companies replied to the question on the cost of obtaining additional capital. The mean internal rate of return for obtaining additional capital is 15.7 per cent and the median is 15 per cent. The minimum cost of obtaining additional capital is 7 per cent and the maximum is 30 per cent.

Firms were asked for their opinion on the appropriateness of the *current* regulatory rules on capital requirements. Thirty companies responded to this question: 17 (57 per cent) believed that capital requirements were appropriate; 12 (40 per cent) did not think that current capital requirements were appropriate; and one was uncertain. The main reason why current capital requirements were not considered appropriate is because regulatory capital does not distinguish high-risk from low-risk firms.

Comments include the following.

- Company A: 'Capital requirements underestimate operational risks and are not based on actual operational volumes.'

- Company B: 'Capital requirements allow an asset management company to settle its expenses during a full quarter, even if it earns no management fee.'

- Company C: 'Regulatory capital requirements are not applicable to fund-management businesses. There are no capital requirements for the US fund managers.'

- Company D: 'Capital requirements are not appropriate for eventual misdealing. However they may be appropriate for funds if capital is separated from company capital.'

- Company E: 'The regulator has a risk profile of each investment manager. However, this profile does not have any impact on capital requirements. A higher capital requirement should be required for high-risk investment managers.'

Compliance

Firms were asked to report the number of workers that were employed in the compliance department (in terms of full-time equivalents).

Thirty-eight firms responded to this question. Statistics on the number of workers employed in compliance are reported in Table 9.19.

The minimum was one person employed in compliance, and the maximum was 80. The mean number of employees in the compliance department is approximately eight people. The mean number of employees in the compliance department as a percentage of the total number of employees is 5.1 per cent and the median percentage is 2.2 per cent. This ranges from 0.3 to 27.3 per cent.

Respondents were asked to report expenditure on formal compliance activities. Details of expenditure on compliance and the ratios of the actual and anticipated expenditure to the total number of employees are reported in Table 9.20.

Firms were asked to report which activities were included as part of their risk-management process and the number of internal and external workers employed in each activity. Table 9.21 reports the number of firms that responded to this question and the proportion of those that responded that provide these activities.

Table 9.21 shows that all firms have compliance departments and the majority of firms include other activities as part of the risk-management process. A relatively low proportion of firms have a derivatives control team, and, in general, the explanation for this result is that these firms do not deal in derivatives. Some firms noted in their completed questionnaires that some activities were performed at a group level. Furthermore, one firm replied that, for some compliance activities, all employees in the company were involved. Other organizations include daily general manager control, formal risk committee, and global risk structure as part of the risk-management process.

Table 9.19. The number of employees in compliance department

	Mean	Median	Minimum	Maximum
Employees	8.1	5	1	80

Table 9.20. The annual actual and anticipated expenditure on formal compliance activities

	Number of responses	Mean	Median
Actual expenditure (€m)	30	1.11	0.54
Anticipated expenditure (€m)	31	1.41	0.68
Actual expenditure per employee (€)	29	3276	2381
Anticipated expenditure per employee (€)	30	3942	2903

Table 9.21. The activities in risk-management process

	Total number of respondents	Percentage of respondents
Compliance department	39	100
Internal audit	38	95
Operational risk management	34	79
Credit risk management	34	76
Market risk team	34	74
Legal support	37	92
Portfolio risk and performance management	36	97
Product approval team	33	85
Derivatives control team[1]	34	47
Control self-assessment processes[2]	24	58
Staff training development on risk-management issues[2]	23	70
FRAG21[3]	33	70

Notes:
[1] From follow-up interviews, it can be concluded that, in some cases, firms do not have a derivatives control team because they do not trade in derivatives.
[2] Firms that responded to the pilot questionnaire were not asked whether they employed control self-assessment or staff training as part of risk management.
[3] A FRAG21 or SAS 70 is a report on a company's internal control systems, produced by auditors. Although originally produced by non-group custodians, FRAG21 documents may also be produced by asset management companies and distributed to clients.

Table 9.22. The number of internal and external employees

	Internal employees		External employees	
	Number of respondents	Mean	Number of respondents	Mean
Compliance dept[1]	38	8.1	—	—
Internal audit	22	7.6	4	3.5
Operational risk management	14	8.5	—	—
Credit risk management	12	8.0	—	—
Market risk team	9	9.1	—	—
Legal support	20	5.2	4	2.5
Portfolio risk and performance management	22	9.6	—	—
Product approval team	15	10.1	—	—
Derivatives control team	6	13.4	—	—

Note:
[1] This includes a firm which reported that all its employees were involved in some activities.

Table 9.22 reports the mean number of internal and external workers employed in each of the activities listed in Table 9.21.

Firms employ external institutions only for internal audit and legal support.

The Parent-firm Guarantee

Firms were asked whether their parent company provided an explicit or implicit guarantee for the case in which the asset management company becomes financially insolvent. Of the 35 firms that belong to a larger group, 29 per cent replied that they had specific guarantees from their parent company. The type of guarantee varied across firms, and those mentioned include:

- specific guarantees for funds;
- an implicit guarantee to bail out the asset management company in order to protect the reputation of the group as a whole;
- a letter of comfort from the parent company;
- a guarantee from the parent for a small number of clients to provide additional protection in the event of the asset manager being liable;
- a guarantee for the liabilities of the asset management subsidiary; and
- a guarantee of due investment or operational performance for certain clients.

Although one company replied that it did not receive a guarantee from its parent company, the parent does provide a declaration of backing. This is a form of implicit guarantee that is not required to be entered on the balance sheet, as a guarantee would. Therefore, this declaration of backing is not subject to a regulatory capital charge.

Non-group Custodianship

Firms were asked to provide information on the proportion of clients' assets that were held by custodians outside the firm's group. The mean percentage of clients' assets held by non-group custodians is 63 per cent. The median percentage is 85.5 per cent. Table 9.23 reports the proportion of clients' assets held with non-group custodians according to the activity of the parent firm.

The proportion of clients' assets held with a custodian outside the group is lower for asset managers which are part of banks.

Figure 9.13 provides statistics on the percentage of clients' assets held by custodians outside the group according to country of head office.

Table 9.23. The non-group custodianship of clients' assets according to institution (%)

	Mean	Median
Bank	39.6	25
Insurance	88.1	100
Banking and insurance	91	91
Asset management	90	100
Broker	0	0
Independent	90	100

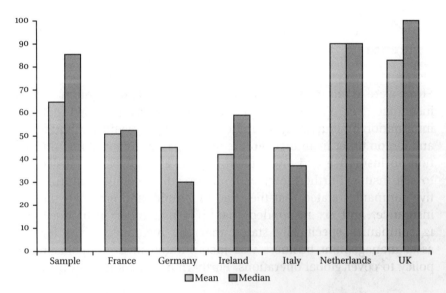

Fig. 9.13. The non-group custodianship of clients' assets according to country (%)

Asset managers operating in the UK outsource the custodianship of a large percentage of their clients' assets to external parties (that is, parties outside the holding group, of which asset management is an activity). This is consistent with the finding in the recent British Invisibles report (British Invisibles 2000) that the proportion of funds in the UK using independent custodians has risen from 50 per cent in 1997 to 71 per cent in 1999. Conversely, in Italy, a lower proportion of clients' assets is outsourced to non-group custodians. This is not surprising, given that more than 70 per cent of Italian firms in the sample are owned by banks, which usually act as custodians or sub-custodians. It should be noted that separation of clients' assets was widespread across all countries.

Firms were asked whether they had delegated any functions to parties inside or outside their group. Twenty-seven companies replied to the first part of this question, 59 per cent of which had delegated functions within their group. The remainder replied that they had not. These functions included settlement, fund administration, and custody. Twenty-five companies replied to the second part of the question: 68 per cent of companies responded that they had delegated some activities to parties outside their group. Custody was the activity that was most frequently outsourced to external parties.

Insurance

Firms were asked to report on the value, excess, and premium of their insurance (see Figure 9.14). Twenty companies provided detailed information on indemnity insurance; 15 on employee fidelity and fraud; and ten on other insurance. Fourteen companies reported no information on insurance and one replied that, as a result of size, it decided to self-insure. Furthermore, without providing detailed information, five companies stated that they had indemnity and employee fidelity insurance, and six responded that they had other insurance. Also 12 companies specifically stated that the insurance cover for the asset management business was incorporated in a group insurance policy to cover global operations. Furthermore 14 companies provided

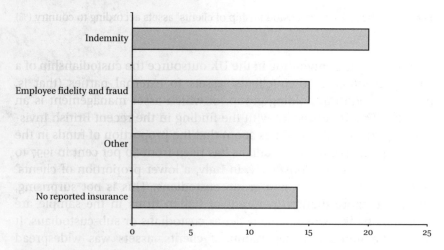

Fig. 9.14. The number of firms with insurance

information on the companies with which they insure. Most of the smaller asset managers did not have insurance policies.

Table 9.24 provides detailed information on the value, excess, and premium on indemnity insurance.

For one firm, this is the Errors & Omissions policy (E&O); for another, this is the sum of indemnity insurance/employee fidelity and fraud insurance.

Detailed information on employee fidelity and fraud insurance is reported in Table 9.25.

One firm commented that employee fidelity and fraud insurance was necessary under the Employee Retirement Income Security Act 1974.

Table 9.26 reports the value and premium for indemnity and employee fidelity insurance as a proportion of OPEX and assets under management.

According to the mean ratios in Table 9.26, firms have insurance coverage that exceeds their OPEX. The cost of obtaining this insurance as a proportion of OPEX is less than 2 per cent.

Table 9.24. Indemnity insurance

	Sample	Minimum (€m)	Maximum (€m)	Mean (€m)
Value	19	4.4	480	100.5
Excess	16	0.04	12.7	2.4
Premium	11	0.2	1.8	0.5

Table 9.25. The employee fidelity and fraud insurance

	Sample	Minimum (€m)	Maximum (€m)	Mean (€m)
Value	15	0.5	880	117.5
Excess	11	0.04	10	1.8
Premium	7	0.06	1	0.3

Table 9.26. The ratios of value and premium to the OPEX and assets under management (%)

Ratio of	Indemnity insurance		Employee fidelity and fraud	
	Mean	Median	Mean	Median
Value to OPEX	347.93	118.20	420.36	43.62
Premium to OPEX	1.69	0.95	0.62	0.27
Value to assets under management	33.97	0.11	0.41	0.10
Premium to assets under management	0.14	0.001	0.001	0.0003

Details of any other types of insurance reported by firms are contained in Table 9.27.

Other types of insurance quoted by respondents included fraud, civil responsibility, real estate, and Directors & Officers (D&O).

Firms were asked whether they had ever made a claim on their insurance. Twenty-one companies replied to this question, and six (29 per cent) responded that they had made a claim. Of the claims, three were paid in full, one 'as agreed', one received all compensation apart from the amount of the excess, and one firm did not provide details of the payment of the claim. For four claims, the companies said that they were paid promptly. Compensation for another claim that was reported was paid with a delay of approximately 12 months. During interviews, asset management companies raised significant concerns about the failure of insurance companies to pay compensation in full, and about the length of time before the compensation was determined.

Firms were asked to report the value of claims on insurance (Table 9.28).

The value of four claims on insurance was reported. These claims were primarily as a result of misdealing and failure to collect all income.

The Means of Financing Losses

Firms were asked to rank the most frequently used method of financing losses arising from operational failure. Those listed were (regulatory)

Table 9.27. Other insurance

	Sample	Minimum (€m)	Maximum (€m)	Mean (€m)
Value	9	0.63	68	38.1
Excess	2	0.15	10	5.1
Premium	4	0.03	0.4	0.14

Table 9.28. The reported claims on insurance

	Mean value of (non-zero) claims (€m)	Total value of (non-zero) claims (€m)
Misdealing	7.2	7.2
Failure to collect all income (including corporate action failures)	1.4	4.1

Table 9.29. The mean ranking of methods of financing losses

	Capital	Insurance	Parent-firm guarantees	Internal profits
Misdealing	2	2.7	2.3	1
Failure to best execute	2	2.4	2	1
Settlement problems	2.2	2.3	1.7	1.1
Counterparty failure	2.3	2	2	1.1
Breach of client guidelines	2.5	2.2	3	1
Fraud	2.6	1.3	3	1.2
IT systems failure	2.2	1.8	2	1.1
Failure to meet guarantees	2.5	3	3	1
Unit trust mispricing	2.3	2.3	2	1
Failure to reconcile assets under custodianship and internal records	2.2	1.7	2.5	1
Failure to collect all income (including corporate action failures)	2.2	2	2.5	1
Stock lending failures	3	2		1
Financial insolvency	1.4	1.5	1	1

capital, insurance, parent-firm guarantees, or internal profits, and Table 9.29 reports the mean ranking of the methods of financing risks. A ranking of one is an indication that that particular method of funding losses is used most often.

According to Table 9.29, firms would use internal profits to finance losses more often than any of the other methods identified. For some risks, such as fraud, insurance is more likely to be used to finance losses than internal profits, parent-firm guarantees, or capital. Note also that, in the case of financial insolvency, firms reported that parent-firm guarantees are an important means of financing losses.

9.8 SUMMARY

Almost 90 per cent of the companies that responded to the questionnaire are subsidiaries of a larger group. These larger groups are mostly banks or insurance companies. Asset managers operating in Continental Europe are more likely to be part of the financial conglomerates.

The majority of assets under management in the sample are in the form of mandates. Pooled funds are relatively more prevalent in Continental Europe.

Most clients are institutions, in particular pension funds.

The majority of transactions are conducted in money market instruments, although equities and bonds also account for a significant proportion.

Most companies that responded to the questionnaire do not lend stock or offer guaranteed products.

Most clients receive discretionary services from asset managers.

Most transactions are conducted with parties outside the group of the asset manager.

The operational risks that were ranked as most likely to occur or to result in the largest loss were breach of client guidelines and mis-dealing. In fact, the largest loss reported by the asset managers that responded to the questionnaire amounted to €7.2 m as a result of misdealing. The total losses for those firms that provided information on losses was €40 m.

On average, losses in the year (1999) amounted to a little over €1 m. However, interviews helped to determine that losses from misdealing could amount to over €20 m under specific circumstances (for example, during periods of significant stock-market downturns).

Firms reported that the level of actual capital held was larger than regulatory capital requirements. During interviews, firms stated that this was a result of strategic decisions, such as acquisition activity, and not due to the risk profile of the company.

All companies have a compliance department. The majority of firms have also adopted other activities involved in the risk-management process.

Twenty-nine per cent of firms have a guarantee from their parent firm.

In general, and particularly in the UK, clients' assets are held with non-group custodians (that is, outside the group to which the asset manager belongs). This statistic is particularly important, given that the focus of this analysis is on discretionary asset management of assets under mandates, and not unit trust management.

A significant number of firms have insurance, although relatively few claims are reported.

Most respondents were persuaded that regulatory capital was not the main means of financing losses arising from operational risks. The main reason why some companies stated that regulatory capital was not the appropriate way to deal with operational risks is that regulatory capital does not distinguish between high- and low-risk companies. Typically losses were offset against annual income and, for larger, infrequent losses, insurance was the main method.

Appendix

9A.1 QUESTIONNAIRE ON REGULATORY CAPITAL AND OPERATIONAL RISKS OF ASSET MANAGERS

QUESTION 1: CHARACTERISTICS OF FIRMS

A: Background Information

1) Name of company _____

2) Your name and telephone number _____

3) Position _____

4) Types of activity performed by your investment management firm

   _____

   _____

5) How many people are employed in your investment management business? (Please state the most recent figures as number of full-time equivalents.)

   _____

6) Please categorise your assets under management, giving the date at which they are measured. (Please note that if the information is not readily available, an indication of ranges would also be suitable.)

Total assets under management

By type of vehicle Unit trusts Open-ended investment companies Closed-ended funds Segregated Others (Please specify)		
	Percentage actively managed	**Percentage passively managed**
By client *Institutional* Pension funds Insurance companies Charities Government Other institutional (please specify) *Private clients*		

B: Structure of Ownership

6) Is your company part of a larger group?   YES/NO

If so, please give the name and main activity of your ultimate parent company

_____

_____

Please give brief details where there are more complex ownership arrangements

_____

_____

7) Do you have any guarantees from your parent company?   YES/NO
   If so, what are they?

_____

_____

8) What is your main regulatory body?_____

9) What is the main regulatory body (if any) of the parent firm of your group?

_____

C: Organisation of Business

10) Please analyse the total transactions that you have executed in terms of value over the past 12 months under the following headings. (Please note that if the information is not readily available, an indication of ranges would also be suitable.) 12 months to: _____ (please give date)

	Value of transactions (Euro million)
Equities Domestic Other Euro Emerging markets Other (please specify)	
Corporate bonds Domestic Other Euro Emerging markets Other (please specify)	
Government bonds Domestic Other Euro Emerging markets Other (please specify)	
Money market instruments	
Options and futures	
Commodities	
Other (please specify)	

12) What proportion of the value of transactions do you conduct within your parent group or outside the group?

	% of the value of transactions
Within parent group	

Outside group: (broken down into the following categories if possible)
    Major international institutions
    Regional institutions
    Other	

13) Do any of the funds you manage include an implicit or explicit guarantee of return (eg, principal protection or equity participation)? YES/NO

If so, please indicate types and sizes (Euro million)

_____

14) Have you hedged the risk of these guarantees? YES/NO

If so, what was the cost of this hedging over the last 12 months (Euro million)?

(Please state the dates to which this refers.) _____

15) Do you lend stock? YES/NO

If yes, what value of stock is available for lending (Euro million)?

_____

What are the key internal controls in place for lending stock?

_____

_____

16) What is the percentage by value of your clients that receive

(a) advice only from your firm? _____

(b) execution only from your firm? _____

(c) full discretionary services from your firm?_____

17) What proportion of clients' assets are held by custodians outside your group? _____

18) Has your firm delegated any function (eg, settlement) to third parties

a) inside your group? YES/NO

b) outside your group? YES/NO

If so, what are these functions?

_____

_____

What are the key controls in place for these functions?

_____

_____

D: Risk Control Functions

19) How many people do you employ to ensure formal compliance with regulatory requirements? (Please state as the number of full-time equivalents.)

_____

20) What were the expenditures that you incurred on formal compliance activities over the last 12 months? (Please state the dates to which this refers.) Note: Compliance costs include fees paid to (internal and external) professionals, such as lawyers and accountants.

_____

_____

21) How much do you anticipate spending on formal compliance activities over the next 12 months?

_____

22) Does your firm (or group) have the following as part of its organisational structure? Please state the number of employees involved in each activity, distinguishing between internal and external (ie, outside the group) employees.

	YES	NO	Number of employees	
			Internal	**External**
Compliance department				
Internal audit				
Operational risk management				
Credit risk management				
Market risk team				
Legal support				
Portfolio risk and performance management				
Product approval team				
Derivatives control team				
Control self-assessment processes				
Staff training development on risk-management issues				
FRAG21 (or equivalent)[1]				
Other (please specify)				

Note: [1] FRAG21 refers to the internal document produced by a company, which details the internal control mechanisms for risk management subject to external audit.

E: Capital

23) Please state your capital (Euro million), and the date to which this refers.

_____

24) What is the value of your own capital at risk (ie, position risk) (Euro million)?

_____

25) What are your capital requirements under regulatory rules (Euro million)?

_____

26) Do you think that the current regulatory rules for capital are appropriate? YES/NO

If not, please state why

_____

27) What is the internal target rate of return/cost of capital for obtaining additional capital?

_____

28) If your capital requirements were to increase by, say, 25%, would it restrict the amount of business you could do?   YES/NO

29) What were your operating expenditures (gross of depreciation) over the last 12 months (Euro million)? (Please state the most recent figure.) _____

30) How much working capital (the cash plus net debtors required to run the business) did you require to finance your business over the last 12 months (Euro million)? (Please state the date to which this refers.) _____

31) What are your fixed costs (Euro million)? (Please state the most recent figures available.) Note: Fixed costs refer to costs that do not vary with output, for example rent. _____

32) What is the value, excess and premium of your insurance as categorised below (Euro million). If not available, please state whether you have insurance for these categories. Please give the dates at which these figures are measured.

	Value	Excess	Premium
Indemnity insurance Employee fidelity and fraud insurance Other insurance (Please specify)			

33) Please state the company/companies with which you are insured.

_____

34) Have you ever made a claim against your insurance?   YES/NO
    If so, what was the proportion of the claim that was paid out by the
    insurance company? _____

    Was this compensation paid out promptly?   YES/NO

QUESTION 2: OPERATIONAL RISKS BORNE BY FIRM[1]

Type of risk	A Please rank the risks starting with 1—most likely to occur	B Please rank the risks starting with 1—largest possible loss	C Largest loss incurred by the following parties over the last year for each risk (Euro million)		D Please list the total losses resulting from the risks listed below over the last year	E Number of complaints over the last year	F Claims on insurance over the last year (Euro million)
			Asset management firm	Investor			
Misdealing[2]							
Failure to best execute[3]							
Settlement problems							
Counterparty failure							
Breach of client guidelines							
Fraud							
IT systems failure							
Failure to meet guarantees							
Unit trust mispricing[4]							
Failure to reconcile assets under custodianship and internal records							
Failure to collect all income (including corporate action failures)							
Stock lending failures							
Financial insolvency							
Risks arising in the process of taking over new business							
Other risks (please specify)							

Notes: [1] Direct financial risks refer to operational risks borne by the firm. [2] Misdealing refers to errors in buying or selling. [3] Failure to best execute refers to a failure to obtain the best price. [4] Unit trust mispricing refers to an incorrect valuation of client or fund assets.

Birmingham City University - Kenrick Library
Self Service Receipt for items borrowed

Title: Multi asset class investment strategy
Item: 6139831639
Due: 08/01/2008 23:59

Title: Asset management and investor protection

Item: 6132586507
Due: 08/01/2008 23:59

Total items: 2
04/12/2007 12:23

Week loan items CANNOT be renewed

If the information on value of losses required to complete Question 2 is not readily available, please answer either Question 2a and/or 2b.

2a) Were there any losses over the last 12 months?   YES/NO

If so, what is the total of these losses? Please tick the appropriate box.

☐ Less than Euro 100,000
☐ Between Euro 100,000 and Euro 500,000
☐ Between Euro 500,000 and Euro 1 m
☐ Greater than Euro 1 m

2b) What is the provision for losses in your company accounts?

_____

QUESTION 3: MECHANISMS FOR MITIGATING RISKS[1]

Please list the internal control for each of these risks and rank the means of financing any resulting losses from these risks, **starting with 1 for the most used.**

Type of risk	A — Please list the KEY internal control for each of these risks	B — Means of financing losses		
		Capital	Insurance	Parent firm guarantees	Internal profits
Misdealing					
Failure to best execute					
Settlement problems					
Counterparty failure					
Breach of client guidelines					
Fraud					
IT systems failure					
Failure to meet guarantees					
Unit trust mispricing					
Failure to reconcile assets under custodianship and internal records					
Failure to collect all income (including corporate action failures)					
Stock lending failures					
Financial insolvency					
Other risks (please specify)					

Note: [1] Mitigating risk means reducing risk to customers by employing certain measures, such as capital or insurance.

How do you rank the potential success of this questionnaire at achieving the goals set out in the introduction? (Please tick.)

☐ Very poor
☐ Poor
☐ Fair
☐ Good
☐ Very good

Other comments:

_____

_____

_____

_____

_____

_____

9A.2 THE RESPONSES TO QUESTIONNAIRE

Respondents were asked to state their main regulatory body and that of their group. The table below reports the results to this question.

Authorities supervising sample of asset management companies

Regulator	Number of asset management companies	Number of parent firms
Italy		
Bank of Italy	7	5
Consob	5	2
Ufficio Dei Cambi		
La Commissione di vigilanza sui fondi pensione	1	1
Istituto per la vigilanza sulle assicurazioni private e di interesse collettivo		1
France		
COB	7	1
Conseil marchés financiers	1	
Commission Bancaire		3
Commission de Contrôle des Assurances		5
UK		
IMRO	15	
Personal Investment Authority	1	2
FSA		3
Germany		
Bundesaufsichtsamt für das Kreditwesen	3	1
Bundesaufsichtsamt für das Versicherungswesen		1
Bundesaufsichtsamt für das Wertpapierhandel	2	1
Ireland		
Central Bank of Ireland	4	2
The Netherlands		
STE	1	
Dutch Central Bank	1	1
Verzekeringskamer (Dutch insurance regulator)		1
USA		
SEC	2	4
US insurance agencies/regulatory bodies		1
Department of Corporations of the State of California		1
Japan		
Ministry of Finance	1	
Belgium		
Belgian Banking and Finance Commission		1

Thirty-six firms responded to this question. However, the total number of firms regulated by the authorities above is larger because several companies reported that they were regulated by more than one authority.

10

A Case Study in Authorized Collective Schemes

In this chapter, a case of large losses is examined in detail. The case took place in the unit trust management industry, and not in the discretionary asset management under mandates, which is the main focus of the research. Nevertheless, it raises generic issues for investor protection, and illustrates:

- the way in which failures in the investment management process can occasionally create large losses;
- how parent firms with deep pockets and reputational capital at stake can provide investor protection;
- potential deficiencies in the protection provided by separate custodians and trustees;
- that capital requirements may not be an appropriate regulatory response to the occasional large losses described in this chapter.

This chapter begins by summarizing the key points of the case study. It then analyses the origins of failure, the role of internal control systems, and the role of other parties, such as trustees and auditors, in the supervision process.

The entire chapter is based on official information from the IMRO press releases. It is not intended to indicate inappropriate behaviour by any individual or company.

10.1 THE KEY FACTS

In September 1996, dealings in three Morgan Grenfell funds were suspended after the discovery of irregularities in the management of the funds. Trading resumed after Deutsche Bank, the parent company, injected £180 m into the funds.

For a period of time, the irregularities that took place remained undetected by the internal control system of Morgan Grenfell Asset Management Ltd. (MGAM) and the external supervision by the trustees. IMRO brought forward charges against the Morgan Grenfell's fund management subsidiaries, responsible senior employees and compliance staff, and the funds' trustees.

Investors in the three funds were compensated directly by the MGAM for the difference between the investment return from their Morgan Grenfell fund and the investment return provided by a specially compiled index of comparable funds. The total compensation costs borne by the firm for losses amounted to more than £210 m.

10.2 BACKGROUND

MGAM was the UK asset management arm of Deutsche Morgan Grenfell and part of the Deutsche Bank Group. Its subsidiary, MG Unit Trust Managers (MGUTM), was the appointed fund manager of the MG European Growth Trust and the MG Europa Fund. MGUTM delegated the day-to-day management of the two unit trusts to another subsidiary, MG International Fund Management (MGIFM). MGIFM was also delegated responsibility to manage the MG European Capital Growth Fund, a Dublin-registered investment fund.

10.3 THE ORIGINS OF THE FAILURE

After taking over the management of the funds in 1994, the individual fund manager started changing the nature of the funds' investments. From being well diversified, the portfolios in due course became increasingly concentrated in high-risk holdings of unlisted securities.

While pursuing this investment strategy, the fund manager faced two primary barriers arising from unit trust regulations:

- the regulatory rule that restricted unit trust holdings in unapproved securities (that is, securities which were not listed in an eligible securities market and which were not issued on terms that a listing would be applied for within 12 months) to 10 per cent of a fund; and
- the rule that prevented unit trusts from acquiring more than 10 per cent in securities issued by one issuer.

To assist in circumventing these regulations, the fund manager set up holding companies, mainly in Luxembourg. These companies were used as special purpose vehicles to hold or acquire problem securities in the funds. They created an indirect exposure to unapproved securities in excess of that permitted by strict adherence to the spirit, as well as the letter, of the rules. In addition, the funds held bonds that had been structured to exploit loopholes in the regulations (IMRO 1997). By April 1996, the fund manager had increased the proportion of unlisted, risky companies in the European Growth portfolio to 33 per cent and thus far above regulatory concentration limits (IMRO 1999).

Overall, it may be claimed that the funds were managed in a way that abided by the letter rather than the spirit of the regulations, leading to a risk and investment profile that was inappropriate for retail funds and could have created liquidity problems.

10.4 THE IMRO'S INVESTIGATION

The problems in the management of the Morgan Grenfell funds were discovered by the IMRO towards the end of August 1996, and dealings in the funds were suspended on 2 September 1996. Trading in the funds resumed on 5 September after the Deutsche Bank, MGAM's parent institution, injected approximately £180 m into the portfolios by buying the particular securities out of the funds.

The fund manager was suspended and, on 16 September, finally dismissed. In mid-October, the chief executive of MGAM and four other senior employees left the company.

On 20 December 1996, the IMRO and MGAM finalized the investor compensation package. All investors in the three funds at any time between August 1995 and September 1996 were compensated directly by the MGAM for the difference between the investment return from their Morgan Grenfell fund and the investment return provided by a specially compiled index of comparable funds. In addition, MGAM paid interest on the compensation payments from April 1997. The total compensation costs borne by the firm for losses in this case amounted to more than £210 m.

10.5 THE FAILURE OF INTERNAL CONTROL SYSTEMS

For its part, the IMRO spent the next eight months investigating and imposing penalties for what it perceived as ineffective controls at Morgan Grenfell, and the lack of effective oversight on the part of the funds' trustees. The fund manager himself became, and at the time of writing still is, the subject of a continuing investigation by the Serious Fraud Office.

According to the IMRO, the fact that the fund manager's actions continued for a lengthy period of time, and that MGAM's management and its compliance staff failed to ensure that the funds were managed according to the regulations and their prospectuses, was largely owing to a lack of adequate internal control and monitoring procedures (IMRO 1997, 1999). In particular, investigations revealed problems related to inadequate documentation requirements and record keeping. The lack of control allowed the fund manager to build up excessively risky portfolios and push the investments beyond existing regulatory limits on unit trust holdings in unquoted equities or securities of a single issuer. Due diligence was not sufficiently exercised to avoid the assets of the funds being used or invested contrary to the unit trust regulations—for instance, it was not recognized that some of the holding companies were not genuine investments but special purpose vehicles used to circumvent regulatory rules (IMRO 1997, 1998c).

By no later than April 1996, however, it was known to the board of MGAM that the risk and investment profile of the European Growth Trust managed by the fund manager was inappropriate and could lead to liquidity problems. The chief executive of MGAM and his management team were informed that the unit trust held 33 per cent in unlisted securities and that full documentation about those unlisted securities was not available (IMRO 1999). Steps were taken to instigate an internal review of the portfolio holdings and implement management changes aimed at dealing with the situation.

The IMRO argued that the chief executive should have done more to satisfy himself personally that the advice and progress reports he was receiving were correct. Moreover, the IMRO argued that he should have required the compliance department to investigate and report to him on how the state of affairs with the European Growth Trust had been allowed to occur. Furthermore, the chief executive failed to inform the IMRO in April 1996, when he was informed about the situation, or two months later, when he knew that, despite the internal review and management changes instigated by him, the level of investment in unlisted securities in the fund remained high and full documentation was still not available (IMRO 1999). As a result of the IMRO's findings, the chief executive was reprimanded and charged the IMRO's investigation costs and a contribution to its disciplinary costs.

On 16 April 1997, the IMRO also fined Morgan Grenfell's subsidiaries, MGIFM and MGUTM, £2 m for mismanagement of the European funds (IMRO 1997). In addition to the £2 m fine, the investment firms had to pay £1 m to defray the IMRO's investigation costs. In deciding on an appropriate fine, the IMRO took into account the number of investors affected, the potential losses, and, in mitigation, Morgan Grenfell's quick action to compensate investors in the funds.

Phillip Thorpe, the IMRO's Chief Executive, commented:

The mismanagement of these funds has caused unnecessary concern to an enormous number of investors. It is right that this is being corrected promptly and thoroughly.

The firm has paid dearly as a consequence of inadequate management control. This affair plainly illustrates the dangers of ignoring clear and repeated warnings. We expect that other investment managers will ensure that they are not exposed to the same risks. (IMRO, 1997)

10.6 OTHER PARTIES' FAILURES

The IMRO investigation and proceedings extended to the funds' trustees. Under the UK regulation, trustees have two main functions:

- to take the assets of a unit trust into custody and hold them in trust for unit-holders;

- supervision to ensure that unit trust managers comply with regulatory rules and investment objectives. This function extends to reporting to unit-holders on manager compliance.

General Accident was trustee of a number of unit trusts managed by MGUTM, including the European Growth Trust and the Europa Fund. When General Accident resigned in early 1996, The Royal Bank of Scotland took over the trusteeship of the funds. Both General Accident and The Royal Bank of Scotland agreed to a settlement of the disciplinary proceedings and to fines of £120,000 and £290,000, respectively. The trustees were also charged the IMRO investigation costs of more than £247,416 for General Accident and £143,020 for The Royal Bank of Scotland. The fines were brought on the basis that the trustees did not exercise an appropriate level of supervision of the MGUTM's operation of the unit trusts, and did not identify and report that the trusts' investments in unapproved securities were in excess of the concentration limits permitted by the regulations. In addition, General Accident was charged for not taking into its custody or providing safe custody for bearer share certificates[1] in two companies acquired by the European Growth Trust on 2 August 1995 for £16 m (IMRO 1998*a* and *b*).

10.7 SOME LESSONS

The events at MGAM show that much larger losses can occur than those reported in the previous chapter, which described losses reported in the survey from operational risks. They also raise questions about the nature of the contract between the asset manager, in this case a unit trust manager, and the trustee and custodian. The concern is that, if MGAM had not had a parent with a deep pocket and a valuable reputation, investors might not all have received adequate compensation. While the compensation fund would have provided some recompense to investors, it is not obvious that it would have provided full compensation to all investors. It is also unclear to what extent the trustee and custodian would have been obliged by the nature of their contract, and the duty of care inherent in it, to contribute. In other words, the concern is that the implied duty of care in these contracts is

---

[1] A bearer share certificate is not registered in the name of the holder, who can sell it or claim dividends upon presentation of the certificate to a bank or broker.

not clear and unambiguous, and therefore may not provide the investor protection. Setting capital requirements at several hundred millions of euros for many asset management firms would seriously limit competition within Europe and make the industry uncompetitive with the USA.

11

Literature Review

This chapter reviews the various strands of academic literature that are relevant to a study of capital regulation of asset managers. There are three that are of particular significance. The first is the corporate finance literature on how firms make capital structure decisions in an unregulated environment. The second examines the role of capital adequacy requirements in the banking sector. The third is regulation of quality and the professions.

The capital structure literature (Section 11.1):

- establishes when capital structure is and is not relevant to the value of a firm;
- emphasizes the importance of asymmetries in information and corporate control in determining a firm's optimal capital structure; and
- demonstrates that the imposition of regulatory capital requirements that differ from the firms' optimal levels is costly.

The banking literature (Section 11.2):

- identifies the 'market failures' that can arise in banking;
- evaluates possible responses to systemic risks in banking;
- describes the role of capital requirements in providing protection against systemic failures; and
- establishes the costs of imposing capital requirements that differ from banks' preferred levels, and the actions that banks may take to diminish these costs.

Since systemic risks are not the primary market failure that arises in asset management, this literature may be less relevant to the current study than that on regulating professions (Section 11.3). The literature on professions (Section 11.4):

- describes the market failures that arise from imperfect information ('adverse selection' and 'moral hazard'), and how these can undermine the operation of markets;
- discusses alternative responses in the forms of quality licensing, certification by regulators, and capital requirements;
- evaluates the costs that these regulations impose in the form of barriers to entry and restrictions on customer choice; and
- suggests that capital requirements will rarely be an appropriate form of investor protection in asset management.

11.1 THE CAPITAL STRUCTURE

Capital requirements that are low relative to a firm's chosen level are ineffective. Very high requirements may impose excessive costs on firms by forcing them to choose capital structures that are different from the preferred ones. Thus, corporate finance theory, which explains how corporate capital structure decisions are made, is a central part of a study of capital regulation of investment managers.

Modern theory of capital structure began with the seminal paper of Modigliani and Miller (Modigliani and Miller 1958) that under certain conditions, capital structure decisions are irrelevant. The Modigliani and Miller proposition contrasts with the intuitive notion that a firm with risk-free debt could borrow at an interest rate below the required return on equity, thereby reducing its weighted-average cost of capital and increasing its value by substituting debt for equity. However, the arbitrage arguments employed by Modigliani and Miller demonstrate that market prices will compensate for any leverage decision the firm takes.

Borrowing increases the expected rate of return on shareholders' investment, but it also increases the risk of the firm's shares. Modigliani and Miller show that the risk increase exactly offsets the increase in expected returns, leaving shareholders no better or worse off. The cost of equity increases just enough to keep the weighted-average cost of capital constant. Also, debt is priced at levels that reflect risks of encountering financial difficulties. Higher interest rates will have to be paid to debt-holders as a compensation for risks of default on interest and principal obligations. In the case where costs of debt and equity adjust to reflect the risks that are incurred by different classes of investors, the capital structure decision is a matter of indifference to firms.

The implications of the Modigliani and Miller proposition in the context of regulatory capital requirements are twofold. First, if any capital structure is as good as any other, regulators have an easy task: they can set capital ratios arbitrarily high at no costs and thereby eliminate the risks associated with corporate failure. Equally important, the proposition suggests that the mere existence of risk would not present a problem since it would be fully reflected in the market prices. Risk per se would not call for regulatory intervention.

However, the irrelevance of the capital structure proposition only applies in a perfect world of full information and complete markets. Subsequent corporate finance research has focused on deviations from the Modigliani and Miller frictionless world that make capital structure relevant (see, for example, Bradley et al. 1984 and Scott 1976). Much of the banking literature described below is built on, or related to, these extensions (see Berger *et al.* 1995). Banks are seen as having an 'optimal' capital structure that maximizes their value in the absence of regulatory capital requirements. Regulators therefore face a trade-off between achieving their regulatory objectives and the cost, which higher regulatory capital levels impose on the firms.

Informational frictions are one of the main reasons why capital structure may not be a matter of indifference to firms. Two types of asymmetric information are important: first, firms have an informational advantage *vis-à-vis* their investors; and, second, information differs between different types of investors.

Managers generally have more information about earnings prospects and the financial condition of their firms than capital markets. Because of this asymmetry, the market will draw inferences from the actions of firms. Capital structure decisions may be one of the tools available to managers to signal information to the market. If optimistic managers find it less costly to signal good earnings prospects through increased gearing than managers who are pessimistic about prospects, a signalling equilibrium may exist in which firms that expect to have better future performance have less equity capital (Ross 1977).

Asymmetric information combined with transactions costs of new issues may also influence the relative costs of internal versus external finance and the relative costs of debt and equity. In Myers (1984) and Myers and Majluf (1984), managers use private information to issue shares when they are overpriced. Investors are aware of this asymmetric information problem and discount the firm's new and existing shares when equity issues are announced. Because managers anticipate these price discounts, they are reluctant to issue equity. This reluctance is reinforced by the costs of issuing equity. Managers therefore, prefer to finance projects with retained earnings, which involve no asymmetric information problem and no issue costs. If internal funds are exhausted, debt is preferred to equity because its issuing costs are usually lower. Equity will be issued only when the debt capacity is running out and financial distress threatens. The result is the so-called pecking order of finance.

A significant part of the literature concentrates on models in which capital structure decisions are explained by agency conflicts that emerge under asymmetric information. On the one hand, there is a conflict of interest between equity-holders and debt-holders. Debt contracts are such that, if an investment yields large returns, equity-holders capture most of the gain.

However, if the investment fails, because of limited liability, debt-holders bear the consequences. If creditors do not have sufficient information to react, equity-holders have a moral hazard opportunity to exploit creditors by investing suboptimally and substituting riskier assets for safer ones (Jensen and Meckling 1976). In addition, when firms are likely to go bankrupt in the near future, shareholders may lack the incentives to contribute new capital, since most of the benefits would be captured by the debt-holders (Myers 1977). The greater the risk of creditor expropriation, the higher the costs of bonding firms to their creditors and the lower the levels of gearing will be.

On the other hand, debt may reduce agency conflicts between shareholders and managers that result from the separation of ownership from control. Where the owners of equity have imperfect information about managerial actions, managers may have an incentive to exert insufficient effort in managing firm resources (Jensen and Meckling 1976). They may also want to invest all available funds, even if paying out cash is better for investors (Jensen 1986; Stulz 1990). In these cases, increasing the fraction of the firm financed by debt raises firm value by mitigating agency conflicts. Debt limits managerial discretion because payments to service debt reduce the free cash flow of the firm.

In these agency models, shareholders are confronted with two offsetting effects. Higher capital avoids expropriation problems between shareholders and creditors, but aggravates conflicts of interest between shareholders and managers. The optimal capital structure then emerges as the trade-off between the costs and benefits of debt relative to equity.

Capital structure theories based on asymmetric information provide explanations for why firms may have a preferred debt–equity choice. The theories also imply that deviating from the optimal choice, for example because of statutory capital requirements, imposes costs on firms and reduces firm value. However, none of the theories provides a rationale for government intervention. Government intervention cannot reduce the distortions in capital structure that result from the asymmetric information problems listed above.

The corporate finance literature also considers corporate control as a determinant of capital structure. In a world where financial contracts are inherently incomplete, firms must determine how investment and operating decisions left out of the corporate charter ought to be taken. The corporate control literature argues that financial structure acts as a determinant of the allocation of control rights among claim-holders, and, in particular, when and how these claim-holders can intervene in management. The capital structure decision thus becomes a problem of selecting an efficient structure of corporate governance (see, for example, Berkovitch and Israel 1996).

Shareholders are not only the residual claimants on the firm's earnings, but also the owners of the firm's assets. Therefore, shareholders have the right to determine how a firm's assets are managed. Creditors generally do not have such a right, unless the firm is in default, in which case control passes to the creditors. Bankruptcy is seen as a mechanism for transferring control rights between claim-holders (for example, Aghion and Bolton 1992; Dewatripont and Tirole 1994).

In this view, debt provides a mechanism of allocating control rights contingent on corporate financial performance. If performance (reflected in earnings) is so low that a firm cannot meet its debt obligations, the firm defaults, and creditors obtain the right to liquidate the firm. Alternatively, creditors may agree to a reorganization. If financial performance is adequate, shareholders remain in control. When is the transfer of control rights from shareholders to creditors justified? It is justified at the point when shareholders have demonstrated that they are less competent than creditors at running the firm. Therefore, if the performance of the firm is informative about the ability of shareholders and their managers, then there exists an optimal level of debt that determines a minimum performance of the firm.

The corporate control theories emphasize the important point that a preferred financial structure only exists where financial performance is related to the underlying quality of firm management. If there is no correlation between the financial performance and quality of management, then there would be no reason for using financial structure to effect changes in control. That is, capital structure only has a role to play where financial returns assist in distinguishing between the good and bad management.

11.2 THE CAPITAL REGULATION FOR BANKS

In contrast to non-bank financial services, the economic literature has extensively examined the role of banking regulation. The principal concern raised is systemic risk. Prudential regulation of banks ensures the stability of the financial system, which would otherwise be undermined by widespread bank failures.

The instability inherent in banking is a reflection of the composition of bank assets and liabilities. Banks transform short-term deposits into long-term loans. This leaves them exposed to withdrawals that necessitate the premature liquidation of long-term assets. If the net realizable value of assets falls below deposits, then banks are unable to service withdrawals in full and insolvency may result. Depositors perceive this risk of bankruptcy. When they observe large withdrawals from their bank, they may respond by withdrawing their own deposits, even if the bank is solvent. This may be rational either because depositors are uncertain that a bank is in fact solvent, or because they fear that a solvent bank can be made insolvent by the uninformed actions of other depositors. In addition, depositors may take the view that, while the probability of a bank failure is low, it would nevertheless be serious to them if it were to occur. Furthermore, if insolvency does occur, claims are paid on a first-come, first-served basis such that those who withdraw early are paid in full whereas latecomers are not. The seminal article providing a model of how a sound bank can be forced into bankruptcy by a pure panic run on deposits is Diamond and Dybvig (1983).

Withdrawals in excess of the current expected demand for liquidity not only generate a negative externality for the bank experiencing the liquidity shortage, they can also generate an externality for the whole banking system. Public information about the condition of individual banks is highly imperfect. When a number of banks fail, it may be difficult to tell whether the cause is idiosyncratic shocks to individual banks or a more widespread shock that jeopardizes the financial system. Thus, the news that some banks failed may create panic runs from other solvent, but illiquid banks (Bhattacharya and Thakor 1993). In particular, if the ability of other banks to rescue troubled banks is dependent on their own financial condition, then investors may correctly infer information about the soundness of the financial system (Aghion *et al.* 1988). In addition to these confidence-related effects, failure of one bank might have direct contagion effects through liabilities to other financial institutions (Guttentag and Herring 1987). In these cases, bank runs, which affect individual firms, may develop into a bank panic, which concerns the whole banking industry.

While not all observers agree that systemic risk is an important issue (see, for example, Benston and Kaufman 1995), widespread banking failure may inflict heavy social costs. These costs comprise reductions in credit availability, bottlenecks in the payments system, less effective monetary policy, or the general collapse of confidence in the macroeconomy (Bernanke 1983; Bernanke and Blinder 1992).

Several remedies to the risk of bank runs have been put forward in the literature. The obvious way to prevent instability of the banking system is to require that, under any possible circumstance, all banks can fulfil their contractual obligations. Since the risk arises from bank deposits being liquid and callable at notice, while bank assets are illiquid or realizable only at substantial cost, safety could be ensured by the 'narrow bank' proposal, according to which the maturity structure of bank assets is perfectly matched with that of bank liabilities (Friedman 1960; Litan 1987). However, these requirements are seen to be too restrictive and antagonistic to the primary function of a bank to transform short-term liabilities into long-term assets.

An alternative solution to eliminate inefficient bank runs is to insure depositors. In this case, even if the bank is not able to fulfil its obligations, depositors receive the full value of their deposits, the difference being paid by the deposit insurance scheme, financed by taxes if the system is publicly run. This removes loss of confidence in banks and incentives for premature withdrawal, at least as long as insurance is 100 per cent.

However, considerable analytical attention has been paid in the literature to the problem of moral hazard in deposit insurance. Regulatory guarantees on the value of deposits remove incentives for depositors to monitor the portfolio allocations or to seek a return that compensates for the risks of liquidation. Deposit institutions are induced to pursue inefficient concentration of risk or to accept an uncomfortably large probability that their firm will fall into an economically insolvent condition (Merton 1978; Buser *et al.* 1981).

Various measures have been proposed to offset directly the moral hazard effects of deposit insurance, by enhancing incentives for monitoring of banks and improving market discipline. These measures include capping of statutory insurance limits at lower levels, introducing more co-insurance, making more use of market-priced subordinated debt, ensuring extensive disclosure of the banks' financial conditions, and making insurance fees more risk-based.

In this context, some have argued in favour of private insurance schemes because competition between companies provides incentives for information extraction and accurate pricing (for example, Kareken 1986). However, the market mechanism may not be sufficient to provide banks with insurance against liquidity shocks. Weakness in reserve availability and enforcement powers may undermine private insurance schemes (Kane 1989; Calomiris 1992). Since runs create risks of simultaneous bank failures, insurers could face devastating claims. Moreover, private insurance lacks credibility unless backed by the government, which, in turn, casts doubt on the incentives of private companies to look for accurate pricing of deposit insurance. In addition, theoretical papers show that, in the presence of asymmetric information, fairly priced deposit insurance may not be feasible (Chan *et al.* 1992) or, in some cases, not socially desirable (Freixas and Rochet 1995).

As regards the monitoring solution, while bank supervision is widely believed to be important, it is imperfect in many ways. For example, one question that has been addressed in the literature is whether regulators have incentives to perform adequately the monitoring role (for example, Kane 1995; Campbell *et al.* 1992).

It is for these reasons that regulators consider capital requirements. Capital requirements achieve a higher safety for banks and reduce the social costs from a systemic crisis. In the presence of deposit insurance, capital requirements have the additional role of protecting regulators and taxpayers against the costs of banking failures. Essentially, the ability to default and the right to sell the bank's assets to the insurer for the face value of insured deposits is a put option on bank assets (Merton 1977). This put option becomes 'in the money' whenever stockholder-contributed capital falls below zero. The value of the option increases with the risk of investments made by the bank, and falls with the capital that the bank holds. As capitalization approaches 100 per cent, both the amount of deposits and the value of the option fall to zero. To keep risks of default below certain levels, banks should be required to hold capital.

However, if banks do have an optimal capital ratio (for reasons explained in the literature on capital structure), regulatory requirements to increase capital beyond the unconstrained optimal level reduce the value of banks and increase the cost of financing. In the long run, regulatory capital costs are likely to be passed on to bank customers. Thus, capital regulation is seen to involve a trade-off between the benefits of reducing the risk of the negative externalities from bank failures and the social costs of higher prices for financial services (Santomero and Watson 1977).

Since this trade-off differs across banks, the ideal regulatory system would reflect these differences and tailor capital requirements for each bank. Similarly, the ideal system would continuously update the requirements to reflect changes in the risk position and the external costs of these risks. Implementation of such an ideal system would be too costly, if not impossible, to operate. Therefore, real-world capital regulation can at best be an approximation to the ideal.

Actual capital standards in place have been subject to extensive comment and criticism in the literature. In this respect, particular attention has been paid to the impact of the 1988 Basel Accord on bank behaviour. The Basel capital requirements oblige banks to maintain equity and quasi-equity funding equal to a risk-weighted proportion of their asset base. The most obvious undesirable distortion is that excessive differentials in the weights applied to different categories of assets might induce banks to substitute away from assets with high risk-weights. This may cause a credit crunch (Berger and Udell 1994; Hancock and Wilcox 1994). Commercial loans are assigned high risk-weights, which provides incentives to substitute from commercial lending into lower risk-weighted categories, thereby inducing a credit reduction of both weakly and well-capitalized banks.

The other concern is that capital requirements may have the perverse effect of exacerbating risk-taking because, within each category, banks may shift towards riskier assets. Kim and Santomero (1988) show formally how a bank that maximizes risk–return preferences and faces uniform proportional capital requirements may substitute towards riskier assets. Other theoretical contributions include Keeley and Furlong (1990) and Rochet (1992).

Recently, concern has been expressed about what is termed 'regulatory capital arbitrage' (Jones 2000). This may take the form of banks restructuring traditional balance-sheet positions through the use of securitization or credit derivatives so as to place the positions within lower-risk-weighted classes. Alternatively, banks can artificially inflate capital by devices such as gains trading or under-provisioning for loan loss reserves. The problem, as perceived by regulators, is that, through capital arbitrage, a bank may achieve an overall regulatory capital ratio that is nominally high, but may mask capital weakness—that is, despite a high capital ratio, the bank may have an unacceptably high probability of insolvency. Mingo (2000) views the 1988 Basel Accord as a 'lose–lose' proposition. From the regulator's perspective, high risk-based capital ratios may have been achieved, but there is no guarantee that banks are sound. Meanwhile, regulatory capital arbitrage is costly, therefore deflecting banks from achieving their goal of maximizing firm value. Additionally, competitive inequities may emerge to the extent that regulatory capital arbitrage is not equally available to all banks.

Empirical evidence of the impact of the Basel capital requirements on the behaviour of banks is mixed (Basel Committee 1999*a*). While the effects on risk-shifting and the credit crunch are uncertain, there is strong evidence that the volume of regulatory capital arbitrage is large and growing rapidly, especially among the large banks. New proposals have been put forward to redress the possible deficiencies of the 1988 Basel Accord. These give a priority to ensuring that the economic risks of financial transactions are better captured by capital charges (Basel Committee 1999*b*; European Commission 1999).

While the analysis of problems associated with actual capital requirements in the banking sector is relevant to the present discussion, it is important to stress again that, in prudential bank regulation, capital requirements have the role of protecting against systemic risks of banking failures.

11.3 THE CAPITAL REGULATION FOR NON-BANK FINANCIAL INSTITUTIONS

Systemic risks are considerably less evident or non-existent for the non-banking financial sector (for example, Llewellyn 1999). Contagion is less likely because of the nature of the contracts involved. Asset managers, for example, do not usually offer debt contracts that guarantee particular rates of return. Instead, they act as agents for investors who delegate portfolio selection and administration to an asset manager. Brokers and dealers merely effect transactions on behalf of others.

In neither case are there similar externalities between investors to those that exist in banks. In addition, while banks rely on potentially volatile, unsecured, short-term deposits for the bulk of their funding, most other financial institutions have a much higher proportion of long-term funding. Dale (1996) points out that other financial institutions, in particular insurance companies, have the reverse maturity transformation from banks: marketable, and, hence, liquid assets and long-term liabilities. The marketability of assets also means that, in contrast to banks, the value of firms in liquidation differs little from the value on a going-concern basis. If an investment firm fails and client funds are held separately from the firm's own assets, portfolios under management can be transferred at a low cost from one manager to another (Franks and Mayer 1989). Moreover, provided that asset managers do not take positions on their own account, interlinkages between firms are limited. There is therefore little reason to believe that financial collapse of one asset manager should have repercussions elsewhere.

In the case of brokers and dealers, failure can have more contagious effects, since client assets are closely associated with those of the firm. Since brokers and dealers take investment positions on their own account, a financial collapse elsewhere can endanger assets and threaten solvency. Moreover, brokers and dealers enhance liquidity and accelerate the execution of transactions. A disruption of this function may be of broader significance outside the financial sector if securities markets are of wider relevance to economic activity. There is therefore, stronger justification for prudential regulation to protect systemic failures in brokers and dealers than in asset management, but even then it is not as compelling as with banks.

One argument for extending capital requirements to non-banks is to ensure a level playing field between banks and other financial institutions by equalizing the regulatory costs across all suppliers of financial services. However, Schaefer (1992) and Dimson and Marsh (1995) point out that there is no case for a level playing field if the socially optimal capital requirement for a particular type of institution depends on the systemic costs imposed on society by its failure and if these costs differ across firms.

It is therefore not surprising that the theoretical literature advocates, or at least considers, capital requirements mainly in the context of banks. As argued in Franks and Mayer (1989) and Mayer and Neven (1991), the case for financial regulation of non-banking financial institutions is based on arguments that are different to those found in the banking literature. In particular, non-banking regulation is more concerned with investor protection than the prevention of systemic failure. These arguments are further explored in the literature on the regulation of quality and the professions.

11.4   **THE REGULATION OF QUALITY AND THE PROFESSIONS**

Microeconomic theory suggests that markets fail in the provision of quality due to the existence of asymmetric information. Suppliers of goods and services know their business better than their customers. This asymmetry gives rise to two well-known types of problems: adverse selection, which results from the fact that customers are imperfectly informed about the quality of the suppliers or the products purchased; and moral hazard, which results from hidden actions of the suppliers.

Faced with a risk that product quality may be low, customers' willingness to pay falls. If customers are uninformed about the quality of different firms and their products, they will attribute the average quality to all firms. So firms that offer low quality and firms that offer high quality will all be able to sell their products at the same price because customers cannot distinguish between them. Assuming that providing quality is costly, this implies that high-quality firms expect to earn less than similar firms offering low quality. In fact, prices may be so low that high-quality firms leave the market. In this case, the proportion of low-quality firms in the market increases, and customers' willingness to pay falls further in appreciation that the quality of the market is poor. The market steadily declines as the quality of firms deteriorates. The bad firms drive out the good. This is the essence of Akerlof's (1970) model of the used-car market. Buyers are unable to distinguish between the quality of cars, and the average quality on the market determines the price. Owners of high-quality cars are discouraged from putting their vehicles on the market, and the average quality declines further. In the extreme, adverse selection may cause the market to break down completely.

The second problem relates to the moral hazard that arises because actions of suppliers cannot be perfectly observed. Although actions could in principle be monitored, customers may find it too costly to establish firm behaviour individually and rely on other customers to engage in monitoring. Free-riding in the collection of information thus aggravates the moral hazard problem. Suppliers are given leeway to act in a way detrimental to the customer. The additional problem that emerges is that 'good' firms are induced to behave badly because they either see bad behaviour in others, or have no assurance that their competitors behave well.

The application to financial institutions is immediate if 'poor quality' is defined in terms of negligence, incompetence, mismanagement, or dishonesty in the provision of financial services (Mayer and Neven 1991). Investors cannot, or find it too costly to, establish the quality of a financial institution or the services it provides. Since asymmetric information between the institutions and investors may result in sub-optimally low quality levels if left to the free market, a case can be made for the intervention of a public agency to regulate the financial sector.

Benston (1998) argues that, although customer protection can be a valid justification for regulation, there is no reason for regulating financial institutions or products more than other firms or products. However, Mayer and Neven (1991) and Llewellyn (1999) point out that most financial products are 'credence goods', for which neither before nor after the purchase of the product does the quality become fully known to the investor. By their very nature, financial services involve investments whose quality cannot be evaluated *ex ante*. *Ex post*, investors find it difficult to establish the quality of services, both because financial performance is difficult to measure and because negligence and incompetence are often indistinguishable from bad luck. These features exacerbate the risks of adverse selection and moral hazard that investors face in the financial sector compared to most other sectors.

The other issue that has been addressed is whether private markets are, by themselves, capable of overcoming the main consequences of informational problems. In particular, firms may refrain from acting badly so as to maintain good reputation and ensure continuing demand for their financial services (Benston 1998). If reputation rectifies market failures, external government intervention is not necessary. Indeed, theoretical models show that firm incentives may be improved by repeat purchases and reputation (Shapiro 1983; Kreps and Wilson 1982; Milgrom and Roberts 1982). In these models, consumers repeat purchases of firms as long as they are not deceived about quality. Firms then choose to supply high quality to avoid being classified as low-quality firms. This strategy is profitable if the value of the reputation of being high quality exceeds the costs saved by cutting quality and deceiving consumers.

Reputation as a disciplinary mechanism may work well in wholesale financial markets where those involved are professional and well informed, and where the provider of the financial services wishes to be involved in many repeated contracts. However, it may not work well for small investors where the risks of losing reputation are lower (Goodhart 1988). Moreover, if the quality of financial services cannot be established *ex post* as well as *ex ante* (credence goods), reputation may be inadequate to sustain good behaviour. Indeed, as firm reputation improves, incentives to cheat may increase. Turning the argument around, if investors cannot evaluate quality, reputations are vulnerable to incorrect assessments, and firms may suffer from unwarranted loss of reputation. Finally, reputation takes time to acquire and requires experimentation on the part of the investors (Diamond 1989). If investors fear that wealth can be appropriated by dishonest firms, they are unlikely to engage in experimentation. Thus, reliance on reputation may also create barriers to entry. It is for these reasons that reputation may have to be supplemented by regulation.

The most straightforward type of market intervention is the introduction of a minimum quality standard that prevents firms from selling products of a quality level lower than the standard, or that excludes firms with a low quality from entering the market in the first place. The first model that explicitly addresses this issue is Leland (1979) within a typical Akerlof-type framework. The argument is that the prices suppliers receive for services provided reflect the average level of quality, not the marginal level. Thus, so long as the average quality exceeds the marginal, there is an incentive for firms to enter the market, thereby depressing the average quality supplied. In this case, a minimum quality standard prevents quality from being driven down.

However, the literature emphasizes the important point that regulation does not come without risk. If the professions set regulation, Shaked and Sutton (1980) show that there are incentives to impose barriers to the entry of new members into the profession. Rents thereby accrue to existing members to the detriment of consumers, who are forced to pay higher prices.

Shapiro (1986) compares licensing and certification as different methods of regulating entry to ensure quality. Licensing sets a minimum level of (human capital) investment that all producers must make; this leads to excessive training by providers of low quality and induces more producers to supply high-quality goods. With certification, high-quality producers have an incentive to undertake excessive training to signal their quality. Both policies increase the average quality level, but the cost of doing so may be so high that the total welfare is reduced. The policies may also have undesirable distributional implications: those who require the provision of high-quality services may benefit, but those who do not will lose out because low-quality services will not be available at a low price.

In Gehrig and Jost (1995), firms cannot credibly signal a higher quality of products individually, but have an incentive to self-regulate market conduct. A self-regulatory club emerges that sets minimum standards. The club has a strong incentive credibly to enforce these standards because, if one member of the club deviates from the prescribed standard, all club members lose credibility. The problem is that self-regulation is costly to society as it confers some degree of monopoly power to the club. Nevertheless, self-regulation is of potential social value whenever the club members have better access to information about rivals' product qualities than an external regulator. In this sense, the desirability of self-regulation is shown to depend on the trade-off between the costs of false statutory regulatory action and those of granting monopoly power. The example provided by the authors is the self-regulation of Swiss banks.

Another application to the financial sector can be found in Mayer and Neven (1991). In their model, quality affects the performance of firms as measured by their profits. However, instead of supplying services honestly, firms can cheat and earn higher returns entirely at the expense of investors. Two classes of regulation to protect investors are considered: capital requirements, and direct penalties if misbehaviour of firms is observed. Capital requirements are imposed to prevent financial institutions, which would otherwise behave badly, from entering the industry. The problem is that capital requirements may also exclude some honest firms from the industry. This is because of possible misperceptions on the part of regulators about the degree of dishonesty in firms. Thus, there is a trade-off between allowing dishonest firms to enter and the exclusion of honest firms. The closer the correspondence of capital with the actual and acceptable quality levels, and the lower the precision in imposing direct penalties, the more advantageous are capital requirements. However, capital requirements that are unable to distinguish between firm quality are undesirable. They exclude too many honest firms from the market.

Instefjord et al. (1998) examine the role of regulation in the context of recent cases of securities fraud. It is argued that regulators who attempt to limit fraud by firm insiders can operate only by encouraging firms to improve their control environments. In this context, capital requirements may be important, not so much because of the cushion they provide against losses, but because variations in their level give regulators a lever to persuade firms to improve controls. Other types of *ex-ante* regulations to prevent fraud include the issuance of guidance concerning systems and controls, inspections, audits, or more intensive monitoring. However, the difficulty of observing the firms' internal operations and the considerable costs that such interventions may impose on firms reduce the attractiveness of *ex-ante* regulation. Instead, it is much more cost-effective for regulators to penalize frauds *ex post* than to prevent frauds by *ex-ante* controls. Regulators should therefore impose *ex-post* penalties that provide incentives to improve internal control systems or operate existing systems in an appropriate fashion. The theoretical analysis by Instefjord *et al.* further shows that, in order to prevent fraud, it is crucial to penalize those in the hierarchy who are responsible for the fraudster, not just the fraudster.

While the literature of quality regulation suggests that imperfections in the operation of markets may call for government intervention, it equally stresses that regulation does not come without risks. Asymmetric information does not only involve the customer, but the regulator as well. This may result in false and costly statutory actions. Where informational problems are severe, control may best be self-administered. No matter whether self-administered or publicly regulated, in seeking to correct the distortions that result from asymmetric information, other distortions may be introduced. In particular, regulation may restrict the supply side of the market, thereby reducing choice, raising price, and conferring rents to incumbent firms. The wrong type of regulation may also impose excessive costs on firms without achieving the desired result of improving quality.

11.5 SUMMARY AND CONCLUSIONS

The three branches of literature that have been discussed emphasize different issues that are relevant to the study of capital regulation of investment firms. The literature on capital structure is important when assessing the costs that capital requirements impose on firms. If firms have an optimal capital ratio, any statutory capital regulation that forces a deviation from the optimal choice is costly to firms. However, while the literature explains why asymmetric information or other market imperfections may give rise to particular types of capital structure, it generally does not provide any justification for capital regulation to correct the distortions.

The banking literature shows that the general issues that legitimize prudential regulation of banks do not apply for most other parts of the financial sector. In particular, risks of systemic failures associated with banks are less important or non-existent in other parts of the financial sector. The literature also highlights that, for capital requirements to have the desired effects, they need to reflect the underlying economic risks of financial transactions.

Government intervention may be justified in cases where asymmetric information causes markets to fail in providing adequate quality. This is important in financial services, where investors cannot distinguish honest from dishonest, competent from incompetent, and conscientious from negligent firms. However, the literature warns that quality regulation may not always increase social welfare. Distributional problems may arise, in that consumers with a lower willingness to pay are often penalized by a quality-increasing regulation; regulation may create barriers to entry; and when informational asymmetries involve the regulator's ability to observe quality levels, the power of regulation is reduced even further. In particular, rules that cannot distinguish between firms of different quality are inefficient.

The literature review, therefore suggests that the case for capital requirements in asset management is limited. Asset managers simply manage portfolios whose values may diminish without imposing any risk of default on the asset manager. Moreover, provided that asset managers do not take positions on their own account, interlinkages between firms are limited. In the case of default, the risk of losses to investors is small if client funds are strictly separated from the firm's own assets and can be transferred at no or low cost to new management. Unlike other parts of the financial sector, there is therefore little evidence of systemic risks and large costs of financial failures in asset management. This weakens the theoretical case for capital requirements.

Regulation of investment businesses is more concerned with investor protection than the prevention of systemic failure. Where client funds are separated and risks of default are limited, investors are mainly exposed to the risks of fraud, theft, incompetence, or negligence on the part of the investment managers. In these cases, capital regulation may have a role if capital is informative about, or correlated with, the quality performance of investment firms. In general, however, capital requirements are unlikely to be cost-efficient ways of protecting investors from the risks of poor or fraudulent management. This suggests that the appropriate regulation of investment firms is very different from that of other financial institutions, and may not involve the traditional regulatory tool of capital charges.

GLOSSARY

Bonds: a loan agreement with a company or the government whereby an arranged repayment is made to the investor upon maturity of the loan and the investor receives interest payments throughout the life of the loan.

Capital Adequacy Directive: this EC directive came into effect on 1 January 1996, setting minimum levels of capital for firms offering investment services.

Closed-ended funds: investment companies that have a fixed capitalization. To buy the shares of a closed-ended fund, there must be someone willing to sell their shares. An investment trust is an example of a closed-ended fund. See 'Investment trusts'.

Collective investment scheme: an investment scheme (company) that offers to invest funds raised from investors in a mix of securities. In Spain, these are referred to as Instituciones de Inversión Colectiva. See 'Investment companies'.

Defined-benefit pension scheme: a pension scheme where the benefits are defined in advance by the sponsor, independently of the contribution rate and asset returns, as where a pension is related to the final salary.

Defined-contribution pension scheme: a pension scheme where only contributions are fixed, and benefits depend on the return on the assets of the fund.

Derivatives: financial instruments, such as futures and options. The value of derivatives depends on other commodities, indices, or individual shares.

Endowment life assurance: a form of life assurance that is taken out for a term less than the whole life, and in which payment is due either on death during the term, or in any case at the end of the term. A variation is endowment assurance with profits, in which the payment is raised in line with the growth in profits through the allocation to the policy of bonuses.

Equity: also known as shareholders' funds.

External management: fund management conducted by a company other than the sponsor.

Fonds communs de placement: open-ended investment funds in France that have a contractual form and represent co-ownerships of transferable securities. They qualify as UCITS.

Funds: an alternative, more general, way of referring to investment funds.

Hedging: protecting an existing position or commitment by using one type of investment to offset adverse market movements.

Index funds: funds that attempt to match exactly the day-to-day fluctuations of a market index. These are sometimes called 'tracker funds'.

Internal management: fund management conducted under the auspices of the sponsor.

Investment advisers: asset managers in the USA.

Investment companies: companies engaged in the business of investing the pooled funds of investors into various investment outlets, including stocks, bonds, options, commodities, property, and money market securities. There are two types of companies: closed-ended and open-ended investment companies (funds).

Investment funds: a general term for collective investment vehicles. See 'Investment companies'.

Investment trusts: closed-ended investment companies that issue shares to investors and invest the proceeds in a portfolio of securities and shares in other companies. Like unit trusts, they are regulated by a trust deed, the trustees being separate from the management. They differ from unit trusts in that for example, the capitalization is fixed and shareholders share in the profits of the company managing the trust.

Large exposure: refers to any exposure to a counterparty or group of connected counterparties that exceeds 10 per cent of a firm's own funds.

Managed accounts: accounts set up and managed on behalf of private clients as, for example, in Italy.

Mandated portfolio management: discretionary asset management on behalf of a third party.

Market failure: occurs when the interests of firms and society fail to coincide. Essentially, there are three reasons why markets may fail. These are referred to as problems of asymmetric information, problems of externalities, and problems of monopoly power. Regulation may be justified if any of these market failures exist.

Mutual funds: the US terminology for investment funds.

Open-ended investment companies: investment funds that sell their shares directly to investors and are ready to buy back their old shares at their current net asset value. The capitalization of open-ended funds is not fixed; they expand and contract as investors invest in or leave the funds. Typically, open-ended investment companies are structured as a company rather than as a unit trust. They are common in Continental Europe and the USA, and have been permitted in the UK since 1997. They qualify as UCITS.

Open-ended investment funds: see 'Open-ended investment companies'.

Open-ended investment vehicles: see 'Open-ended investment companies'.

Operational risks: are risks that arise in the process of discretionary management of clients' assets. These risks are described in Section 9.6.

Organismes de placement collectif en valeurs mobilière (OPCVMs): the French term for UCITS. In France they comprise fonds communs de placement and SICAVs.

Pension funds: funds that are set up to pay pension benefits to retired employees of a corporation, government entity, or of other organisations.

Pooled investment scheme: see 'Collective investment scheme'.

Portfolio management companies: entities that undertake all types of discretionary asset management. In France they are referred to as sociétés de gestion de portefeuille.

Public funds: German open-ended investment funds that issue their shares to the general public. In addition, there are special (institutional) funds.

Put option: an option providing the holder with the right to sell an investment at a future date at a price agreed now.

Segregated funds: funds that are managed for a single client and therefore not pooled. See 'Mandated portfolio management'.

SICAV: open-ended investment company (see 'Open-ended investment companies'), for example in France and Italy.

Società di gestione del risparmio: a company that engages in individualized portfolio management in Italy. It is also permitted to manage assets on behalf of mutual funds.

Società di intermediazione mobiliare: refers to securities houses in Italy.

Société de gestion de portefeuille: a French portfolio management company that manages individual mandates as well as UCITS.

Société de gestion d'OPCVM: a French portfolio management company that exclusively manages UCITS (OPCVM).

Special funds: German open-ended investment funds that issue their shares to institutional or corporate investors only.

Systemic risk: this refers to a situation where financial difficulties in an institution could spread to other market players.

Tracker funds: see 'Index funds'.

UCITS (undertaking for collective investment in transferable securities): open-ended collective investment vehicles that fall under the 1985 European Community UCITS Directive. By definition, UCITS may extend to all entities that offer to invest the funds raised in a mix of transferable securities and to repurchase or redeem units from the common fund on demand. UCITS encompass the UK or Irish unit trusts, as well as the Continental equivalent of contractual common funds (fonds communs de placement) and open-ended investment companies.

UCITS Directive, 1985: the purpose of Council Directive No85/611/EEC of 1985 as amended by Council Directive No 88/220/EEC of 1988 is the coordination of laws, regulations, and administrative provisions relating to UCITS. It is primarily designed to harmonize investor protection in the EU and to ensure that a UCITS established in one member state can be marketed freely in another.

Unit-linked life assurance: a form of life assurance, in which policy-holders receive, in return for their premiums, a unit of a fund invested directly by the insurance company in securities or in property. This enables policy-holders to switch the investment of their premiums.

Unit trusts: open-ended collective investment vehicles that invest funds subscribed by the public in securities, and in return issue units that they will repurchase at any time. The trust is regulated by a trust deed, the trustees being separate from the management. Each investor owns a unit, the value of which depends on the value of the funds owned by the fund. Unit trusts in the UK and Ireland are similar to mutual funds in the USA or the open-ended investment companies in Continental Europe. They qualify as UCITS.

REFERENCES

AFG-ASFFI (1998). 'Statistical overview of collective investment', and forthcoming for 1999.
—— (2000). 'Annuaire de la gestion financière 2000'.
Aghion, P. and Bolton, P. (1992). 'An incomplete contracts approach to financial contracting', *Review of Economic Studies*, **59**, 473–94.
—— —— and Dewatripont, M. (1988). 'Interbank lending and contagious bank runs', mimeo, Delta, Paris.
Akerlof, G. (1970). 'The market for "Lemons": Qualitative uncertainty and the market mechanism', *Quarterly Journal of Economics*, **84**, 488–500.
Banca d'Italia (1999). 'Annual report 1999'.
Basle Committee on Banking Supervision (1988). International Convergence of Capital Measurement and Capital Standards, Basel Committee Publications No. 4, July.
—— (1999a). 'Capital requirements and bank behaviour: The impact of the Basel accord', *Working Paper 1*, April.
—— (1999b). 'A new capital adequacy framework', Consultative Paper, Basel Committee Publications No. 50, June.
—— (2001a). 'The new Basel capital accord: An explanatory note', January.
—— (2001b). 'Operational risk: Supporting document to the new Basel capital accord', January.
—— (2001c). 'Working paper on the regulatory treatment of operational risk', September.
—— (2001d). 'Potential modifications to the committee's proposals', November.
—— (2001e). 'Sound practices for the management and supervision of operational risk', Basel Committee Publications No. 86, December.
Benston, G. J. (1998). *Regulating Financial Markets: A Critique and Some Proposals*. London: Institute of Economic Affairs.
—— and Kaufman, G. (1995). 'Is the banking and payments system fragile', *Journal of Financial Services Research*, **9**, 209–40.
Berger, A. N., Herring, R. J. and Szego, G. P. (1995). 'The role of capital in financial institutions', *Journal of Banking and Finance*, **19**, 393–430.

Berger, A. N. and Udell, G. F. (1994). 'Did risk-based capital allocate bank credit and cause a "Credit Crunch"?', in M. Klausner and L. J. White (eds), *Structural Changes in Banking*. Homewood IL: Irwin Publishing.

Berkovitch, E. and Israel, R. (1996). 'The design of internal control and capital structure', *Review of Financial Studies*, **9**, 209–40.

Bernanke, B. S. (1983). 'Non-monetary effects of the financial crisis in the propagation of the great depression', *American Economic Review*, **73**, 257–76.

—— and Blinder, A. (1992). 'The federal funds rate and the channels of monetary transmission', *American Economic Review*, **82**, 901–21.

Bhattacharya, S. and Thakor, A. V. (1993). 'Contemporary banking theory', *Journal of Financial Intermediation*, **3**, 2–50.

Board of Governors of the Federal Reserve System (2000). 'Flow of funds accounts of the United States: Flows and outstandings second quarter 2000', September, Washington DC.

Bradley, M., Jarrell, G. A. and Kim, E. H. (1984). 'On the existence of an optimal capital structure', *Journal of Finance*, **39**, 857–78.

British Invisibles (1997). 'Fund management', City Business Series, Statistical Update.

—— (2000). 'Fund management', City Business Series, Statistical Update.

Bundesbank (1994–8), *Financial Accounts*.

—— (1998). *Capital Market Statistics*.

Buser, S. A., Chen, A. H. and Kane, E. J. (1981). 'Federal deposit insurance, regulatory policy and optimal bank capital', *Journal of Finance*, **36**, 51–60.

Calomiris, C. W. (1992). 'Getting the incentives right in the current deposit insurance system: Successes from the Pre-FIDC era', in J. R. Barth and R. D. Brumbaugh (eds), *Disciplining Government and Protecting Taxpayers*. New York: Harper Collins.

Campbell, T. S., Chan, Y. S. and Marino, A. M. (1992). 'An incentive-based theory of bank regulation', *Journal of Financial Intermediation*, **2**, 255–76.

Chan, Y. S., Greenbaum, S. I. and Thakor, A. V. (1992). 'Is fairly priced deposit insurance possible?', *Journal of Finance*, **47**, 227–45.

Commission des Opérations de Bourse (1998). *Facts and Figures*.

—— (1999). *Facts and Figures*.

Dale, R. (1996). 'Regulating the new financial markets', in M. Edey (ed), *The Future of the Financial System*. Sydney: Reserve Bank of Australia.

De Nederlandsche Bank (2000). 'Statistical bulletin', March.

Dewatripont, M. and Tirole, J. (1994). 'A theory of debt and equity: Diversity of securities and manager–shareholder congruence', *Quarterly Journal of Economics*, **109**, 1027–54.

Diamond, D. (1989). 'Reputation acquisition in debt markets', *Journal of Political Economy*, **97**, 828–62.

Diamond, D. V. and Dybvig, P. (1983). 'Bank runs, deposit insurance, and liquidity', *Journal of Political Economy*, **91**, 401–19.

Dimson, M. and Marsh, P. (1995). 'Capital requirements for securities firms', *Journal of Finance*, **50**, 821–51.

European Commission (1999). 'A review of regulatory capital requirements for EU credit institutions and investment firms', MARKT/1123/99-EN-Rev.1, November.

—— (2001). 'Commission services' Second Consultative Document on Review of Regulatory Capital for Credit Institutions and Investment Firms, February, MARKT/1000/01

Franks, J. and Mayer, C. (1989). *Risk, Regulation and Investor Protection: The Case of Investment Management*. Oxford: Oxford University Press.

Freixas, X. and Rochet, J. (1995). 'Fairly priced deposit insurance? Is it possible? Yes. Is it desirable? No.', Finance and Banking Discussion Paper Series 16, Universitat Pompeu Fabra, Barcelona.

Friedman, M. (1960). *A Program for Monetary Stability*. New York: Fordham University Press.

Fund Managers' Association (1999). 'Fund management survey 1999', October.

Gehrig, T. and Jost, P.-J. (1995). 'Quacks, lemons and self regulation: A welfare analysis', *Journal of Regulatory Economics*, **7**, 309–25.

Goodhart, C. (1988). *The Evolution of Central Banks*. Cambridge, Mass.: MIT Press.

Guttentag, J. and Herring, R. (1987). 'Emergency liquidity assistance for international banks', in S. Portes and A. K. Swoboda (eds), *Threats to International Financial Stability*. Cambridge: Cambridge University Press.

Hancock, D. and Wilcox, J. A. (1994). 'Bank capital and the credit crunch: The roles of risk-weighted and unweighted capital regulations', *American Real Estate and Urban Economics Association Journal*, **22**, 59–94.

ICI Mutual Insurance Group (1999). 'Annual report'.

ICI (2000). *Mutual Fund Fact Book*.

IMRO (1997). press release, Ref. 05/97.

—— (1998*a*). press releases, Ref. 03/98.

—— (1998*b*). press releases, Ref. 04/98.

—— (1998*c*). press releases, Ref. 07/98.

—— (1999). press release, Ref. 01/99.

—— (2000). 'Report & Accounts 1998–9'.

—— (2001). 'Report & Accounts 1999–2000'.

—— *Rulebook*.

Instefjord, N., Jackson, P. and Perraudin, W. (1998). 'Securities fraud', *Economic Policy*, **27**, 587–623.

Investors Compensation Scheme, '1999 annual report' and '2000 annual report'.

Jensen, M. C. (1986). 'Agency costs and free cash flow, corporate finance and takeovers', *American Economic Review*, **76**, 323–39.

—— and Meckling, W. (1976). 'Theory of the firm: Managerial behaviour, agency costs, and capital structure', *Journal of Financial Economics*, **3**, 305–60.

Jones, D. D. (2000). 'Emerging problems with the Basel accord: Regulatory capital arbitrage and related issues', *Journal of Banking and Finance*, **24**, 35–58.

Kane, E. J. (1989). 'Changing incentives facing financial-services regulators', *Journal of Financial Services Research*, **2**, 263–72.

——(1995). 'Three paradigms for the role of capitalisation requirements in insured financial institutions', *Journal of Banking and Finance*, **19**, 431–59.

Kareken, J. (1986). 'Federal bank regulatory policy: A description and some observations', *Journal of Business*, **59**, 3–48.

Keeley, M. C. and Furlong, F. T. (1990). 'A reexamination of mean-variance analysis of bank capital regulation', Federal Reserve Bank of Kansas City, *Working Paper*, December.

Kim, D. and Santomero, A. M. (1988). 'Regulation of bank capital and portfolio risk', *Journal of Finance*, **43**, 1235–44.

Kreps, D. and Wilson, R. (1982). 'Reputation and imperfect information', *Journal of Economic Theory*, **3**, 285–351.

Leland, H. (1979). 'Quacks, lemons and licensing: A theory of minimum quality standards', *Journal of Political Economy*, **87**, 1328–46.

Litan, R. E. (1987). *What Should Banks Do?* Washington: Brookings Institution.

Llewellyn, D. (1999). 'The economic rationale for financial regulation', FSA Occasional Paper Series, 1. London: Financial Services Authority.

Mayer, C. and Neven, D. (1991). 'European financial regulation: A framework for policy analysis', in A. Giovannini and C. Mayer (eds). *European Financial Integration*. London: Centre for Economic Policy Research.

Merton, R. C. (1977). 'An analytical derivation of the cost of deposit insurance loan guarantees: An application of modern option price theory', *Journal of Banking and Finance*, **1**, 3–11.

——(1978). 'On the cost of deposit insurance when there are surveillance costs', *Journal of Business*, **51**, 439–52.

Modigliani, F. and Miller, M. (1958). 'The cost of capital, corporation finance, and the theory of investment', *American Economic Review*, **48**, 261–97.

Milgrom, P. and Roberts, J. (1982). 'Predation, reputation and entry deterrence', *Journal of Economic Theory*, **27**, 280–312.

Mingo, J. J. (2000). 'Policy implications of the federal reserve study of credit risk models at major US banking institutions', *Journal of Banking and Finance*, **24**, 15–33.

Myers, S. C. (1977). 'Determinants of corporate borrowing', *Journal of Financial Economics*, **5**, 147–75.

——(1984). 'The capital structure puzzle', *Journal of Finance*, **39**, 575–92.

——and Majluf, N. S. (1984). 'Corporate financing and investment decisions when firms have information that investors do not have', *Journal of Financial Economics*, **13**, 187–221.

Office of National Statistics (1994–8). 'Financial accounts'.

Risk Management Group of the Basel Committee (2001). 'Working paper on the regulatory treatment of operational risk', September.

Rochet, J. (1992). 'Capital requirements and the behaviour of commercial banks', *European Economic Review*, **36**, 1137–78.

Ross, S. (1977). 'The determination of financial structure: The incentive signalling approach', *Bell Journal of Economics*, **8**, 23–40.

Santomero, A. and Watson, R. (1977). 'Determining an optimal capital standard for the banking industry', *Journal of Finance*, **32**, 1267–82.

Schaefer, S. M. (1992). 'The regulation of banks and securities firms', *European Economic Review*, **34**, 587–97.

Scott, J. H. (1976). 'A theory of optimal capital structure', *Bell Journal of Economics*, **7**, 33–54.

SEC (2000). 'Annual report 1999'.

—— (2001). 'Annual report 2000'.

Shaked, A. and Sutton, J. (1980). 'The self-regulating professions', *Review of Economic Studies*, **48**, 217–34.

Shapiro, C. (1983). 'Premiums for high quality products as rents to reputation', *Quarterly Journal of Economics*, **98**, 659–80.

—— (1986). 'Investment, moral hazard and occupational licensing', *Review of Economic Studies*, **53**, 843–62.

STE (2000). 'Annual report 1999'.

Stulz, R. (1990). 'Managerial discretion and optimal financing policies', *Journal of Financial Economics*, **26**, 3–27.

The Investment Ombudsman, 'Annual report 1999/2000'.

INDEX